New Horizons in Asian Management

Palgrave Macmillan Asian Business Series

Series Editor: **Harukiyo Hasegawa** is Professor at Doshisha Business School, Kyoto, Japan, and Honorary Professor of Japanese Business at the University of Sheffield's School of East Asian Studies, where he was formerly Director of the Centre for Japanese Studies.

The Palgrave Macmillan Asian Business Series seeks to publish theoretical and empirical studies that contribute forward-looking social perspectives on the study of management issues not just in Asia, but by implication elsewhere. The series specifically aims at the development of new frontiers in the scope, themes and methods of business and management studies in Asia, a region which is seen as key to studies of modern management, organisation, strategies, human resources and technologies.

The series invites practitioners, policy-makers and academic researchers to join us at the cutting edge of constructive perspectives on Asian management, seeking to contribute towards the development of civil societies in Asia and further afield.

Titles include:

Glenn D. Hook and Harukiyo Hasegawa (*editors*)
JAPANESE RESPONSES TO GLOBALIZATION IN THE 21st CENTURY
Politics, Security, Economics and Business

Diana Rosemary Sharpe and Harukiyo Hasegawa (*editors*)
NEW HORIZONS IN ASIAN MANAGEMENT
Emerging Issues and Critical Perspectives

Sten Söderman (*editor*)
EMERGING MULTIPLICITY
Integration and Responsiveness in Asian Business Development

Palgrave Macmillan Asian Business Series
Series Standing Order ISBN 1–4039–9841–8

You can receive future titles in this series as they are published by placing a standing order. Please contact your bookseller or, in case of difficulty, write to us at the address below with your name and address, the title of the series and the ISBN quoted above.

Customer Services Department, Macmillan Distribution Ltd, Houndmills, Basingstoke, Hampshire RG21 6XS, England

New Horizons in Asian Management

Emerging Issues and Critical Perspectives

Edited by

Diana Rosemary Sharpe

and

Harukiyo Hasegawa

First published 2007 by
PALGRAVE MACMILLAN
Houndmills, Basingstoke, Hampshire RG21 6XS and
175 Fifth Avenue, New York, N.Y. 10010
Companies and representatives throughout the world

PALGRAVE MACMILLAN is the global academic imprint of the Palgrave Macmillan division of St. Martin's Press, LLC and of Palgrave Macmillan Ltd. Macmillan® is a registered trademark in the United States, United Kingdom and other countries. Palgrave is a registered trademark in the European Union and other countries.

ISBN-13: 978-0-230-01365-0 hardback
ISBN-10: 0-230-01365-1 hardback

This book is printed on paper suitable for recycling and made from fully managed and sustained forest sources. Logging, pulping and manufacturing processes are expected to conform to the environmental regulations of the country of origin.

A catalogue record for this book is available from the British Library.

A catalog record for this book is available from the Library of Congress.

10   9   8   7   6   5   4   3   2   1
16   15   14   13   12   11   10   09   08   07

Printed and bound in Great Britain by
Antony Rowe Ltd, Chippenham and Eastbourne

Contents

List of Figures and Tables

Figures

Tables

Notes on the Contributors

Michelle C. Barker is Professor of Management, Griffith Business School and Deputy Director of the Centre for Work, Leisure and Community Research, Griffith University, Australia. She has an international reputation as a scholar in the areas of intercultural adjustment, and workplace bullying and violence. Michelle has achieved national recognition for her innovative approaches to teaching by winning Australian Awards for University Teaching in 2003 and 2005. She has co-led the development of an intercultural skills programme (The ExcelL Intercultural Skills Program) which is used in many countries to assist migrants and international students to achieve employment, social and educational goals in new cultural contexts. Her recent publications include a chapter with Billett and Smith on 'Relational Interdependence as Means to Examine Work, Learning and the Remaking of Cultural Practices', in *The Learning Potential of the Workplace* (2006); and a chapter with Branch and Ramsay on 'The Bullied Boss: a Conceptual Exploration of Upwards Bullying', in *Advances in Organizational Psychology: an Asia-Pacific Perspective* (2006).

Julia Brandl is postdoctoral researcher and lecturer in management and organizational behaviour at the Vienna University of Economics and Business Administration, Austria, and regular visiting professor at the Arhus Business School, Denmark. Her research focuses on legitimacy, power and the use of formal accounting instruments in organizations. In her current research project she investigates legitimation processes in a cross-cultural perspective.

Jeremy Cresswell is an energy journalist and analyst who specializes in upstream oil and gas and renewable energy. He holds an MBA degree awarded by The Robert Gordon University and writes primarily for Britain's oldest daily newspaper, the *Press and Journal* of Aberdeen, as editor of the specialist supplement *Energy*. He is the author of three books and has co-authored a significant number of energy-related reports and publications. He is an associate of economists Mackay Consultants, chairman of the private–public partnership, Aberdeen Renewable Energy Group, and is on the management committee of the Institute of Energy,

Aberdeen branch. His research interests include the potential impact of offshore oil and gas on the Faroese business community.

A.R. Goddard is Professor of Accounting, and Director of Postgraduate Education at the School of Management, University of Southampton. He is a qualified charatered accountant, being a Fellow of the Institute of Chartered Accountants of England and Wales and a member of the Chartered Institute of Public Finance and Accountancy (FCA and CIPFA). He worked in the public sector, including local government and housing, for several years before joining the accounting firm KPMG. He completed his PhD entitled 'Financial and Organisational Control in the Public Sector – a Paradigmatic Exploration', at the University of Southampton. He has researched extensively in public sector financial control, including local government, health and NGOs. He is Chair of the British Accounting Association Special Interest Group in Public Service Accounting Research. His current research interests include: researching the relationship between accounting, accountability and governance, and between accounting, strategy and performance management in the public services; researching contextual aspects of accounting, using grounded theory; historical analyses of the development of accounting in the public sector; strategic management accounting and auditing.

Harukiyo Hasegawa is Professor of Global Management and Human Resource Management at Doshisha Business School in Kyoto and Honorary Professor of Japanese Business of the University of Sheffield. His recent major publications include *Steel Industry in Japan: a Comparison with Britain* (1996); *Japanese Business and Management: Restructuring for Low Growth and Globalization* (co-editor/contributor, 1998); *The Political Economy of Japanese Globalization* (co-editor/contributor, 2001); *Japanese Responses to Globalization* (co-editor/contributor, Palgrave Macmillan, 2006). He is general editor of the international journal, *Asian Business & Management* (Palgrave Macmillan) and series editor of Palgrave Macmillan Asian Business Series.

Dr Chutarat Inma currently holds the position of Postdoctoral Fellow for the Division of Health Sciences at Murdoch University in Western Australia. She coordinates collaborative research projects in assessing the effectiveness of the ageing workforce in regional organizations funded by the Australia Research Council between the Peel Campus and the industry partners in regional Southwest of Western Australia. Her research interest falls into many aspects of business ethics, occupational health and safety and international human resource management. She is now researching into factors impacting business ethics in the Asia Pacific region.

Ulrik Jørgensen is Professor at the Department of Manufacturing Engineering and Management at the Technical University of Denmark, working within the fields of technology studies, design engineering, and environmental policy and management. His recent publications include 'Cleaner Technology in Denmark – Support Measures and Regulatory Efforts', in Theo de Bruijn and Vicky Norbert Boehm (eds), *Industrial Transformation: Environmental Policy Innovation in the United States and Europe* (2005); 'Energy Sector in Transition – Technologies and Regulatory Policies in Flux', in *Technology Forecasting and Social Change*, 2005; *Green Technology Foresight about Environmentally Friendly Products and Materials – Challenges from Nanotechnology, Biotechnology and ICT*, with M.S. Jørgensen, M.M. Andersen (2005); 'Environmental Professional Competence – the Role of Communities of Practice and Spaces for Reflexive Learning', with Erik Hagelskjær Lauridsen, *Greener Management International* (2006); and 'Historical Accounts of Engineering Education', in *Rethinking Engineering Education: The CDIO Approach* (2007).

Doo-Jin Kim is Professor of Political Economy and Korean Studies at Frankfurt University. He was also the Chair of Korean Studies and Professor of Political Economy at Sciences Po in Paris. He gained his first PhD from Korea University in 1992. Afterwards he held a second doctoral degree from the University of Sussex, UK, on Contemporary European Studies. He has written extensively on international competitiveness, EU trade policy, East Asian security issues, and Korean FDI in the EU. His recent work includes *Newly Industrialising Economies and International Political Economy: Market Power and Korean Electronics Multinationals* (2006), and *10 Years After the Asian Crisis* (forthcoming 2007).

Young-Chan Kim is Senior Lecturer of International Business and Economics at Greenwich University, and Senior Research Fellow in Chinese Research Network in the same University. He gained his PhD in International Business and Strategy and Trade Policy at Royal Holloway, University of London. He is co-founder of the Anglo-Korean Economic Institute and is Chief Consultant for the Asian Desk, Department of Trade and Industry, UK. He has written extensively on foreign direct investment and has contributed numerous papers to edited volumes and journals. He also participated in an ESRC-funded research project and co-organized the 10th anniversary edition of *Asia Pacific Business Review*. His recent publications include *Japanese Inward Investment in UK Car Manufacturing* (2002), *Globalisation and Korean Foreign Direct Investment* (2004), *Newly Industrializing Economies and International Competitiveness: Market Power and Korean Electronics Multinationals* (2006), and *10 Years After the Asian Crisis* (forthcoming 2007).

Erik Hagelskjær Lauridsen is Assistant Professor at the Department of Manufacturing Engineering and Management at the Technical University of Denmark. His main interest is in the dual issues of how to support environmental competences and how environmental agendas are constituted as arenas where technical solutions, policy regimes and professional practices are translated. Using approaches from science and technology studies he is currently working on how to stimulate environmentally improved innovation and design. Recent publications include: 'Disciplinary Fragmentation in Comprehensive Issues: A Literature Survey on the Environment of the Songkhla Lakes', in the Proceedings *Integrated Lake Management*, Prince of Songkhla University, Hai Yai, Thailand, August 2004; '*Industrial Developments Challenging Planning and Research Endeavours Around Songkhla Lak*', with U. Jørgensen, paper for the Greening of Industry Network conference, Hong Kong, November 2004; *Environmental Impact of the Use of Natural Resources (EIRES)*, with P. Nielsen, A. Tukker, B. Weidema and P. Notten, European Commission Joint Research Centre, 2004. 'Environmental Professional Competence – the Role of Communities of Practices and Spaces for reflexive learning', with U. Jørgensen; and *Waste Prevention, Waste Policy and Innovation*, with M.S. Jørgensen, U., report from the ESTO-WASTE project, Dept. of Manufacturing Engineering and Management, 2007.

Fuan Li (PhD Florida International University) is an associate professor of marketing in the Christos M. Cotsakos College of Business at William Paterson University. His current research interests include business ethics, cross-cultural research on consumer choice, brand trust, and customer relationship management. His work has been published in the *Journal of Marketing Science,* the *Journal of Advertising,* the *Journal of Business Psychology,* the *Journal of Marketing Management,* the *European Journal of Marketing,* the *Asia Pacific Journal of Marketing and Logistics,* and others.

Daniel W. Lund is a sessional lecturer and PhD candidate in the Department of Management, Griffith Business School, Griffith University, Australia. He has an MBA from the Schulich School of Business at York University in Canada and has taught business in the ITESM University system in Mexico and was the head of a business school in China. His research interests are in the areas of expatriate adjustment in China, immigrant adjustment, young overseas Chinese entrepreneurs, diversity management, and intercultural skills training. His recent publications include a 2006 chapter titled 'Young overseas Chinese entrepreneurs in Australia', in *Experiences of Transnational Chinese Migrants in the Asia-Pacific*.

Florentine Maier is research assistant in nonprofit management at Vienna University of Economics and Business Administration, Austria. Her research interest is the spread of managerial ideas and practices in organizations. In her current research, she examines how managerialism permeates nonprofit organizations.

Vesa Peltokorpi is Project Director of the COE (Center of Excellence) in the Graduate School of International Corporate Strategy at Hitotsubashi University in Japan. He received his PhD in International Business at the Swedish School of Economics and Business Administration in Finland, an MA in International Relations at Flinders University of South Australia, and a BA in International Economics at Boise University in the USA. His research interests include cross-cultural psychology, group and shared cognition, and knowledge management. His recent and forthcoming studies have been published in international reviewed journals, such as *Journal of Management Studies, Employee Relations, Asian Business & Management*, and the *International Journal of Technology Management*.

A.R. Abdul Rahman is Associate Professor at the Department of Accounting, International Islamic University Malaysia. He obtained his bachelors degree in Accounting and Finance from University of East London, UK, Masters and PhD degree in Accounting from University of Southampton, UK. His PhD thesis title was 'An Interpretive Inquiry into Accounting Practices in Islamic Organisations in Malaysia'. He is currently the Director of the IIUM Institute of Islamic Banking and Finance. He has published his work in academic journals, including *Financial Accountability and Management, Managerial Auditing Journal, American Journal of Islamic Social Sciences, International Journal of Islamic Financial Services*, and *IIUM Journal of Economics and Management*. His current research interests include: accounting and accountability in public services and religious organizations; accounting for Islamic financial institutions; Islamic banking and finance; and corporate governance.

Diana Sharpe is an Associate Professor of Management at Monmouth University, New Jersey and an Affiliated Fellow of the Centre for Women and Work, Rutgers University. Her research interests include the comparative analysis of organizations, work organization and control processes in the multinational and the transfer of organizational practices across contexts. She has published in the field of Japanese management practices with R. Whitley and G. Morgan and has carried out ethnographic research on Japanese shopfloor work practices. The research has been published in the *Journal of Management Studies,* the *International Journal of Human Resource Management* and the *Journal of International Management.*

Yi Tan is currently a business analyst and advisor for energy and high-tech industries and non-for-profit organizations. She read strategic management in East Asia for both her PhD and MBA degrees at The Robert Gordon University. Prior to this, she worked in China for nine years in a variety of management roles, including in the energy sector. Her main research interests include corporate and business strategies, business process, and the assessment of business environment and business performance in an international context such as China. She has published in a number of international academic journals and the outcome of her academic research work has been utilized by BBC World and BBC News 24. She is now an active writer on businesses in China and provides regularly analytical reports for press and industrial publications.

Robert Taylor is Reader in Modern Chinese Studies and Co-Director of the Centre for Chinese Studies at the University of Sheffield. His research interests concern contemporary Sino-Japanese Relations and Chinese business management, especially corporate social responsibility, in the context of the growing globalization of Chinese companies in the wake of the WTO, and China's foreign policy. His recent publications include *Greater China and Japan* (1996), and 'China's Human Resource Management Strategies: The Role of Enterprise and Government,' *Asian Business and Management* (2005), 4(1): 5–21.

Preface

We would like to thank all the contributors to this book whose work follows through on the editors' concerns for attention to emerging issues in Asian Business and Management and Critical Perspectives of the field, which as yet remain relatively underdeveloped in the literatures on Asian Business and Management.

We would also like to thank Palgrave Macmillan for supporting this project and Jacky Kippenberger for her input and encouragement.

1
Introduction

Diana Rosemary Sharpe and Harukiyo Hasegawa

New Horizons in Asian Management brings together empirical and theoretical research that provides critical perspectives and contextual analysis and reflection to the study of management practices in organizations across the Asian region. The chapters contribute to understanding the ways in which wider contextual factors such as institutional, social and cultural influences impact on organizational structures and processes. The book also raises critical reflection on the ways in which firm choices in working across contexts have not only economic implications, but also ethical and social implications. Research on the comparative analysis of business systems (see, for example, Whitley 1992, 1999) has examined how business systems are socially structured and firms embedded in a wider societal context that influences organizational forms, strategic choices and wider management practices. Drawing on such a sociological approach to the study of organizations, a further strand of research is opened up into the ways in which internal organizational processes and social relations within firms and across institutional contexts are influenced by contextual factors. In this way there has been growing interest in examining the ways in which organizational structures and processes are embedded, enabled and resisted by wider contextual factors at the local, regional and international level.

This line of enquiry tends to reject mainstream economic approaches to the study of organizations that ignore the influence of context and that assume economic rationality in contrast to contextual rationality. Further, it raises research questions of how management practices that have evolved in one institutional context are translated, sustained or resisted in other contexts. It also encourages a focus on management practices as social processes. This edited book brings together recent research focusing on cultural and institutional factors interacting with and influencing internal firm processes, including management strategy and decision-making.

The book also brings a critical perspective to the appreciation of how firms are embedded in wider communities and stakeholder relations and the ways in which organizational decision-making and strategic processes impact on stakeholder groups, including workers, local communities and the environment. Several chapters look at the ways in which managerial practices are being introduced into the specificities of an Asian context, including Malaysia, China, Korea and Thailand, and how they are appropriated, resisted, adapted and sustained in different institutional contexts. A critical perspective also sensitizes analysis to the power relations between the stakeholders involved and the ways in which power is distributed, enacted and institutionalized in specific business systems. This is taken up in the chapter by Kim and Kim on the relationship between Korean state power and corporate power. A critical perspective also encourages attention to the ways in which multinational corporations as political actors on a global scale can impact on local socioeconomic structures and value systems, as shown in the work by Inma on employment practices in Thailand, Brandl and Maier on Audit Objectives in China and Lauridsen and Jørgensen on Environmental Management Systems in Thailand. The authors demonstrate that whilst multinationals and international regulatory institutions seek to transfer specific practices across contexts, the ways in which they are interpreted, received, resisted, adapted and sustained depends on the institutional context into which they are being introduced and the specificities of power relations between stakeholders in that context. In this way processual analysis of how management practices are introduced, sustained, adapted and resisted over time are particularly important emerging areas for research.

The chapter by Peltokorpi focuses on intercultural conflicts from the point of view of contextual actors. Drawing on a constructivist approach in which conflict in intercultural settings is conceptualized as emerging from individual and situation-specific factors and cultures of individuals engaged in social interactions, the chapter brings in a processual analysis, addressing not only sources of intercultural conflict but also processes and consequences. It focuses on conflicts between Nordic expatriates and local Japanese employees. The research on foreign expatriates in Japan provides an interesting compliment to previous research on Japanese expatriates overseas. Peltokorpi highlights the ways in which multinational organizations may engage in international operations without understanding how the local context influences local expectations and systems of management. From a critical perspective it considers how headquarters' openness to learn from subsidiaries can be restricted by a closed approach (Beechler and Bird, 1999) to organizational learning and a stance that knowledge flows from headquarters to subsidiary (Mir, 2001). In this way change being articulated in terms of 'concessions' and perceptions of being a weak expatriate. As noted by Morgan *et al.* (2003), the strategic approach to internationalization and role of the expatriate is influenced by headquarters' own institutional context as well as organizational and industry-level factors and history.

A further related issue raised by the chapter is that of the organization as a political arena in which power relations between locals and expatriates are constantly enacted. The research indicates the structural power bases of local Japanese managers who had control of customer bases and customer relations, a strategic contingency for the business. It also raises the issue of local managers' being embedded within their own institutional context, finding it difficult to consider how alternative management practices may translate easily into the local context, despite market and legislative changes. In this way, the chapter highlights how local managers' behaviour is influenced by the wider institutional context shaping employment relations – this also impacts upon the strategic management choices that are made in specific contexts. Whilst there may be initiatives in the education sector through professional bodies and other transnational organizations to transfer one best 'professional way' of working, or best practice, across contexts as noted by one expatriate, local recipes of organizing and managing continue to be practiced.

The social constructivist methodological approach adopted in the research provides further insights into how members make sense of and experience their own location within international diverse work groups and organizational structures The experience of power relations and identity, including race and gender, are areas that are under-researched in such organizational contexts in looking at organizational processes and outcomes.

In chapter 3 Fuan Li reflects on how moral principles, behavioural standards and ethical values may be influenced by the underlying cultural context. Focusing on the Asian context the collectivist culture – displayed, for example, in Chinese relationalism – is seen as requiring a methodological collectivism to gain insight into moral thinking. With an emphasis on relationships and circumstances, collectivists may change ethical judgement according to the party involved in a particular situation. Li draws on Triandis (1995) to argue that in interpersonal relationships, the norms and values for in-group members are different from and sometimes opposite to the norms for outsiders. Equality or needs are the basis for allocating resources among in-group members who are expected to cooperate, reciprocate, make sacrifices, and protect each other's interests. However, such behavioural norms and the emphasis on collective welfare and duties are seen to apply typically only to the in-group and not out-groups. When dealing with out-group members, collectivists, just like individualists, are seen primarily to use the equity norm (to each according to his/her contribution). Working across contexts, for example in a multinational organization, Li argues that the notion of a self-regulated profession seems to be based on an individualistic value that professionals should maintain their allegiance to a professional code. Given their emphasis on relationship networks and tendencies to identify themselves with the in-group, family or company, Li argues that collectivists may more readily break the rules of professional codes when it is in the best interest of the in-group. This suggests that for example international codes of ethics may be perceived in different ways in collectivist as compared to individualistic cultures.

Lund and Barker's chapter focuses on the factors influencing the performance of western expatriate managers in small Chinese-owned organizations in China. The findings indicate that perceptions of effectiveness are very much tied into the wider cultural context in which the organization is embedded and the manager has to manoeuvre. In the context of the small Chinese-owned college in China maintaining a sense of organizational and cultural harmony and establishing strategic relations with those both higher and lower in the organization's power and influence structure were seen as important for the western expatriates. More research is needed to understand how concepts of effectiveness and failure also emerge and are influenced by specific social, institutional and cultural contexts within which organizations are embedded.

Taylor's chapter highlights the challenge of developing a corporate culture where a sense of corporate social responsibility frames strategic decision-making. The research provides an interesting institutional context within which to examine the attempts to introduce a philosophy of environmental sensitivity and corporate social responsibility, focusing on the political, social and economic factors influencing firm behaviour, including government, customer and international regulatory influences. As examined in Taylor's chapter, China's transition from a command to a market economy has enhanced the strategic

decision-making powers of management and heightened the consciousness of corporate social responsibility among Chinese state collective
and private enterprises. There is an examination of the holistic approach
of newly created enterprise groups that seek integration through a
'green' supply chain. Taylor notes that whilst the Ecological Industrial
Park has been introduced in China, the original concept of the park,
to protect the natural resources of a whole region by having a group of
enterprises and a neighbourhood residential community encompassed,
with the sharing of waste recycling skills and collaboration between
diverse industries, has not always been honoured in practice. Competition to establish parks for economic gain is seen as one of the factors
leading to neglect of the environment. Taylor notes that it is not a foregone conclusion that Chinese and Asian norms will necessarily replicate
those in the Anglo-American tradition. In the environmental sphere, as
in other spheres, as discussed by many authors in this book, solutions
may prove to be uniquely Chinese or Asian or a hybrid born of a blend
of different cultures and practices.

Tan and Cresswell's chapter continues the focus on the institutional
context of organizations through a conceptual and empirical study of
environmental uncertainty. Through a study of organizational environments in the energy service sector in China, Singapore and Malaysia the
chapter both conceptualizes and assesses environmental uncertainty.
This is done by analysing organizational environmental influences in
terms of environmental complexity, dynamism and hostility. In this way
the chapter provides a contribution to the organizational and strategic
management literature by providing a means of assessing the nature
of the environment confronting organizations in different environmental sectors. This in turn can inform strategic decision-making within
the organization. The chapter provides an example of a comparative,
cross-national environmental analysis research methodology containing
both qualitative and quantitative analytical techniques.

Lauridsen and Jørgensen reflect on the process of appropriation of
new management standards in the context of Thai industry. Focusing
on the interpretation and incorporation of environmental standards
into management practices (EMS) in a number of sectors, the chapter
examines the changes in the environmental agenda in the business
community and develops a contextual analysis of the interaction
between the stakeholders involved. The chapter adopts a critical stance
to the implicit assumptions of 'modernization', in other words, that
Thai industries and society have to 'catch up' with the western model
of management principles and standards of environmental regulation

as if these are universal and have met their final destination rather than being constantly contested. Through the examination of empirical case studies the chapter argues that the specific content and function of environmental management relies on the interaction between companies and their stakeholders. The changing environmental objectives that are constituted and prioritized in the management practices are seen as a reflection of the changing societal context of Thailand with regards to management style, regulatory regimes and available technologies and competences.

The chapter introduces a theoretical approach drawing on Actor–Network Theory, stressing how the outcomes of EMS depends on the ability of company management to enroll diverse actors in the development of new or changing environmental agendas. The chapter raises some general points for consideration concerning how the appropriation of management systems such as EMS across contexts may spur the development of specific new local regulatory and social interactions concerning the issues and problems to be addressed. Secondly, from the new interactions and relations developed, in this case the new customer and ownership dependencies, new innovative competencies and capabilities for strategic development of technology, markets and products may emerge.

In chapter 8 Rahman and Goddard, through an analysis of research on religious organizations in Malaysia, show how broader social, historical and religious contexts in which organizations are embedded, together with the power relationships within them, resulted in unique accounting *verstehen* and, in turn, accounting practices.

The chapter provides a contribution to understanding financial management and accounting in religious organizations in general and in Islamic organizations in particular, showing how the sacred/secular divide which prior studies had identified as an important aspect of Christian organizations, was not evident in the Muslim context. Rather, the Islamic *verstehen* is characterized by Islamic values and beliefs concerning the all-encompassing nature of Islam and also by the *Taklif* notion of personal accountability to God. Adopting a grounded theory approach the research examines accounting as a social practice, describing two case studies of accounting practices as embedded in two religious, public service organizations in Malaysia. In this way the chapter addresses a comparatively under-researched topic, that of accounting as a situated social practice in Islamic religious settings.

The study showed that important differences in accounting practices occur between organizations within the same religious denomination.

These differences were explained by the different accounting *verstehen* in each organization which emerged from the differences in the contexts of power and other cultural influences within which the organizations were located. There is an examination of three interrelated areas: accounting *verstehen* and culture, accounting *verstehen* and power, and accounting *verstehen* and accountability.

Brandl and Maier's chapter notes how different local environments may lead to variations in auditing instruments and practices, needing to be related to specific institutional contexts (that is, integrated with other practices). At the individual level the chapter reflects on how the integration of auditing into normative orientations means that people use audit techniques to evaluate others – for example, through individual performance appraisals. Furthermore, the integration of auditing into the cognitive level means that auditing becomes a general, unquestioned way of reflection about issues, which Scott (1995) describes as taken-for-grantedness. Once implemented, auditing is seen to gain a state of irreversibility because it structures the interests of stakeholders and is manifested in the institutional order (Power 1997). In other words, it becomes an unquestioned element of management, a rationalized myth (Meyer and Rowan 1977). The chapter conceptualizes how the institutionalization of auditing occurs over different time horizons in different contexts as institutional contexts are seen to slow down the expansion of management knowledge (Sahlin-Andersson and Engwall 2002). Taking the example of the People's Republic of China (PRC), the authors argue that audit objectives develop cumulatively rather than consecutively from a focus on fraud detection to that of a legitimating activity and through to use as a management decision support. The growing presence of western companies and the centralized bureaucracy are seen to facilitate the expansion of auditing knowledge in the PRC.

As noted by the authors, the conceptual framework drawing on institutional analysis can be used to examine the spread of other types of management knowledge or rationalized myths in the Asian context such as human resource management (see chapter 10) and corporate social responsibility (see chapter 5).

Inma's chapter highlights the role of the multinational corporation (MNC) as a political actor on a global scale. Drawing on the example of age discrimination in employment, the chapter studies the practices of domestic firms as well as Asian, American and European MNCs in Thailand and finds that the propensity to discriminate against older candidates in the Thai employment market was found not only in local Thai firms but also extensively in the MNCs studied – even though these firms worked within anti-discriminatory age legislation in their home countries. In a study of the Thai institutional context Inma notes that employment discrimination is prohibited in Thailand under a Labour Protection Act. However, when cases of discrimination practice in employment occur, Thai employees often avoid legal institutions for dispute resolution. Among the contextual factors that are seen to sustain this situation were argued to be legal resources, heavily skewed in favour of employers and relationships between Thai employers and their employees that tend to be paternalistic. Individual employees rarely have significant bargaining power and the unionization in the country is fragmented and fractionalized. In this context the legislation towards employment discrimination practice is deemed to be only a *'paper tiger'* in the Thai labour market, with a lack of mechanisms to establish fairness between employers and employees. The chapter raises some important issues concerning the power and practices of multinationals across institutional contexts and the vulnerability of host nations to the impact of MNCs on local socioeconomic structures and value systems.

In the closing chapter Kim and Kim also focus on business as a political power through a case study of Korean state-corporate power, or *chaebol* governance. The chapter discusses the relationship between international competitiveness and shifting state and corporate power, examining how Korean big business can be regarded as a political power rather than as a mere market agent with Korean corporate power emerging as the countervailing force against Korean state power. The chapter examines how the increasing significance of international trade barriers in advanced markets since the early 1980s and the growing importance of international competitiveness has tended to increase the market power of indigenous big corporations.

Through a historical examination of the evolving interaction of state, market and firm the chapter argues that Korean big businesses have come to emerge as political actors, whether in world markets responding to a new international trade regime, or, more specifically, in the process towards European integration. Individual MNCs incorporating knowledge-intensive technology have begun to emerge as market coordinators, individually or collectively. The authors argue that 'market power' originating with Korean major MNCs has tended to pave the way for political power, because multinational companies intrinsically translate economic activities in international markets into political leverage. This chapter's analysis of Korean firms in the context of globalization indicates how Korea's *chaebol*-governance gives rise to 'market power' (economic actor) as well as 'political power' (political actor).

The chapter considers how and to what extent the *nature* of industry has transformed the state–corporate power relations, in political and economic terms, in the context of the growth of knowledge-intensive industries. In this way the analysis highlights why *chaebol* big firms may be seen as exercising *political* power rather than as mere market agents exercising economic power.

References

Beechler, S.L. and Bird, A. (1999) *Japanese Multinationals Abroad: Individual and Organizational Learning*. Oxford: Oxford University Press.

Meyer, J.W. and Rowan, B., (1977) 'Institutionalized Organizations: Formal Structure as Myth and Ceremony', *American Journal of Sociology*, 83(2): 340–63.

Mir, R.A. (2001) *Migrating Ideas: An Empirical Study of Intra-Organizational Knowledge Transfer*. Doctoral Dissertation, University of Massachusetts, Amherst.

Morgan, G., Kelly, B., Sharpe, D., and Whitley, R. (2003) 'Global Managers and Japanese Multinationals: Internationalization and Management in Japanese Financial Institutions', *International Journal of Human Resource Management*, 14(3): 1–19.

Power, M. (1997) *The Audit Society: Rituals of Verification*. Oxford: Oxford University Press.

Sahlin-Andersson, K. and Engwall, L. (2002) 'The Dynamics of Management Knowledge', K. Sahlin-Andersson and L. Engwall (eds), *The Expansion of Management Knowledge: Carriers, Flows and Sources*. Stanford: Stanford University Press, pp. 277–96.

Scott, R.W. (1995) *Institutions and Organizations*. Thousand Oaks, CA: Sage.

Triandis, H. C. (1995) *Individualism and Collectivism*. Boulder, CO: Westview Press.

Whitley, R. (1992) *Business Systems in East Asia*. London: Sage.

Whitley, R. (1999) *Divergent Capitalisms: The Social Structuring and Change of Business Systems*. Oxford: Oxford University Press.

Part I
Cultural and Strategic Issues

2
Intercultural Conflicts: Evidence from Nordic Subsidiaries in Japan

Vesa Peltokorpi

Introduction

Corporate internationalization has created an environment in which an increasing number of employees are working in foreign locations and encountering workforce diversity in its richest form. Intercultural work interaction is often taking place in foreign subsidiaries, the fastest-growing type of international organization (Stage, 1999). While conflicts are a normal part of daily organizational reality in all cultures, the ways they are perceived, manifested and managed are subject to cultural variations (Leung *et al.*, 2002). In addition to personality differences and situational factors, complications in intercultural settings can occur due to a varying array of needs and conflict resolution styles (Lebra, 1985; Ting-Toomey, 1988).

Scholars have studied the 'East–West differences' in conflict behaviour by comparing subjects in the USA and Japan (e.g., Tinsley, 1998; Oetzel and Ting-Toomey, 2003). As context-specific interaction, not comparison, is the essence of organizational behaviour in foreign subsidiaries, more focus needs to be directed toward intercultural processes (Adler and Graham, 1989). Consistent to the overarching objective of this book, this chapter contributes to the literature on expatriate management in Asia and conflict management by providing a critical perspective on intercultural conflicts from the contextual actors' point of view. Drawing from the constructivist approach (Hong and Chiu, 2001; Morris and Fu, 2001; Hong *et al.*, 2003), conflicts in intercultural settings are conceptualized as an emergent property influenced by individual and situation-specific factors and cultures of individuals engaged in social interactions. The research questions are: (1) 'What are the sources of intercultural conflicts?'; (2) 'How are the intercultural conflicts managed?'; and (3) 'What are the consequences of intercultural conflicts?' Interviews with 30 Nordic expatriates and eight Japanese managers are used to describe the sources, processes, and consequences of intercultural conflicts in Nordic subsidiaries in Japan.

The rest of this chapter is structured as follows. The following section discusses intercultural conflicts. While conflicts may occur between headquarters and subsidiaries and between subsidiaries, the emphasis here is on conflicts between expatriates and local employees. The third section discusses the research sample and methods. The fourth section describes intercultural conflicts in Nordic subsidiaries in Japan. The findings and implications are discussed in the fifth and sixth sections, respectively. The chapter ends with conclusions and suggestions for future research.

Intercultural conflicts

Conflict, an inevitable part of human relationships, refers to 'the perceived and/or actual incompatibility of values, expectations, processes, or outcomes between two or more parties over substantive and/or relational issues' (Ting-Toomey, 1994: 360). Conflicts, often divided into task/substantive and person/relational issues[1] (see, for example, Jehn, 1995), stem from disagreements during which different views are made explicit and escalate to conflicts when the disputing parties give greater priority to their own views rather than to engaging in problem-solving behaviours (Smith *et al.*, 1998). Thus, while all conflicts entail disagreements, not all disagreements entail conflicts. Individuals display conflicts in various ways, such as aggressive demands, reluctant concessions, long silences, and emotional outbursts (Morris and Fu, 2001). In comparison to intracultural conflicts (that is, conflicts between members of the same culture), intercultural conflicts (that is, conflicts between members of different cultures) tend to be more complicated due to the different ways of exhibiting and managing conflict (Doucet and Jehn, 1997).

A trait approach in cross-cultural psychology examines how general cultural values influence conflict behaviour (Morris and Fu, 2001). While useful to examine differences in conflict behaviour across cultures, cross-cultural studies say little about the dynamics of intercultural encounters because they examine the similarities and differences between two or more cultures on some *a priori* construct. In contrast, intercultural studies based on the constructivist approach focus on the penetration by a member of one culture into another culture (Landis and Wasilewski,

1999), and show that individuals in intercultural interaction do not always behave in line with their cultural values. Instead of acting and reacting in a predetermined, uniform manner to the social environment, scholars in the constructivist approach claim that people through interactions actively create their own environment (Hong and Chiu, 2001). In support, individual variations have been detected in conflict research. For example, a study by Weldon and Jehn (1995) indicated that individual differences influence the individualism–collectivism value dimension in the conflict management style measure.

How much can value orientation explain individual behaviour? According to an influential research study (Keller *et al.*, 1992), 40 per cent of an individual's values are genetic and 60 per cent are environmentally based, indicating that people can display substantial variance in the extent to which they subscribe to their culture's pivotal norms and values. In contrast to static, deterministic views of cultures in macro-level cross-cultural studies, the constructivist approach is built on the assumption that cultures are dynamic systems that evolve through social interaction over time (Hong and Chiu, 2001). In this view, each individual's social world is constituted within a framework of pre-acquainted, familiar knowledge about various situations. Schemas used to interpret environmental events are dynamic; they grow from accumulated experiences and vicarious learning resulting in the formation of organized knowledge (Austin, 1997). Individuals develop schemas, for example, through social interactions with people of the same culture, and activate these schemas when a new situation seems similar to those encountered in the past. As the incoming information is processed through the schema, individuals, at least in initial intercultural interactions, may engage in behaviors consistent with their cultural values (Brannen and Salk, 2000). However, scholars emphasizing the impact of social learning propose that a person who has extensive experiences in two cultures might have learned the conflict frames in both cultures (Morris and Fu, 2001). In the constructivist approach, people consequently respond to stimuli by knowledge structures that are both accessible (meaning easy to retrieve) and applicable (meaning that it structurally fits the stimulus that an individual is interpreting) (Hong and Chiu, 2001; Morris and Fu, 2001; Hong *et al.*, 2003). The stimuli-response does not need to be consistent to a person's cultural values.

A brief description of cross-cultural differences before intercultural ones is useful as conflicts are partly culturally defined, regulated events, and cultural differences between the Nordic countries and Japan are likely to be greater than within-culture variances. In-group harmony and conflict avoidance are common themes in discussions about conflicts in Japan. For example, Moran *et al.* (1994) proposed that the Japanese management system prevents conflicts rather than actually resolving generated conflicts. Several other scholars have adopted a more pragmatic approach, arguing that conflicts are expressed in culture-specific ways in Japan (Krauss *et al.*, 1985; Eistenstadt, 1990). Conflict avoidance behaviour can be explained by *honne* (true motives and sentiments) and *tatemae* (proper and conventional display) in social relationships in Japan (see Doi, 1986). Because *honne* is often subordinated by *tatemae*, the Japanese may not explicitly disagree or voice conflicting opinions, especially with those higher in the hierarchy. The Japanese may avoid saying 'no' for face concerns or to foster a harmonious atmosphere (Tinsley, 1998). The word 'yes' is not necessarily a sign of approval, but maintenance of the communication line (Miyahara *et al.*, 1998). Facing conflict avoiding behaviour of Japanese employees, Nordic expatriates, who tend to use a more direct approach toward conflict resolution and are accustomed to factual-inductive conflict management styles (Gydykunst *et al.*, 1988), may, at least initially, consider their Japanese counterparts to be passive, lacking in initiative, and unwilling to challenge ideas (Peltokorpi, 2006, 2007).

Conflict avoidance is not a sign of low intercultural or intergroup conflict frequency in Japan. Strong and salient in-group/out-group[2] boundaries are distinctive features of social interaction in Japan (Triandis, 1986). Strong in-group identification encourages people to overlook or downplay differences between themselves and their fellow group members to make stereotypical distinctions between in-groups and out-groups (Nakane, 1971; Matsuda, 1985). While all people are ethnocentric to some degree and use their cultures as bases to judge other cultures, it is claimed that cultural, linguistic, and racial homogeneity facilitate ethnocentricity and in-group/out-group categorization in Japan (e.g., Feldman and Arnold, 1983; Triandis, 1986). As intercultural conflicts take place and escalate, the internal cohesiveness of the groups increases, and so do the negative images of an out-group among in-group members. If cultural differences between conflicting parties are large, even trivial types of behaviour – such as eye contact, body language, speech rhythms, and punctuality – can aggravate stereotypes (LaFrance and Mayo, 1978). These reinforced stereotypes tend to intensify conflicts and lead to situations in which the exchange of information beyond group boundaries is rationed and/or deliberately distorted (Feldman and Arnold, 1983; Hambrick *et al.*, 2001).

In addition to cultural values as schematic frames to interpret environmental events, scholars in the constructivist approach claim that intercultural conflicts are influenced further by individual and situational factors (Morris and Fu, 2001). While disregarded in cross-cultural studies, individuals vary in their experiences and ability to use knowledge acquired in social interactions. In support, expatriate studies indicate that experiences in similar countries facilitate interactions with the host country nationals (Takeuchi *et al.*, 2005). Various situational factors can also initiate and aggravate intercultural conflicts. In foreign subsidiaries, conflicts may be linked to work roles and unequal distribution of power. Expatriates, normally working in subsidiaries from two to five years, are at the top of the organizational hierarchy (Harzing, 2001). Their possible strong identification with headquarters policies can be in contrast to local preferences. Also time pressures tend to create situations wherein disagreements, backed by local preferences, escalate to conflicts. Hogg and Terry (2000) propose further that when power distances are small, the less powerful manager may refuse to accept his lower status, causing and escalating conflicts. The number of expatriates should also be considered. Being in the minority, expatriates may lack the ability to use social control mechanisms to, such as exclusion, to manage conflicts (Yamagishi, 1988). In Japan, the threat of isolation and exclusion are used to make people accept their roles as a part of a group/organization (Ohbushi, 1998). Lacking these methods, expatriates can either use their formal power or comply with the majority.

In summary, the constructivist approach acknowledges that individual traits, cultural differences, and situational factors can all influence conflicts and their management in intercultural settings. In addition to differences in cultural values, intercultural conflicts can be influenced by the number and training of individuals involved in the transactions, the balance of power and influence of national cultural groups, language and cultural fluency, and the ability to use knowledge acquired in daily interactions. While small, task-related conflicts can increase information exchange and facilitate decision-making (Jehn, 1995), differences in language, nonverbal behaviour, values, norms, attitudes, roles, and power are likely to intensify the division between Nordic expatriates and Japanese employees, resulting in a negative influence on collaborative behaviour. As conflicts can be managed only when they are perceived as conflicts (Pinkley and Northcraft, 1994), the latent nature of conflicts in Japan can put expatriates into a disadvantageous position. Instead of mitigating conflicts, the cultural value of social harmony increases latent hostility and intensifies conflicts (Lebra, 1985). Harmony may initially be observed where there is actually deep-seated antagonism.

Methodology

An interview-based study was conducted to investigate the sources, management, and consequences of intercultural conflicts in Nordic subsidiaries in Japan. The data were derived during 2002 and 2004 in Japan. The interviews were carried out with 30 Nordic expatriates [Finnish (n = 7), Danish (n = 7), Norwegian (n = 2), and Swedish (n = 14)] and eight Japanese managers. All interviewees were male, holding subsidiary president (87 per cent) or divisional/functional manager (13 per cent) positions. Most expatriates (83 per cent) have been in Japan more than five years. The sample consists of 38 subsidiaries, with one expatriate or Japanese manager interviewed per subsidiary. These subsidiaries had 28 expatriate presidents. Most of these subsidiaries (95 per cent) are in sales-related businesses: engineering (47 per cent), computer (28 per cent), and shipping (25 per cent) industries. These subsidiaries are rather small (with an average of 37 employees) and have been in Japan an average of 17 years. Most expatriates (67 per cent) reported not to be fluent in Japanese.

The interviewee's lead was followed during the interviews. Although most questions addressed intercultural interaction, all interviewees were asked the following questions: What kinds of disagreements or conflicts, if any, have taken place in this subsidiary? Describe these disagreements or conflicts. How did these disagreements or conflicts affect intercultural interaction? How were these intercultural conflicts solved? Active listening, including suspending judgment, listening attentively, and using eye contact, was used to motivate subjects to provide more descriptions and explanations. Among the local managers, two disagreements and one conflict were indicated to have occurred. Among the expatriates, 27 disagreements and 23 conflicts were indicated to have occurred. Among the conflicts, nine have continued without resolution. The interviews revealed that four employees have left and seven employees have been fired because of conflicts. The interviews further showed that most intercultural conflicts occur between expatriates and local managers.

The length of the tape-recorded interviews, conducted on the subsidiary premises, ranged from 30 to 90 minutes. All Danish, Norwegian, and Swedish expatriates and five Japanese managers were interviewed in English. Based on recommendations to conduct the interviews in native languages when possible (Marchan-Piekkari and Reis, 2004), all Finnish expatriates and three Japanese managers were interviewed in their native languages. To ease data comparison, the author translated these interviews into English. All interviews were transcribed and supplementary field notes were made within one day after the interview. In line with the established qualitative research protocol (Yin, 1994), the interviews were supplemented with observations and field notes. Individual or subsidiary names are not revealed as the managers were assured of confidentiality.

The interviews were analysed on the basis of guidelines provided by Miles and Huberman (1994). During the data reduction phase, the interviews were simplified to categories. In order of importance, categories for Research Question 1 were organizational changes, ethnocentricity, and differences in power and status and work behaviour; for Research Question 2, verbal persuasion, accommodation, and managerial changes; and for Research Question 3, separation and normalization. During the data display phase, the information was organized to draw conclusions. The regularities and patterns were used in the verification and conclusion drawing phase.

Intercultural conflicts in Nordic subsidiaries in Japan

Sources

Research Question 1 identifies the sources of intercultural conflicts in the visited Nordic subsidiaries. Interviews indicate that the sources of conflicts are organizational changes, ethnocentricity, differences in power and status, and work behaviour. These sources of conflicts were often interrelated.

Organizational changes

The attempts to initiate organizational changes or inability to implement them successfully were indicated as being one of the sources of intercultural conflict. While some changes are initiated as a natural part of the global agenda, expatriates identified several areas of organizational processes that were not according to their preferences. As one expatriate president explained: 'When a new president comes in, new things happen. I came into a situation in which things were not set up according to my management style.' Sources of several conflicts were changes in seniority-based promotion and compensation. One expatriate president, for example, noted that, 'Since last year there is no longer any salary revision for people over 40 years old, except if they are getting a promotion or doing an exceptionally good job.' Local managers resisted the changes in which compensation was tied to annual evaluations.

Accustomed to working in organizations with flat hierarchies, several expatriate presidents have sought to make structural changes, often unsuccessfully. According to one expatriate president:

> We have taken off organizational layers and tried to make this organization as flat as possible. However, it takes time because old local managers are still clinging to a seniority system that was abolished several years ago. Old managers here do not change their attitudes easily [...] they just wait.

Efforts to implement change were often unsuccessful simply because employees refused to change their behaviour. While several expatriates valued flat structures, verticality was identified by some experienced expatriates as an important element of well-functioning interaction in Japan. According to one expatriate, 'After working here for 20 years, my experience tells me it is better not to remove the hierarchy as the Japanese need a hierarchy to know who they are.' In addition to causing conflicts, flat structures were seen to create more confusion than increase organizational efficiency. Consequently, several expatriates expressed their deep frustration at being unable to transfer management systems because of cultural differences.

Expatriate roles of headquarter representatives were indicated as sources of conflict. Expatriates were sometimes placed in the unpleasant position of acting according to the headquarters' policy, even if this policy was not appropriate to the situation in Japan. An expatriate, working in a recently acquired company, indicated that he periodically received directives to hire and fire people. According to him:

> This does not fit with the Japanese mentality. Employees are negative about it and I have to act as a buffer between the headquarters and the Japanese operations. I have to justify our operations to the Americans and try to explain things to the Japanese. This is like being a middleman.

While expatriates can bargain with headquarters, some changes are executed uniformly as a part of global policies. Local employees in some cases were told by the expatriates to identify these 'irrational' organizational changes with them, thereby linking work roles to conflicts. The unfavourable attitudes and related conflicts tended to reinforce negative stereotypes and potentially increase divisions between local employees and expatriates.

Ethnocentricity

Ethnocentricity, defined as an attitude of superiority and uniqueness of one's home country, was indicated as a source of conflict. The attitudes of both expatriates and local employees can be considered ethnocentric. According to the expatriates, their ideas were frequently resisted or rejected based on the uniqueness of the Japanese market. As one expatriate president commented:

> I say that they [Japanese managers] are very concentrated on their home market instead of getting ideas from the outside and bringing them in. They think that Japan is special and things cannot be brought here from the outside.

The sources of conflicts were 'what can be implemented' and 'to what extent they can be implemented' in Japan. In several cases, local managers accepted little. For example, expatriates noted that 'the problem here is the "it-cannot-be-done-here syndrome," ' and that 'when you initiate changes, you hear people here saying that it will not work in Japan.' Although the expatriates note that they welcomed constructive task-related debates, disagreements backed by ethnocentric arguments were indicated as leading to gridlock situations. In contrast, some local managers said that especially inexperienced expatriates are insensitive to the local market requirements and often implement their ideas without respecting the opinions of more experienced local managers.

Several expatriate presidents shared their frustration with the constant and persistent resistance, often initiated by senior local manager(s). An expatriate president remarked that:

> It was resistance to all things. Resistance is not even the right word. It was shown by shrugging shoulders and saying 'difficult' or 'this is not the Japanese way' [...] all things have to be open for discussion. Shrugging shoulders and saying that 'we have tried that before' is unacceptable.

The market and legislative changes were seen by the expatriates to have opened up opportunities to foreign companies, requiring flexibility and the ability to make fast operational changes. One way to compete is to be faster than Japanese companies at capturing these new opportunities. Instead of seeking to capture the opportunities, local managers were described as being passive, past-oriented, and tended to cling to old practices. Although several expatriates acknowledged the importance of context sensitivity in Japan, they reasoned that similar business logic applied in all countries. It should be noted that few expatriates said that local managers became more open to external ideas because of the lengthy economic slow-down.

Customer relations are one area over which expatriates and Japanese managers often had conflicts. Local managers were described as establishing customer relations through frequent social interaction that was not always based on economic rationality. While the expatriates understood the importance of trust in customer relations, Japanese managers were seen as spreading resources too thinly to please a wide array of customers. Several expatriates noted that limited resources require an emphasis to be placed on customer segmentation with the focus on a few key customers. As one expatriate president reasoned, 'We have potentially 10,000 customers in Japan, but we cannot go after all of them.' He outlined that concentration on a few key customers made it possible to deliver better services.

Power

Expatriates are at the top of the organizational hierarchy, causing power to be unequally distributed between expatriates and local employees. Power alternations were indicated to occur when expatriate presidents replaced local manager(s). Both an unwillingness to accept the expatriates as subsidiary presidents and the local president's reluctance to accept his lowered status were sources of conflict in subsidiaries. As one expatriate president explained:

> We have a 60-year old Japanese general manager who has worked for this subsidiary for 30 years. He has been passed over three times. Because of our company's expatriate policy, he will not be promoted as a subsidiary president. He has told me: 'Why do we need foreigners? Why do we need you?'

While most subsidiaries can select either expatriates or local managers as presidents, positions are often filled by expatriates. Reasons for this, according to the expatriates, include problems with promoting local sales managers as presidents because of their lack of administrative experience, incomplete understanding of global operations due to lack of international experience, and inability to communicate with headquarters. As put by one expatriate president: 'While they are very good sales managers, they do not know how to make budgets and deal with human resources.'

Power changes and unequal distribution of power were frequent sources of conflict between expatriate presidents and the replaced local managers. Several expatriates outlined that the local managers were reluctant to accept a lower position in the hierarchy, sometimes creating a situation wherein 'expatriates find themselves in the middle of power battles when they are sent to Japan'. As one expatriate president commented:

> I knew from several discussions with him that my status was a problem. It was simply because I was the boss rather than him. It [conflict] was all about status.

Interviews show that replaced managers could seek to maintain their position informally. In one subsidiary, the former local president who had started up the operation and hired most of the employees remained as an executive director. The new expatriate president clashed with the old president at all levels. The expatriate president outlined that because of their dual roles, 'Employees did not really know what they should do with me.' Initial interactions with the expatriate president were cautious and some employees continued to report to both managers. According to the expatriate, 'I understand part of the problem as he started operations and was asked to move away. He has tried to retain control [...] I did not accept it, and this caused the conflicts.'

Work behaviour

Differences in work behaviour were indicated sources of conflict. As one expatriate reported, 'because people are used to working in a different way here, it is possible to go wrong from the beginning... frustration is what expatriates share because we are not used to working in the Japanese way'. Interviews indicate that slow decision-making and risk avoidance irritated especially young expatriates and those who had recently arrived. An expatriate president, accustomed to working for a multinational high-tech company, explained:

I am a very direct person and like to move fast. The Japanese are reluctant to take risks and make mistakes. Sometimes the result is that they do not do anything. That is not acceptable. It is a challenge to make things happen in that kind of environment.

Because of their work roles and desire for rapid decision-making, the expatriates tended to dominate discussions in meetings, often frustrating local managers used to consensus decision-making and informal consultation. One local manager expressed his frustration as: 'Expatriates are pushy and going for hasty decisions.' This manager noted in leaving the decision-making to the expatriates, along with the responsibility for the decisions.

Although several expatriates acknowledged that consensus decision-making was an important part of Japanese culture, time pressures required expatriates to make fast decisions. According to one expatriate president:

The problem is that expatriate managers cannot wait for a long time. Dictate for a two per cent market share can come [from headquarters] after being in Japan only one year. I get frustrated if changes here take too long.

To several expatriates, consensus decision-making was just an effective way to delay or block changes. Japanese managers were told to delay decision-making in the hope that the expatriates would eventually give up. The tendency for low risk-taking is captured by the statements, 'conflicts started when we started to expand because managers did not want to take any risks', and 'Japanese managers are not as ready to make big decisions as Europeans, causing conflicts.' In particular, managers recruited from large Japanese organizations were identified as not being used to working in subsidiaries with short decision times.

Behavioural differences in meetings were sources of frustration and conflict. Several expatriates commented that little was said to happen in these meetings due to language differences and the general hesitancy to express contrasting ideas. The interviews can be summarized by one expatriate's comment that, 'No one wants to talk about problems. It has to be something that really bothers them before they talk about it.' While lack of a common language was indicated as a reason for low interaction, interviews indicate that problems were not confined solely to language barriers. As revealed by one expatriate president:

There is a tendency in managerial meetings for them to say what I want to hear and then walk out and do something else. I have noticed sometimes that they [Japanese managers] do not do the things agreed upon in the meetings at all.

Considering silence from their Japanese counterparts to be an indication of consent, several expatriates thought that local managers had agreed only to find out later that little had happened after the meetings. Another expatriate noted that, 'I do not think that they [local managers] ever disagreed. This does not mean that they follow what I say.' The interviews indicate that conflicts have often been initiated by gaps between what is agreed upon and what is actually executed. One expatriate manager noted that, 'managers say first "yes" to the expatriate and then tell their subordinates "don't do this" or "I am against this proposal." ' Because of limited language skills and interaction with local employees, informal resistance and conflicts tended to exist unrealized for a long period of time.

The roles of local managers as informal leaders, and their central position in informal communication networks, created conflicts. In contrast to expatriates as formal leaders, local managers as informal leaders understand the goals and needs of local employees and thus frequently play critical roles as opinion leaders. Several frustrated expatriates detached from informal communication networks reasoned, for example, 'information is an important part of power in Japan' and '[Japanese] managers are afraid of giving away too much information.' Direct interaction with local employees was further indicated to create suspicion. An expatriate president explained this as 'passing middle managers is against the Japanese business culture'. In addition, divergent views of work roles were indicated as sources of conflict. An expatriate president noted that, 'When Japanese reach a certain age and managerial position; they feel entitled to not work anymore . . . we had conflicts about this issue.' Although local managers considered differentiated work roles as a hard-earned reward, expatriates tended to compare it to freeloading.

Conflict management

Research Question 2 describes conflict management. Interviews indicate that conflicts could remain unnoticed and their management delayed. When noticed, the expatriates used verbal persuasion, accommodation, and managerial changes to solve conflicts.

Verbal persuasion

Once conflicts were realized, most expatriates indicated that they would start to solve them by using verbal persuasion or other 'soft' methods. To maintain a functioning work relationship and retain important local managers, indirect ways of managing conflict were advocated. As one expatriate president explained:

> Conflicts were solved by talking, and solutions were normally reached within one day. It is also important to persuade other local managers through consensus, compromise-style. Managers start with different viewpoints and slowly shift closer to each other... if there is no harmony, work conditions deteriorate.

Instead of wishing that conflicts would fade away, proactive conflict management was important to restore social relationships. Based on one expatriate, 'I address conflicts as they come up because you do not know when conflicts are going to end.' Subtlety in conflict management was indicated to be important because the Japanese hesitate to talk about personal matters in public. Another expatriate said that, 'It is difficult to talk about conflicts in the office. These matters are talked about over drinks after work.' While several expatriates identified *nomikai* (after-work get-togethers in informal settings) as an effective method for solving conflicts, a few maintained 'dry' relations with local employees. One expatriate president explained, 'I am not active with employees after work... days for *nomikai* are over, at least in our company.' Instead of engaging in after-work interaction, several expatriates used work-related opportunities, such as long business trips, to solve conflicts with local managers.

Cultural differences were indicated to complicate conflict resolution through verbal persuasion, requiring frequent interactions and patience. Several expatriates admitted thinking prematurely that they had reached an understanding with Japanese managers. An expatriate president with 20 years of experience in Japan cautioned:

> It is a trap to believe that people have accepted the changes and go ahead. That is one way of causing confusion. At least you, yourself, get confused. It [persuasion] is a long procedure and requires a lot of communication back and forth. It is time-consuming and requires a lot of patience.

Allowing for some concessions during conflict management was important to show sensitivity to local wishes and to allow Japanese managers to save face. One expatriate noted that, 'There needs to be a balance between accommodation and forced changes.' This expatriate continued, saying, 'There are certain things about which I do not compromise and say that is the way that things are.' Frequent concessions were identified as making subsidiaries too local and creating an image of a weak expatriate president.

Accommodation

Some expatriates accommodated the wishes of local managers at their own expense in order to avoid conflicts and/or retain key managers. Instead of understanding this behaviour as a hesitancy to resolve conflicts in a proactive way, several expatriates complained that they lacked effective sanctioning systems. One expatriate president explained:

> I had two options. One was to cut a lot of heads. That is risky as people are not mean by their nature. There are various reasons for that kind of behaviour. These managers carry a lot of know-how and skills. Kicking them out would mean more damage than good to our business.

In several subsidiaries, key customer relations were controlled by one local manager. As these local managers had frequently started up the operations and created the customer relations, the expatriates considered them to be important to business and in possession of considerable power. One expatriate president explained the situation as, 'His control over business is so strong that if he leaves, it could breakup our operations in Japan. Strength is his bargaining chip.' Due to the lack of effective sanctioning mechanisms and the considerable power of these key local managers, they were able to challenge expatriate presidents and create blocks to organizational changes.

Instead of firing them, several expatriate presidents seek to persuade these managers verbally. One expatriate president explained the situation in this way:

> The only way to try to solve the conflict is to talk a lot with the man who is causing the problems... He is strong, controlling about 50 per cent of the business in this subsidiary. I can try to change him but I can never fire him.

This senior manager was having a negative impact on the organizational climate and was blocking changes. The local manager expressed his disagreement by 'hardly speaking in managerial meetings or looking sarcastic'. Conflict management, mainly through verbal persuasion, was unsuccessful in solving this conflict that had initially stemmed from power differences. The manager was fired after two years of continuing conflicts.

Managerial changes

The interviews indicate that conflicts between expatriate presidents and local managers tend to escalate over time. Verbal persuasion seldom produced desired results in conflicts flavoured by interpersonal animosity. When expatriate-initiated organizational changes were constantly blocked and conflicts continued without viable solutions, options were limited. As one expatriate president explained, 'It is sometimes necessary to take out people who do not change to allow others to grow and to get fresh ideas.' Another expatriate president, whose efforts were constantly blocked by one manager, related his experience:

> I did one thing that solved the problem of persistent resistance. I removed the obstacle. We have now a new manager. Having a new manager was not my original intention, but I came to that conclusion because operations were not going anywhere due to resistance to all new things.

This expatriate was sent to make changes in a subsidiary that was losing its market share. Due to personal animosity, change efforts were persistently resisted by one senior manager based on the 'it-cannot-be-done-here' argument, and the only feasible option was to fire the manager.

While often used as the last option, managerial changes were described as a quick and efficient way to solve conflict. Several expatriates felt that they were too tolerant; hoping that local managers would eventually change their behaviour and the conflicts would fade away. As conflicts reduce intercultural interaction, several expatriates noted that soft conflict management needed to be followed by managerial changes, preferably during the first six months. As one expatriate president expressed:

> It [firing the manager] should have happened a long time ago. We tried to find alternative solutions, but they did not work. People in the headquarters were afraid that customer connections would be severed if he left.

While managerial changes generally had a positive impact, half of the employees in the above case resigned in support of the local manager. The expatriate president explained that, 'He [dismissed manager] had an aura and magnetism to the staff and they left.' In this case, the consequences were greater than expected, largely because the dismissed manager had hired most of the employees and had established the customer networks. It can be assumed that this local manager had established close ties with most employees that expressed their disagreement with the expatriate manager by leaving the company.

Consequences

Research Question 3 identifies the consequences of conflicts. While most conflicts were solved successfully, some were ignored or remained unsolved due to cultural differences or other reasons, occasionally separating expatriates and local employees.

Separation

Unresolved conflicts can separate expatriates and local employees. Due to close local manager–subordinate relations and the lack of a shared language, one expatriate noted that, 'It is easy to keep foreigners outside [...] they [Japanese managers] do not tell him anything, not even the good news.' Another expatriate president warned that unsolved conflicts could create a dual organizational reality:

> If you have a situation, which some subsidiaries have, where the foreign and local sides of the organization are not overlapping, then you have two organizations in which the *gaijin* [foreigner] organization does not really know that there is a mirror organization that is running the business. It just looks like the *gaijin* decides.

One expatriate commented that interaction with front-line employees was limited as subordinates 'willingly or not adopt the same way of thinking' as their supervisors. Due to the gaps between what was agreed upon in meetings and what was executed in the subsidiaries, some expatriate presidents felt it necessary to monitor the subsidiaries to make sure that the changes took place. According to one expatriate, it was important 'to be involved in all the details to find out what is happening. Otherwise they [Japanese managers] mislead you in many ways.'

In subsidiaries with long unresolved conflicts, local employees were frequently allied behind one powerful manager. Because these managers were important for business, the expatriates tolerated the situation and sometimes simply waited for them to retire. One expatriate president described his position as:

> They accept that I am a company president, but they want to have someone on the Japanese side that is my parallel. I do not want this to happen, but they have formed this dual structure. They have the oldest manager as their representative.

In this subsidiary, interactions between expatriates and local employees had become too severed to use soft conflict management methods. The key local manager had emerged as an opinion leader in the subsidiary and was able to block expatriate-initiated changes. The expatriate president decided to wait for the manager's retirement and thereby leave the conflict unresolved. Another expatriate related that, during long conflicts flavoured by interpersonal animosity, 'social relations get frozen', decreasing interaction and making decision-making rigid and mechanical.

Normalization

In most subsidiaries, soft and hard conflict management methods have produced desired results. Based on the interviews, dismissals of dominant local managers have allowed some expatriates to resolve interpersonal conflicts, increase the organizational dynamics and restore their positions as subsidiary leaders. In several cases, external recruiting was effectively used to make organizational changes and increase diversity in management teams. Based on one expatriate president, hiring three managers in their mid-thirties was done in order 'to send a clear message that individuals with abilities are recruited and promoted'. To prevent conflicts from occurring again, several expatriate presidents have formed, for example, work councils, personnel committees, and other arrangements to increase information flows and to detect conflicts early.

Discussion

This chapter draws from the constructivist approach to provide a holistic perspective of the sources, management, and consequences of conflicts in Nordic subsidiaries in Japan. Although cross-cultural studies provide useful guidelines by which to make general predictions about groups of people in particular cultures, the interviews show that they are not accurate in intercultural settings. Instead of assuming that individual behaviour is solely determined by cultural values, this study indicates that intercultural conflicts are also socially situated, richly contextualized, and conditionally expressed.

Although cultural values partly influence an individual's response to external stimuli and guide conflict behaviours in intercultural settings, the interviews indicate that they are also influenced by idiosyncratic individual values and situational factors. On the one hand, this study indicates parallel to cross-cultural research that conflicts are exhibited as passivity and informal resistance in Japan (for example, Ohbushi and Takahashi, 1994; Oetzel and Ting-Toomey, 2003). This culture-specific behaviour can make the expatriates to interpret silence on the part of their Japanese counterparts as a sign of consent and thus fail to recognize conflicts. On the other hand, this study supports the constructionist approach by showing that personal factors and environmental events influence both the frequency and the nature of intercultural conflicts (Morris and Fu, 2001). For example, considerable differences among expatriates in their ability to understand the nuances of Japanese behaviour were detected. Situational factors were found both to initiate conflicts and shape conflict management. For example, the Japanese tendency for risk avoidance and slow decision-making was found to initiate intercultural conflicts when expatriates work under time pressure.

While often overlooked in the trait-based cross-cultural studies, different work roles and power were linked to conflicts and their management. This study indicates that an important task, especially to incoming expatriates, is to change organizational practices towards their preferences and initiate global policies in subsidiaries. While coordination and control are important reasons to transfer managers from the headquarters to foreign subsidiaries (Edström and Galbraith, 1977), several expatriate-initiated changes might have been incongruent to local cultural values. Context-insensitive changes might create conflicts between expatriates and Japanese managers who seek to promote themselves and protect their subordinates. The interviews indicate that work roles provide natural lines to organizational interaction along which conflicts tend to occur. In addition, balances of power and alternations in formal power were sources of conflicts between several incoming expatriate presidents and replaced Japanese managers. If replaced, local managers try to maintain their formal power or use their informal power to block expatriate-initiated change efforts with the consequence that conflicts on task-related issues slowly become more personalized and emotional. Indeed, the interviews indicate that several expatriates have been unsuccessful in combining their formal leadership roles with informal ones to gain support from local managers.

Another important factor shaping interpersonal conflicts is the number of involved expatriates and Japanese employees. Expatriates were numerical minorities in all visited subsidiaries and most conflicts were found to occur in subsidiaries with few expatriates. During conflicts, local managers tend to emphasize their numerical majority to stress their unified preferences and opposition. Expatriates can choose either to promote their preferences and disregard the opposing views or comply with the majority. If both local managers and expatriates promote their preferences without making compromises and the differences between the preferences are wide, there is no middle ground, nor is there a willingness to accept different preferences. A lack of converging preferences might escalate conflicts to a point where the opposing parties sharply reduce their interactions, fail to exchange information, and exhibit rigid decision-making. Another possibility is that expatriates as minorities comply with the majority preferences and act in contrast to their preferences and cultural values. As both approaches were detected, no clear pattern of distinctive Nordic conflict management styles emerged from the interviews.

Consistent with the social identity theory (Tajfel and Turner, 1986) and Japan-specific research (Matsuda, 1985); intercultural conflicts tend to reinforce social categorization. Although cultural differences do not always initiate conflicts, social categories based on cultural differences provide naturally occurring boundaries along which conflicts can be drawn. As most local employees have limited contacts with expatriates, comments from the interacting employees or organizational grapevine can reinforce negative stereotypes and further reduce intercultural interactions. For example, comments from a frustrated local supervisor affect the perceptions of his subordinates who have infrequent contacts with the expatriates. This second-hand information is frequently more exaggerated and polarized than first-hand information obtained through direct social interaction. During conflicts, small differences promote the perception of expatriates as out-group members who are less trustworthy, capable, and cooperative than in-group members. While the Japanese orientation of in-group and out-group categorization was shown in interviews, expatriates frequently engaged in similar behaviour. While several expatriates identified Japanese managers as sources of conflicts, no expatriate was identified as a source of conflicts.

This study shows further that conflict management is shaped by individual, cultural, and situational factors. Although few expatriates give little regard to cultural differences, most expatriates seek to manage conflicts through verbal persuasion, accommodation, and other host culture and/or situation-specific ways. Instead of deducing an assumption from cross-cultural studies that expatriates adopt conflict management styles congruent to their home cultures, most expatriates in this study have adopted conflict management styles contingent to local culture, consistent with the constructivist approach (Hong and Chiu, 2001), and claims that expatriates make efforts to act in ambiguous situations in ways that they think are meaningful to host nationals (Brislin, 1981). This implies that connections between an individual's cultural traits can be loosely connected to behaviour driven by situational factors. Expatriates, emphasizing situational factors, said they used verbal persuasion in situations in which a conflicting party was valuable to business operations and/or they had time to solve conflicts through such methods. The usage of formal power, including managerial changes, is prominent during power battles and time pressure. These findings consequently indicate that cultural values are integrated with situational factors in conflict management.

Overall, this study indicates that the sources, management, and consequences cannot be explained solely through the cross-cultural trait approach. Those studies are based on the assumption that individuals internalize culture in the form of broad motivational or attentional orientations – ever-present lenses that shape all social perceptions (Hong *et al.*, 2003). This assumption makes it hard for the trait approach to explain why people's cultures can affect them in one situation and then have no effect in the next situation. Although the trait approach suggests that intercultural conflicts are unavoidable due to cultural differences and that the conflicts are displayed and managed in culture-specific manners, the constructionist approach proposes that the sources of conflicts cannot be traced to a single source and do not follow the overly deterministic influence of national cultures of thought and action. However, if people tend to make partly contingent rather than culture-specific responses in real-life situations, then it becomes more complex predicting the role of cultural differences in an intercultural setting. While macro-level cultural directives play a role in terms of conflict frames and behavioural patterns, this study indicates that these interact with or are modified by numerous micro-level situational factors. From a critical perspective, an overarching theme of this book, it can be argued that conflict is to be anticipated due to a plurality of interest groups, and that culture mediates and shapes the emergence, manifestation, and resolution of conflicts.

Implications

The interviews provide several implications. First, as conflicts are partly influenced by cultural values, their acknowledgement can help to resolve conflicts before they have a detrimental impact on work relations. While Japan has been portrayed as a country with conflict avoidance and low conflict frequency (see e.g., Moran *et al.*, 1994; Ohbushi and Takahashi, 1994), value differences increase conflicts in Japan. Instead of interpreting conflict avoidance as low conflict frequency, Japanese employees tend to show conflicts in subtle ways, such as low risk-taking, passivity, and low interaction. Interviews show, for example, that several expatriates made the error of reading silence as an indication of consent. These cultural factors should be included as a part of pre-departure training.

Secondly, personality and broad experience-related knowledge should be emphasized in expatriate selection. Consistent with a study in which personality traits were found to be important in conflict management (see Caligiuri, 2000), a certain determination and toughness were indicated as being important in old, male-dominated subsidiaries. One expatriate president recommended, 'Send a manager who is tough to old subsidiaries. If you are too soft, you end up giving in.' A few expatriates indicated the existence of a 'testing period' of incoming expatriate presidents. In addition to masculine personality traits, flexibility, optimism, and humility facilitate conflict management. Instead of sending expatriates to Japan as part of their managerial training, they need to bring value-added knowledge to local operations. As one expatriate president explained, 'you are completely lost if you don't know better than the Japanese what you are doing'. This knowledge goes beyond the technical competence of expatriates.

Thirdly, more attention needs to be paid to establishing close relationships with local managers and to managing conflict. The interviews indicate that task interdependence between expatriates and local managers serves to decrease conflicts caused by cultural misunderstandings. Frequent interactions tend to decrease social categorization and increase the feeling of 'we'-ness characterized by a strong organizational identification. Mediated conflict resolution is a useful alternative to personal attempts to manage conflicts. Based on scholars (Leung, 1987; Ting-Toomey, 1988), collectivists prefer informal third-party conflict mediation. Help should first be sought from someone informed about the conflict situation and whom both parties trust and respect. Internal mediators, however, can be difficult to find, as conflicts tend to divide organizations in two.

Conclusions and limitations

This chapter described the sources, management, and consequences of intercultural conflicts in Nordic subsidiaries in Japan. The findings imply that intercultural conflicts cannot solely be explained using the relatively stable and context-independent effects of cultural values on thought and action. In addition to differences in language, nonverbal behaviours, values, norms, attitudes, rules, and other cultural manifestations, intercultural conflicts are influenced by individual and situational factors. In addition, the minority role of expatriates can potentially increase in-group and out-group categorization, accelerating conflicts and complicating their management. Most expatriates seek to solve conflicts through verbal persuasion and accommodation. Running out of alternatives, expatriates use their formal power to fire managers. While most conflicts have been managed successfully, some conflicts have led to the isolation of expatriates from the Japanese side of the organization.

This study has limitations. First, conflicts and their management are influenced by organizational culture (Schneider and Northcraft, 1999). Although the methodology used does not allow for definite predictions about the impact of organizational culture, it needs to be taken into account in future research. Secondly, people have a tendency to see themselves as being better than others (Miller and Ross, 1975), causing local managers to be perceived as the primary sources of conflicts and vice versa. In order to reduce self-serving biases, the Japanese perspective should be elaborated in future studies. At the beginning of this research, eight local managers were interviewed, but the interviews were terminated because of lack of transparency. While expatriates exhibited little reluctance to discuss conflicts, Japanese managers were hesitant and answered in indirect ways. Thirdly, beliefs that certain cultural characteristics are associated with certain behaviours can become self-fulfilling prophesies (Snyder, 1984) to the effect that perceived linkages between cultural values and behavior reflect stereotypical images. This problem is inherent in all qualitative studies.

Acknowledgements

I thank Patricia Robinson, Diana Sharpe, and Christian Fjäder for their valuable comments on earlier drafts of this chapter.

Notes

1. Task conflict refers to conflicts which arise over substantive issues (such as differences of opinion or ideas about the correct way to approach a task or solve a problem), and relationship conflict refers to socioemotional/interpersonal disagreements that are usually associated with feeling of annoyance and animosity (Jehn, 1995).
2. In-groups are groups of individuals about whose welfare a person is concerned, with whom that person is willing to cooperate without demanding equitable returns, and separation from who leads to anxiety. Out-groups are groups of individuals with which one has something to divide, perhaps unequally, or are harmful in some way, groups that disagree on valued attributes, or groups with which one is in conflict (Triandis, 1995: 9).

References

Adler, N.J. and Graham, J.L. (1989) 'Cross-Cultural Interaction: The International Comparison Fallacy?', *Journal of International Business Studies*, 20: 515–35.
Austin, J.R. (1997) 'A Cognitive Framework for Understanding Demographic Influences in Groups', *International Journal of Organizational Analysis*, 5(4): 342–59.
Brannen, M.Y. and Salk, J.E. (2000) 'Partnering Across Borders: Negotiating Organizational Culture in a German–Japanese Joint Venture', *Human Relations*, 53(4): 451–87.
Brislin, R.W. (1981) *Cross-Cultural Encounters: Face-to-Face Interaction.* New York: Pergamon.
Caligiuri, P.M. (2000) 'Selecting Expatriates for Personality Characteristics: A Moderating Effect of Personality on the Relationship between Host National Contact and Cross-Cultural Adjustment', *Management International Review*, 40(1): 61–80.
Doi, T. (1986) *The Anatomy of Self.* Tokyo: Kodansha.
Doucet, L. and Jehn, K.A. (1997) 'Analyzing Harsh Words in a Sensitive Setting: American Expatriates in Communist China', *Journal of Organizational Behavior*, 18: 559–82.
Edström, A. and Galbraith, J.R. (1977) 'Transfer of Managers as a Coordination and Control Strategy in Multinational Organizations', *Administrative Science Quarterly*, 22: 248–63.
Eisenstadt, PE. (1990) 'Pattern of Conflict and Conflict Resolution in Japan: Some Comparative Indicator', in S.N. Eisenstadt and Ben-Ari (Eds.), *Japanese Models of Conflict Resolution.* London: Kegan Paul International, pp. 51–70.
Feldman, D.C. and Arnold, H.J. (1983) *Managing Individual and Group Behaviour in Organizations.* New York: McGraw-Hill.

Fiske, S.T. and Taylor, S.E. (1991) *Social Cognition*, 2nd ed., New York: McGraw-Hill.

Gudykunst, W.B., Ting-Toomey, S. and Chua, E. (1988) *Culture and Interpersonal Communication*. Newbury Park, CA: Sage.

Hambrick, D.C., Li, J., Xin, K. and Tsui, A. (2001) 'Compositional Gaps and Downward Spirals in International Joint Venture Management Groups', *Strategic Management Journal*, 22: 1033–53.

Harzing, A. (2001) 'Who's in Charge?: An Empirical Study of Executive Staffing Practices in Foreign Subsidiaries', *Human Resource Management*, 40(2): 139–58.

Hogg, M.A. and Terry, D.J. (2000) 'Social Identity and Self-Categorization Processes in Organizational Context', *Academy of Management Review*, 21(5): 121–40.

Hong, Y., Benet-Martinez, V., Chiu, C. and Morris, M.W. (2003) 'Boundaries of Cultural Influence: Construct Activation as a Mechanism for Cultural Differences in Social Perception', *Journal of Cross-Cultural Psychology*, 34(4): 453–64.

Hong, Y. and Chiu, C. (2001) 'Toward a Paradigm Shift: From Cross-Cultural Differences in Social Cognition to Social-Cognitive Mediation of Cultural Differences', *Social Cognition*, 19(3): 181–96.

Jehn, K.A. (1995) 'A Multimethod Examination of the Benefits and Detriments of Intragroup Conflict', *Administrative Science Quarterly*, 40: 256–82.

Keller, L.M., Bouchard, T.J., Arvey, R.D., Segal, N.L. and Dawis, R.W. (1992) 'Work Values: Genetic and Environmental Influences', *Journal of Applied Psychology*, 77: 79–88.

Krauss, E.S., Rohlen, T.P. and Steinhoff, P.G. (1984) 'Conflict and its Resolution in Postwar Japan', in E.S. Krauss, T.P. Rohlen and P.G. Steinhoff (eds), *Conflict in Japan*. Honolulu: University of Hawaii Press, pp. 3–15.

LaFrance, M., and Mayo, C. (1978) *Moving Bodies, Nonverbal Communication in Social Relationships*. Monterey: Brooks/Cole.

Landis, D. and Wasilewski, J.H. (1999) 'Reflections on 22 Years of the International Journal of Intercultural Relations and 23 years in other Areas of Intercultural Practice', *International Journal of Intercultural Relations*, 23: 535–74.

Lebra, T.S. (1985) 'Nonconfrontational Strategies for Management of Interpersonal Conflicts', in E.S. Krauss, T.P. Rohlen, and P. G. Steinhoff (eds), *Conflict in Japan*. Honolulu: University of Hawaii Press, pp. 41–60.

Leung, K. (1987) 'Some Determinants of Reaction to Procedural Models for Conflict Resolution: A Cross-National Study', *Journal of Personality and Social Psychology*, 53: 898–908.

Leung, K., Tramain Koch, P. and Lu, L. (2002) 'A Dualistic Model of Harmong and Its Implications for Conflict Management in Asia', *Asia Pacific Journal of Management*, 19(2/3): 201–20.

Marschan-Piekkari, R. and Reis, C. (2004) 'Language and Languages in Cross-Cultural Interviewing', in R. Marschan-Piekkari and D. Welch (eds), *Handbook of Qualitative Research Methods for International Business*. Cheltenham: Edward Elgar, pp. 224–43.

Matsuda, N. (1985) 'Strong, Quasi- and Weak Conformity among Japanese in the Modified Ash Procedure', *Journal of Cross-Cultural Psychology*, 16: 83–97.

Miles, M.B. and Huberman, A.M. (1994) *Qualitative Data Analysis*. London: Sage.

Miller, D.T. and Ross, M. (1975) 'Self-serving Biases in the Attribution of Causality: Fact or Fiction?', *Psychological Bulletin*, 82: 213–25.

Miyahara, A., Kim, M-S., Shin, H-C. and Yoon, K. (1998) 'Conflict Resolution Styles among "Collectivist" Cultures: A Comparison between Japanese and Koreans', *International Journal of Intercultural Relations*, 22(4): 505–25.

Moran, R.T., Allen, J., Wichman, R., Ando, T., and Sasano, M. (1994) 'Japan', in M.A. Rahim and A.A. Blum (eds), *Global Perspectives on Organizational Conflict.* Westport, CT: Praeger, pp. 33–52.

Morris, M.W. and Fu, H. (2001) 'How Does Culture Influence Conflict Resolution? A Dynamic Constructivist Analysis', *Social Cognition*, 19(3): 324–49.

Nakane, C. (1971) *The Japanese Society.* Berkeley, CA: University of California Press.

Oetzel, J.G. and Ting-Toomey, S. (2003) 'Face Concerns in Interpersonal Conflict: A Cross-Cultural Empirical Test of the Face Negotiation Theory', *Communication Research*, 30(6): 599–624.

Ohbushi, K. (1998) 'Conflict Management in Japan: Cultural Values and Efficacy', in K. Leung and D. Tjosvold (eds), *Conflict Management in Asia Pacific: Assumptions and Approaches in Diverse Cultures.* Singapore: John Wiley & Sons, pp. 49–72.

Ohbushi K. and Takahashi, Y. (1994) 'Cultural Styles of Conflict', *Journal of Applied Social Psychology*, 24: 1345–66.

Peltokorpi, V. (2006) 'Japanese Organizational Behavior in Nordic Subsidiaries: A Nordic Expatriate Perspective', *Employee Relations*, 28(2): 103–18.

Peltokorpi, V. (2007) 'Intercultural Communication Patterns and Tactics: Nordic Expatriates in Japan; *International Business Review*, 16(1): 68–82.

Pinkley, R.L. and Northcraft, G.B. (1994) 'Conflict Frames of Reference: Implications for Dispute Processes and Outcomes', *Academy of Management Journal*, 37: 193–205.

Schneider, S.K. and Northcraft, G.B. (1999) 'Three Social Dilemmas of Workforce Diversity in Organizations: A Social Identity Perspective', *Human Relations*, 52: 1445–67.

Smith, P.B., Dugan, S., Peterson, M.F. and Leung, K. (1998) 'Individualism: Collectivism and the Handling of Disagreement: A 23 Country Study', *International Journal of Intercultural Relations*, 22(3): 351–67.

Snyder, M. (1984) 'When Belief Creates Reality', in M.P. Zanna (ed.), *Advances in Experimental Social Psychology*, vol. 18. Orlando: Academic Press, pp. 247–305.

Stage, C.W. (1999) 'Negotiating Organizational Communication Cultures in American Subsidiaries doing Business in Thailand', *Management Communication Quarterly*, 13: 245–80.

Tajfel, H and Turner, J.C. (1986) 'The Social Identity Theory of Intergroup Behavior', in S. Worchel and W.G. Austin (eds), *Psychology of Intergroup Relations.* Chicago: Nelson-Hall, pp. 7–24.

Takeuchi, R., Wang, M. and Marinova, S.V. (2005) 'Antecedents and Consequences of Psychological Workplace Strain during Expatriation: A Cross-sectional and Longitudinal Investigation', *Personnel Psychology*, 58: 925–48.

Ting-Toomey, S. (1994) 'Managing Intercultural Conflicts Effectively', in L.A. Samovar and R.E. Porter (eds), *Intercultural Communication: A Reader.* Belmont: Wadsworth Publishing, pp. 360–72.

Ting-Toomey, S. (1988) 'Intercultural Conflict Styles: A Face-Negotiation Theory', in Y. Kim and W. Gudykunst (eds), *Theories in Intercultural Communication.* Newbury Park CA: Sage, pp. 213–35.

Tinsley, C. (1998) 'Models of Conflict Resolution in Japanese, German and American Cultures', *Journal of Applied Psychology*, 83: 316–23.

Triandis, H.C. (1995) *Individualism and Collectivism*. Boulder, CO: Westview Press.

Triandis, H. (1986) 'Collectivism vs Individualism: A Reconceptualization of a Basic Concept in Cross-Cultural Psychology', in C. Bagley and G. Vernma (eds), *Personality, Cognition, and Values*. London: MacMillan, pp. 60–95.

Weldon, E. and Jehn, K.A. (1995) 'Examining Cross-Cultural Differences in Conflict Management Behaviors: A Strategy for Future Research', *The International Journal of Conflict Management*, 6(4): 387–403.

Yamagishi, T. (1988) 'The Provision of a Sanctioning System in the United States and Japan', *Social Psychology Quarterly*, 51: 265–71.

Yin, R. (1994) *Case Study Research: Design and Methods*, 2nd edn. Beverly Hills, CA: Sage.

3
Asian Collectivism and Ethical Decision-making

Fuan Li

Introduction

Research concerning the impact of culture on ethics has been largely focused on identifying similarities and differences in moral judgement and ethical behaviours across cultures. By exploring how Collectivism and Individualism (C-I) affect moral thinking and ethical behaviour, this chapter goes beyond simple observations and seeks to formulate a theoretical explanation of cultural effects on ethical decisions. This can enhance our understanding of business ethics across cultures and, accordingly, provide guidance to international and transnational businesses.

This chapter focuses on the relevance of culture to moral and ethical concerns. In recent years, there has been an increase in interest in Asian business ethics amongst both academics and practitioners. Empirical studies reveal that culture and socioeconomic conditions in Asian countries place constraints on codes of ethics and have significant influences on ethical perceptions, values and moral standards (Rashid and Ho, 2003). It has been suggested that the long-term nature of relations among Asians result in an ethics that extend far beyond the limited idea of rights and duties (Koehn, 1999). Different moral principles, behavioural standards, and ethical values may lead to dramatic contrasts in moral judgements and choices when facing ethical dilemmas (Thorne and Saunders, 2002).

To understand the impact of Asian culture on business ethics we need to go beyond identifying similarities and differences across cultures and to focus on the underlying mechanism that explains how culture affects business ethics. This chapter attempts to do that by contrasting individualistic and collectivistic views of ethics and looking into the impacts of collectivism, the dominant cultural orientation in Asia, on ethical decision-making. Collectivism and individualism (C-I) concern one's view of self (identification), others and the world. Individualism takes an atomistic understanding of human beings (Koehn, 1999) and considers each person as a discrete, independent individual who is responsible for his or her own well-being. Social relationships are thus derivatives of the independent individuals who interact with others for mutual benefits and follow mutually agreed-upon principles, such as equality, noninterference (privacy) and equity (Hofstede, 1991; Triandis, 1995). In contrast, collectivism considers individuals as living in a matrix of interrelated, highly determinate relations (for example, parent–child, superior–subordinate, peers and friendship, and so on.). Collectivism emphasizes relationships, interdependence, and social context (Triandis and Gelfand, 1998). To collectivists, the interests and needs of the group assume priority whenever conflicts exist between personal needs and the needs of the group. Given the sharp contrast between individualism and collectivism and the importance of the issues involved, C-I are often considered as the cultural dimension revealing fundamental cultural differences (Triandis, 1995; Triandis and Gelfand, 1998). By concentrating on this single dimension, we attempt to be more focused in our inquiry to achieve a better understanding of the impact on ethics of culture.

Now let us look at the ethical decision process and the role individualism and/or collectivism plays in the process. We will examine two different routes through which C-I affect the ethical decision-making process and discuss the effect of C-I on each component of ethical decision-making.

Ethical decision process and the role of individualism/collectivism

As Rest (1994) describes, a model of moral action involves four components: ethical sensitivity, prescriptive reasoning, deliberative reasoning, and ethical character. Ethical sensitivity refers to the awareness that the resolution of a particular dilemma may affect the welfare of others. Such sensitivity initiates the ethical reasoning process by identifying an ethical dilemma. Following dilemma identification, individuals engage in reasoning that gives rise to prescriptive judgement, which specifies what should or should not be done in solving the dilemma. Next, a person assesses alternative courses of actions and formulates an intention to act through deliberative reasoning. Finally, the ethical choice consistent with his or her prescriptive judgement will lead to ethical behaviour provided he or she has a strong ethical character. The intention to act may not materialize if a weak-willed person is unable to follow through his or her chosen course of actions. Adopting Rest's model of moral action (or moral decision), this chapter proposes that the moral decision process begins with moral dilemma identification, proceeds to prescriptive judgement and assessment of alternative courses of actions, and then moral choice is made that further leads to ethical actions (See Figure 3.1).

As shown in Figure 3.1, C-I may influence ethical decisions through two routes. First, C-I may have direct effects on ethical perception, prescriptive judgment, moral choice and behaviour. Second, C-I may affect the structure of moral judgement through its impact on moral development; thus, indirectly influencing ethical behaviors.

We expect collectivism and individualism to have a direct effect on ethical decision-making. Previous research has revealed sharp contrasts

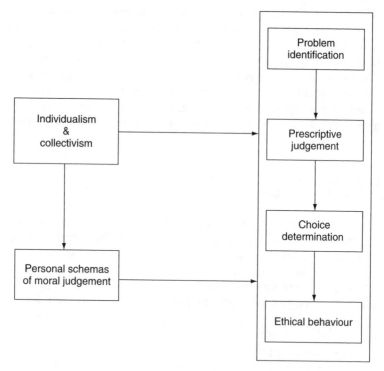

Figure 3.1 The impact of C-I on ethical behaviour

between collectivists and individualists in their value systems. Individualists place great values on autonomy, independence, freedom, self-enhancement, hedonism, competition, the desire to be distinguished and/or simply emotionally distant from the in-group; they emphasize being curious, open-minded, creative and having an exciting and varied life. In contrast, collectivists value personalized relationships, family security, harmonious social relationships, group cohesion, social order, and respect for tradition (cf. Triandis, 1995; Earley and Gibson, 1998; Fukuyama, 1995). Values are enduring beliefs that specific modes of conduct (behaviour) or end states of existence (life goals) are preferable. Thus, the value system has important implications for behavioural standards. Given the discrepancy in value systems between collectivism and individualism, collectivists and individualists may differ from each other in their ethical standards and, consequently, perceived acceptable behaviours. For example, lack of consensus on acceptable behaviours was observed in Swinyard, Rinne and Kau's (1990) empirical study of ethical orientations in software piracy. Since the collectivistic culture in Asia emphasizes sharing and reciprocity, the individual artist or writer is expected to share his or her creation with others. Accordingly, making copies of software is not considered as wrongdoing, but acceptable. This is in contrast to the belief held by individualistic cultures, where emphasis is placed on protecting the artist or writer's copyright. In their experimental study, Singapore management students were found more likely than American students to make copies of software, even though they had greater knowledge of software laws. Therefore, we propose that Asians' collectivistic cultural orientation will directly impact their moral perception, judgement and ethical behaviour.

Secondly, moral psychologists have long regarded ethical behaviour as being determined by moral judgement derived from moral reasoning (Kohlberg, 1969; Trevino, 1992). Building on Kohlberg's moral development model, Rest and colleagues (2000) examine the construction of basic moral categories (for example, justice, duties, legitimate authorities, and rights) and propose three distinctive schemas of moral judgement: the personal interest schema, the maintaining norms schema, and the postconventional schema. Although adhering to Kohlberg's sequential approaches, they argue that different schemas lead to different moral judgements and, consequently, people at various stages of moral development may behave differently. Because moral development as part of the socialization process is primarily a process of acquiring cultural values, norms, and behaviour standards (Narvaez, Getz, Rest and Thoma,

1999), we propose that C-I may affect ethical decisions through its power of shaping the structure of moral judgement. In fact, previous research has revealed that moral judgements differ widely across people, cultures, and historical periods. Cultural psychologists (Shweder, 1990; Shweder and Haidt, 1993) argue that different cultures have different ways of moral talking: some (that is, individualistic cultures) emphasize autonomy – concerns about freedom, rights, harm, and justice while others (that is, collectivistic cultures) stress community – concerns about duty and the collective enterprise. Given the collectivistic nature of Asian culture, we may expect that community-oriented ethical talking are more likely to occur in Asians' moral thinking.

More importantly, difference in moral talking or ethical values may extend to postconventional schemas. According to Rest *et al.* (2000), essential to postconventional thinking is that moral obligations are based on shared ideals or abstract and universal principles. Kohlberg and Wasserman (1980) propose: 'at heart, these are universal principles of justice, of the reciprocity and equality of human rights, and of respect for the dignity of human beings as individual persons' (p. 562). The idea of evaluating morality in terms of universal rights, justice, equality and fairness assumes autonomous individuals who undertake self-imposed obligations that apply to all (Gilligan, 1982). In contrast, collectivists view themselves as inherently interdependent (Triandis, 1995) rather than as independent of others. They attach much value to their relationships with others. When examining Chinese relationalism, Ho (1991, 1998) argues that scholars need to conduct relational analysis and consider how relationships are culturally defined before interpreting individuals' behaviours. This so-called methodological collectivism represents the most recent wisdom in exploring the alternative postconventional thinking. The relational perspective emphasizes a duty to care for relationships with others (Gergen, 1999; Ma, 1988). It seems that the principles of caring, love, brotherhood and community (Shweder and Haidt, 1993) are more likely to be at the heart of collectivists' postconventional moral thinking.

Drawing on previous research, I propose that C-I may affect moral behaviour by influencing the process of moral development and, consequently, the nature of moral schemas (Rest *et al.*, 2000), which in turn determine the structure of moral judgement and affect individuals' moral reasoning. That is, the process of moral development and the nature of moral schemas will mediate the effect of Asian collectivism on ethical decision making as well as behaviour.

Effect of Asian collectivism on moral behaviour

Our fundamental assumption about the direct and indirect effect of C-I on ethical decision processes holds that C-I not only determine the nature of moral schemas but also affect moral behavior along with schemas of moral judgement. Examination of the impact of C-I on each component of the ethical decision process follows.

Ethical sensitivity

First, compared with individualists, collectivists might have different perceptions when faced with an ethical dilemma. Ethical decision-making begins with the perception that a particular problem falls within the moral domain (Rest, 1986; Trevino, 1986). Moral domain refers to a set of activities that are subject to judgements of right and wrong. Thus, recognition of an action subject to moral judgement activates the ethical decision process. Individuals from a given culture may include certain business practices within the moral domain, and exclude others. Thus, C-I influence decision-makers' perception of acceptable or unacceptable business practices.

Given their emphasis on behavioural norms and the importance they assign to virtues (Slingerland, 2001), Asians as collectivists generally have great expectation of ethical behaviours and are more likely to be sensitive to ethical issues. For example, in addition to performance and group maintenance, Chinese leaders are expected to be role models of moral character. Accordingly, not only must he or she have positive attitudes towards and be committed to the job and the organization, but he or she must also be honest and trustworthy, must care about organization members, and must help others solve their personal problems. The high expectation concerning morality perhaps helps to explain the findings of Vitell, Nwachukwu and Barnes (1993) that informal norms and formal codes of ethics are likely to have more influence in collectivistic countries than in individualistic countries.

If collectivists are more likely to take into consideration the vested interest of the collective in a given situation, and if the relationship focus among collectivists leads to greater concerns for the interests of others, then collectivists ought to have a greater tendency to identify ethical dilemmas. This is because an ethical dilemma is based on the premise of a conflict of interest between the parties involved and such a conflict would be more likely when the number of interested parties (multiple stakeholders) increases. Thus, decision-makers in Asia are more likely to identify the existence of an ethical dilemma in a broader range of situations than are those from cultures with individualistic orientations.

Moreover, collectivists are more likely to define themselves in terms of group membership and to place great value on its welfare. Collectivists would perceive a behaviour to be unethical if it impairs relationship harmony or harms group welfare (Triandis, 1995). In contrast, in an individualistic culture, people are more likely to perceive themselves as autonomous and place a higher value on their individual interests. While duty, hierarchy, and interdependency are at the crux of a collectivistic moral domain, harm and rights form the basis of an individualistic moral domain (Shweder, 1990). For example, favouritism in hiring towards children of its own employees is commonly practiced by businesses in India without violating their sense of morality (Donaldson and Dunfee, 1999). Such a practice falls within the moral domain in an individualistic culture because it causes harm to autonomous individuals, specifically qualified candidates for the particular job who are not children of the employees.

The above analysis suggests that although they are generally more concerned with ethical issues, collectivists may be less sensitive to certain ethical dilemmas, especially when a questionable action appears to be in favour of the collective. This is confirmed by Moon and Franke (2000), who demonstrated that Koreans were generally more sensitive to ethical problems in sales practices than US sales personnel. However, Koreans were less sensitive to ethical problems involving questionable fees than were the US practitioners. These findings are consistent with the ethical implications of Hofstede's cultural dimension. Individuals in Asia thus are more likely to be sensitive to questionable business practices, especially those that adversely affect group welfare. In contrast, individuals in an individualistic culture are more likely to be sensitive to business practices that adversely affect personal interests.

Moral judgement and reasoning

Individualists and collectivists should differ in formulating the ideal ethical judgement that ought to occur in a given situation. They may disagree on what is the right thing to do in a variety of ways. First, in individualistic cultures, individuals tend to place priority on achieving personal goals over group goals given their emphasis on self-interest. For individualists, the meaning of life lies in personal success and fulfillment (e.g., self-sufficiency and self-glorification), which are essential for self-esteem and, consequently, more important than his or her relationships with the group. Thus, individualists are more likely than collectivists to activate the personal interest schema in moral reasoning and formulate prescriptive judgement by focusing on personal concerns and, perhaps, concerns for those with whom they have close relationships.

In contrast, collectivists have stronger institutional norms and structures that may reinforce individual's consideration of multiple stakeholders when formulating prescriptive judgement. In collectivistic cultures, individuals are more likely to give priority to group interest. This suggests that individuals in Asia would be more likely to consider the broader needs of society in addition to their own needs. Apparently, C-I influence the formulation of prescriptive judgement. Accordingly, unlike their individualistic counterparts, individuals in Asian collectivistic culture are less likely to use the personal interest schema in moral reasoning.

The maintaining norms schema advanced by Rest and colleagues is equivalent to Kohlberg's conventional moral reasoning, which is based on conformity to socially defined standards (Colby and Kohlberg, 1987). The maintaining norms schema emphasizes social expectations, existing practices and established rules and norms including compliance with duties to uphold the law. In individualistic cultures, decision-makers tend to place priority on personal beliefs and attitudes. In collectivistic cultures, individuals feel a greater obligation to comply with socially shared norms, others' expectations and duties to the in-group (Triandis, 1995). Collectivists tend to respect and accept the customs and ideas of traditional cultures such as humility, devotion, obedience, and self-control. Previous research has demonstrated that members of collectivistic cultures tend to stress impulse control and are more likely to live up to peer expectations and to agree about what constitutes correct actions (Triandis, 1995; Hofstede, 1991). For instance, one of the salient features of Confucianism is its emphasis on virtues – defined as traditionally proper behaviour or the correct way of living. Virtuous behaviour towards others consists of not treating others as one would not like to be treated oneself (Fukuyama, 1995; Ho, 1976). More importantly, being virtuous is to behave according to social requirements and social norms deemed appropriate to a person's social position (Ho, 1976). Virtues are essential to saving face because saving face means to demonstrate virtuous behaviour, such that he or she can meet others' expectation and satisfy what is required by social norms. Being a person of virtues and not losing face are keys to gaining social acceptance, approval, and maintaining harmonious relationships. Given the importance assigned to being virtuous and complying with social norms, the maintaining norms schema should play a significant role in Asian moral thinking. Consequently, compared to individualists Asians may have a greater tendency to utilize the maintaining norms schema. That is, relative to individualists, collectivists are more likely to use the maintaining norms schema in their moral reasoning.

Ethical choice and behaviour

Asian collectivism may moderate the relationship between moral judgement and behavioural choice because of its views concerning the relationship of beliefs and norms. The observed differences in values between collectivism and individualism suggest different attitudes towards social norms. Because a person in a collectivistic culture is supposed to be responsible for his or her family, clan, community, and even society in which he or she lives in addition to taking responsibility for him- or herself, collectivists emphasize the collective interest of the in-groups and feel a moral obligation of conforming to established behavioural norms. As a result, collectivists may be more susceptible to social norms and interpersonal influences than individualists when deliberating on which course of action to take in resolving a particular ethical dilemma. Given that, we expect that individuals in Asia are more likely to choose a course of action that is consistent with social norms and/or others' expectations in a given situation. In contrast, believing in internal locus of control and driven primarily by internal needs, perceptions and attitudes, individuals in an individualistic society are more likely to form ethical intentions consistent with their moral schemas and personal philosophy rather than social norms. In short, compared to individualists, collectivists in Asia are more likely to make a choice with a greater concern for others' expectations and social norms.

The different attitudes towards social norms and personal beliefs imply that Asians may behave differently in carrying through the ethical choice. After a person makes a judgement about whether or not a particular action is ethical, the person engages in behaviour that may or may not be consistent with his or her judgement. In a collectivist society such as China, proper behaviors rather than attitudes are important. As previously stated, Confucianism (Ho, 1976; Hwang, 2000) emphasizes sensitivity to others' perceptions, conformity to norms, and restraint of actions and impulses likely to upset or harm others. Individuals in the Chinese culture would be less likely to carry out a chosen behaviour (ethical choice) if there happens to be a conflict between the choice and social norms or there exists opposition from significant others. In collectivistic cultures, people may have personal beliefs (private self) that differ significantly from the group norm (public self), but still behave in accordance with the group norm. In a similar manner, they also expect others to conform to social norms and are unwilling to tolerate even slight deviations from established behavioral norms.

In contrast, it is internal needs, perceptions (Iwao and Triandis, 1993) and attitudes rather than concerns for group harmony or social norms that determine individuals' behaviour in individualistic cultures. Previous research indicates that there tends to be greater consistency between personal attitudes and behaviours for individuals in individualistic cultures than in collectivistic cultures (Volkema, 1998). People are rewarded for independent actions and creativity; conforming to the established norms and maintaining group solidarity are not particularly encouraged. Moreover, individualistic cultures often have multiple, sometimes conflicting norms about what to do. Those who deviate from norms are thus not necessarily punished. Therefore, in individualistic cultures people are more likely to behave in accordance with judgements formulated as a result of moral reasoning than will their collectivist counterparts. In summary, individuals in Asia are less likely to exhibit consistency between their moral judgment/choice and their behaviour.

Situational influences in moral thinking

Finally, compared with individualists, collectivists' moral behaviour may vary drastically with different situations. Hampden-Turner and Trompenaars (1993) found that a majority of American managers believe that each person has his or her own destiny and moral direction. Because people in individualistic cultures tend to hold the locus of control internal and believe that moral responsibility lies in each individual, they are highly likely to fulfill their intentions to act ethically (Trevino, 1986). In addition, individualism regards individuals as universal entities and advocates understanding, appreciation, and protection for the welfare of all people. As a result, individualists hold that the moral principles and social norms are equally applicable to all individuals. Therefore, individuals from individualistic societies are more resistant to situational influences and more likely to engage in ethical actions that are consistent with their ethical beliefs, judgments and personal moral philosophy.

In contrast, individuals' ethical behaviour in a collectivistic culture may vary with the context and situations. Unlike individualists who value universalism, collectivists' morality is more likely to be 'contextual' (Triandis, 1995: 77). Viewing individuals' behaviours as concrete, relational, and bound in behavioural contexts, collectivists downplay abstract principles and allow moral judgements to vary according to circumstances. For instance, lying violates social norms and is a serious offence to individualists, but it may be acceptable for collectivists. Confucius' (collectivistic) perspective emphasizes social cohesion, conformity to social norms, and stresses harmonious relationship (Hofstede, 1980). Therefore, lying may not necessarily be viewed as unethical, especially in a situation in which it may help achieve social cohesion and/or benefit the in-group. Therefore, it seems reasonable to say whether collectivists carry out a chosen ethical action depends upon whether or not it is consistent with established social norms and/or viewed to be beneficial to the groups.

With their emphasis on relationships and circumstances, collectivists may change ethical judgement according to the party involved in a particular situation. Triandis (1995) argues that in interpersonal relationships, the norms and values for in-group members are different from and sometimes opposite to the norms for outsiders. Equality or needs are the basis for allocating resources among in-group members who are expected to cooperate, reciprocate, make sacrifices, and protect each other's interests. However, such behavioural norms and the emphasis on collective welfare and duties typically apply only to the in-group and do not extend to out-groups. When dealing with out-group members, collectivists, just like individualists, primarily use the equity norm (to each according to his/her contribution). Thus, one who fails to adhere to the equality norm would be held accountable in a situation in which resources are allocated within the in-group, but not when it involves dealing with out-groups.

Previous research also reveals that there are more differences between the public and private settings in a collectivistic culture than there are in an individualistic culture. For collectivists, a transgression of social norms is often seen as an action of little importance as long as the behaviour is unknown publicly and has no impact on a person's in-group. For instance, actions that are considered inappropriate in Japan do not worry most Japanese unless the perpetrator is found out and this leads to public dishonour. Only when the transgression becomes public, and then threatens the in-group's honour, does the transgression assume great importance (Fukuyama, 1995). To recapitulate, relative to individualists' behaviours that are more likely to be consistent across situations, individuals' behaviours in Asia are more likely to be contextual and vary with situations.

Concluding comments

The effect of culture on business ethics has been a great concern for both international businesses and global marketers. Although well documented in the current literature, it has not received as much attention as it deserves. By adopting a New Kohlbergian approach this chapter delineates two different routes in which collectivism and individualism may affect moral thinking and ethical behaviour. In addition to their direct impacts on ethical decision-making, C-I also affect individuals' ethical behaviour through their role in moral development because individuals' schemas of moral judgement that result from the moral development process determine their moral reasoning and ethical behaviours. Moreover, C-I may affect ethical behaviours by moderating the effect of moral schemas on ethical decisions as illustrated by the different tendencies of Asian collectivists in utilizing the personal interest schema and/or the maintaining norms schema. The explicit delineation of different routes through which C-I influence ethical behaviour offers an explanation for observed differences between Asian collectivists and people living in an individualistic society, which should facilitate our understanding of how cultural differences impact moral reasoning and ethical judgement.

Based on the assumption of both direct and indirect impacts of C-I, this chapter further details the impact of collectivism and individualism on moral thinking and ethical behaviours. These discussions have close relevance to ethical practices and may provide valuable insights for international businesses and global marketers. For example, given Asians' selective view of what is ethical and what is unethical, international businesses should pay close attention to the domain of ethics as defined by Asians because what is acceptable in an individualistic culture may be viewed as unethical and, similarly, an action regarded as unethical may be well accepted by Asians. Furthermore, the contextual view of morality held by collectivists implies collectivists may differ from individualists in the extent to which they adhere to the codes of ethics. Given the universalism held by individualists and the emphasis on abstract principles rather than specific context in a given situation, those in an individualistic culture would be less likely to violate international codes of ethics. However, the notion of a self-regulated profession seems to be based on an individualistic value that professionals should maintain their allegiance to the code of a more abstract and more distant profession (Cohen, Pant and Sharp, 1992). Given their emphasis on relationship networks and tendencies to identify themselves with the in-group, family or company, individualists in Asian countries may be less likely to adhere to professional guidance, including the codes of ethics. That is, the differences in role orientation suggest that collectivists may be ready to break rules when it is in the best interest of the in-group. This certainly affects the degree to which they adhere to the international codes of ethics.

In this chapter we have examined the impact of Asian collectivist culture on business ethics, especially ethical decision-making. Going beyond identifying similarities and differences in moral judgement and ethical behaviours across cultures, we have explored different routes through which C-I affect moral thinking and ethical behaviour, thus, providing a theoretical explanation of cultural effects on ethical decisions. This chapter should enhance our understanding of business ethics across cultures and, accordingly, provide guidance to international and transnational businesses who have a presence in Asia or conduct businesses with Asians. Needless to say, the cultural issues discussed here are by no means exhaustive. Further examination of cultural impacts on ethical behaviour is still required.

References

Cohen, J.R., Pant, L.W. and Sharp, D.J. (1992) 'Cultural and Socioeconomic Constraints on International Codes of Ethics: Lessons from Accounting', *Journal of Business Ethics*, 11(9): 687–700.
Colby, A. and Kohlberg, L. (1987) *The Measurement of Moral Judgment*. Cambridge, UK: Cambridge University Press.
Donaldson, T. and Dunfee, T. (1999) *The Ties That Bind: A Social Contracts Approach to Business Ethics*. Boston, MA: Harvard Business School Press.
Earley, P.C. and Gibson, C.B. (1998) 'Taking Stock in Our Progress on Individualism-Collectivism: 100 Years of Solidarity and Community', *Journal of Management*, 24(3): 265–304.
Fukuyama, F. (1995) *Trust: The Social Virtues and Creation of Prosperity*. New York: Free Press.
Gergen, K.J. (1999) *An Invitation to Social Construction*. London: Sage Publications.
Gilligan, C. (1982) *In a Different Voice*. Cambridge, MA: Harvard University Press.
Hampden-Turner, C. and Trompenaars, A. (1993) *The Seven Cultures of Capitalism*. New York: Currency Doubleday.
Ho, D. (1976) 'On the Concept of Face', *American Journal of Sociology*, 81: 867–84.
Ho, D. (1991) 'Relational Orientation and Methodological Relationalism', *Bulletin of the Hong Kong Psychological Society*, 26/27: 81–95.
Ho, D. (1998) 'Interpersonal Relationships and Relationship Dominance: An Analysis Based on Methodological Relationalism', *Asian Journal of Social Psychology*, 1: 1–16.

Hofstede, G. (1980) *Culture Consequences: International Differences in Work-Related Values*. Beverly Hills, CA: Sage.

Hofstede, G. (1991) *Culture and Organization: Software of the Mind*. London: McGraw Hill.

Hwang, K.K. (2000) 'Chinese Relationalism: Theoretical Construction and Methodological Considerations', *Journal of the Theory of Social Behavior*, 30(2): 155–78.

Iwao, S. and Triandis, H.C. (1993) 'Validity of Auto- and Heterostereo Types among Japanese and American Students', *Journal of Cross-Cultural Psychology*, 24(4): 428–44.

Koehn, D. (1999) 'What Can Eastern Philosophy Teach Us About Business Ethics?', *Journal of Business Ethics*, 19(10): 71–9.

Kohlberg, L. (1969) 'Stage and Sequence: The Cognitive Developmental Approach to Socialization', in D.A. Goslin (ed.), *Handbook of Socialization Theory and Research*. Chicago: Rand-McNally.

Kohlberg, L., Levine, C. and Hewer, A. (1983) 'Moral Stages: A Current Formulation and a Response to Critics', in J.A. Meacham (ed.), *Contributions to Human Development*, vol. 10. New York: Karger.

Kohlberg, L. and Wasserman, E.R. (1980) 'The Cognitive–Developmental approach and the Practicing Counselor: An Opportunity for Counselors to Rethink Their Roles', *The Personnel and Guidance Journal*, May, pp. 559–67.

Ma, H.K. (1988) 'The Chinese Perspectives on Moral Judgment Development', *International Journal of Psychology*, 23: 201–7.

Moon, Y.S. and Franke, G.R. (2000) 'Cultural Influences on Agency Practitioners' Ethical Perceptions: A Comparison of Korea and the US', *Journal of Advertising*, 29(1): 51–65.

Narvaez, D., Getz, I., Rest, J.R. and Thoma, S.J. (1999) 'Individual Moral Judgment and Cultural Ideologies', *Developmental Psychology*, 35(2): 478–88.

Rashid, M.Z.A. and Ho, J.A. (2003) 'Perceptions of Business Ethics in a Multicultural Community: The Case of Malaysia', *Journal of Business Ethics*, 43(1/2): 75–87.

Rest, J.R. (1986) *Moral Development: Advances in Research and Theory*. New York: Praeger Publishers.

Rest, J.R. (1994) 'Background Theory and Research', in J. Rest and D. Narvaez (eds), *Moral Development in the Professions* Hillsdale: Erlbaum and Associates.

Rest, J.R., Narvaez, D., Thomas, S.J. and Bebeau, M.J. (2000) 'A Neo-Kohlbergian Approach to Morality Research', *Journal of Moral Education*, 29(4): 382–95.

Rokeack, Milton (1973) *The Nature of Human Values*. New York: Free Press.

Shweder, R.A. (1990) 'In Defense of Moral Realism: Reply to Gabennesch', *Child Development*, 61: 2060–7.

Shweder, R.A. and Haidt, J. (1993) 'The Future of Moral Psychology: Trust, Intuition, and the Pluralist Way', *Psychological Science*, 4(6): 360–5.

Slingerland, E. (2001) 'Virtue Ethics, The Analects and the Problem of Commensurability', *Journal of Religious Ethics*, 29(1): 97–125.

Swinyard, W.R., Rinne, H. and Kau, A.K. (1990) 'The Morality of Software Piracy: a Cross Cultural Analysis', *Journal of Business Ethics*, 9(8): 655–65.

Thorne, L. and Saunders, S.B. (2002) 'The Socio-Cultural Embeddedness of Individuals' Ethical Reasoning in Organizations (Cross-Cultural Ethics)', *Journal of Business Ethics*, 35(1): 1–14.

Trevino, L.K. (1986) 'Ethical Decision in Organizations: A Person-Situation Inter-
actionist Model', *Academy of Management Review*, 11 (3): 601–18.

Trevino, L.K. (1992) 'Moral Reasoning and Business Ethics: Implications for
Research, Education, and Management', *Journal of Business Ethics*, 11(5),
445–59.

Triandis, H.C. (1995) *Individualism and Collectivism*. Boulder, CO: Westview Press.

Triandis, H.C. and Gelfand, M.J. (1998) 'Converging Measurement of Horizontal
and Vertical Individualism and Collectivism', *Journal of Personality and Social
Psychology*, 74(1): 118–28.

Vitell, S.J., Nwachukwu, S.L. and Barnes, J.H. (1993) 'The Effects of Culture on
Ethical Decision-Making: An Application of Hofstede's Typology', *Journal of
Business Ethics*, 12 (October): 753–60.

Volkema, R.J. (1998) 'A Comparison of Perceptions of Ethical Negotiation Behavior in Mexico and The United States', *International Journal of Conflict Management*, 9(3): 218–33.

4
Assignment China: Three Factors Influencing the Effectiveness of Western Managers

Daniel W. Lund and Michelle C. Barker

Introduction

The economic emergence of China in recent years, along with its 2001 entry into the World Trade Organization, has made it a valued destination for business expatriates and brought the issue of cultural adjustment and expatriate managerial effectiveness in China to the forefront of management literature (http://www.wto.org; Lau, 2006). As the differences between Chinese and western organizational management and business practices are considerable, so is the need to have a critical understanding of how western expatriate managers can work with these differences in order to increase their effectiveness as managers in China (Hutchings, 2003; Lund and Barker, 2004; Bond, 1991; Blackman, 1998; Phillips and Pearson, 1996). This need is emphasized by seemingly inconsistent studies, which find western expatriate failures in China to range broadly between 25 and 70 per cent (Ralston *et al.*, 1995; Hendry, 1994; Shay and Bruce, 1997; Valner and Palmer, 2002; Tung, 1981, 1984; Garonzik *et al.*, 2000; Milkovich and Newman, 1996; Harzing, 2002; Selmer, 2002). Such 'failure' is commonly defined as the early departure of expatriates, whereby financial losses can be calculated or inferred, due to disrupted operations or damage to business relationships caused by the expatriate's low commitment levels, or cultural improprieties committed by the expatriate (Garonzik *et al.*, 2000; Harzing, 2002; Hutchings, 2003; Milkovich and Newman, 1996; Selmer, 2002). Short-to long-term costs for expatriate failures are estimated to range between US$250,000 and US$1,000,000 per expatriate, for some larger multinational organizations (Valner and Palmer, 2002; O'Boyle, 1989). Studies examining western expatriate failures and the costs associated with these failures in smaller Chinese-owned organizations, however, are lacking, as are studies examining the factors affecting the managerial effectiveness of western expatriates working in such organizations (Lau, 2006). These failures could detrimentally affect the expatriates, their families, and the organizations and local economies in which they work, along with the business relationships and reputations of expatriate colleagues who remain in the organization, or who are brought in to replace them. Empirical research is needed, therefore, in this emergent area of international business management, to provide a deeper understanding of the factors which influence the managerial effectiveness of western expatriates working in locally-owned organizations in China.

The present study explores the phenomenon of managerial effectiveness, as it relates to a group of western expatriates working in a private, Chinese-owned, academic college in South-east China. Interviews were conducted with the college's six expatriate department and administrative heads. In addition, a survey was administered to 17 of the western expatriate teachers in the organization. The expatriates' perceptions of their own managerial effectiveness and the factors which influence their effectiveness are examined. First, the concept of managerial effectiveness is discussed, followed by an examination of the notions of cross-cultural effectiveness of managers and the effectiveness of western managers in China. Analyses of the interview and survey studies are then presented. As part of a larger study on the cross-cultural adjustment, managerial effectiveness, and organizational commitment of expatriates in China, the present investigation addresses the problem of high expatriate failure rates in China, as it relates to the managerial effectiveness of the participant managers. The data and their analysis incorporate and add to previous research conducted within the larger study (Lund and Barker, 2004).

Managerial effectiveness

The effectiveness of a manager can be viewed in terms of effective or ineffective work-related behaviours that are assessed in relation to a manager's ability to accomplish specified organizational requirements (Drucker, 1967, 2001; Wood *et al.*, 2004). Effectiveness can also be understood as the demonstration of how a manager's proficiency in job-related knowledge, skills, and abilities promotes the advancement of organizational goals (Gillard and Price, 2005; Boyatzis, 1982). The criteria used to assess a manager's effectiveness, however, as well as the choosing of individuals assigned or techniques designed to rate them, can be problematic (Shay and Baak, 2004; Barrett, 1966; Latham and Wexley, 1994;

Gregersen *et al.*, 1996). Intentional or unintentional rater bias may vary widely, depending upon who the rater is and what effect, if any, the assessment outcomes have upon them (Shay and Baak, 2004; Rastogi and Vandana, 2004). Flores and Utley (2000) suggest that assessment techniques alone, although useful, are inadequate for measuring or ensuring managerial effectiveness, which they argue to be a key component of organizational effectiveness. Likewise, Sandholm (1999) argues that adherence to popular assessment techniques, without specific integration into an organization's ongoing strategic plan, may provide only moderate improvements. Although problematic, definitions and assessment of managerial effectiveness can help to determine, at least in part, the health of an organization.

Some authors argue that the most influential factors for determining a manager's effectiveness relate to what a manager does and how they do it (Drucker, 1967, 2001; Wood *et al.*, 2004), while others emphasize the organizational and environmental contexts in which the manager works (Deming, 1982; Page *et al.*, 2003). For example, Deming (1982) argues that organizations need to be transformed into effective working environments in which managerial effectiveness can flourish, before the effectiveness of a manager can be duly assessed. Again, however, rater bias in defining and assessing effective working environments could be problematic. Despite differing perspectives about the nature of effectiveness, it is commonly agreed in the literature that managerial effectiveness results from a manager's efforts to satisfy the strategic goals of the organization. The term 'satisfying' implies that the goals are achieved in such a way that promotes the overall aims of the organization (Page *et al.*, 2003). Managerial effectiveness, therefore, can be broadly defined as the ongoing satisfying of organizational goals through the purposeful efforts of individual managers.

Cross-cultural effectiveness of managers

As with managerial effectiveness, there is little agreement in the literature regarding the factors affecting the cross-cultural effectiveness of managers or of the criteria used to assess such effectiveness. Coleman (1995, 1998, 2000), with the development of the *Emotional Intelligence Index* for determining global managerial leadership competence, contends that 90 per cent of the difference between average and highly effective managers is due to emotional intelligence, as opposed to cognitive abilities. The factors of cross-cultural competence that make up the *Emotional Intelligence Index* are self-awareness, self-regulation, motivation, empathy, and social skills (Coleman, 1995, 1998, 2000). Managers with acceptable attributes in each of these areas are considered more likely to be effective managers and, therefore, have increased suitability for foreign postings.

In contrast, Kraimer *et al.* (2001), building on stress management and social support theories, take a more situational-specific approach to expatriate managerial effectiveness, arguing that perceived organizational support and supervisory support are the most influential factors affecting the managerial effectiveness of expatriates (Feldman and Brett, 1983; Fisher, 1985; Pinder and Schroeder, 1987). Further, Van Der Zee and Van Oudenhoven (2000), using their *Multicultural Personality Questionnaire*, argue that openness, emotional stability, social initiative and flexibility are the four personality traits most pertinent for assessing and predicting international orientation and inspiration and, therefore, cross-cultural managerial effectiveness. However, Black *et al.* (1991) contend that managerial effectiveness is a factor of expatriate adjustment and that the five most influential factors affecting adjustment, and therefore managerial effectiveness, are pre-departure training, previous foreign experience, organizational selection mechanisms, individual skills, and non-work factors. Non-work factors include overall dispositions towards cultural adventuring and the degree of support received from spousal and/or familial relationships (Black *et al.*, 1991). Shay and Baak (2004) argue, however, that studies linking adjustment and effectiveness are largely unsubstantiated and often based on self-assessments, which are inherently susceptible to same-source bias. While such bias could affect data adversely, depending upon the chosen research methodology, it is also recognized that some methodologies construct theory based primarily on interpretations of participants' individual perceptions and self-assessments (Denzin, 2001; Strauss and Corbin, 1998).

A number of studies also identify positive correlations between spousal relationships and expatriate adjustment (Adler, 2002; Aycan, 1997; Black, 1988; Black and Gregersen, 1991; Black and Stephens, 1989; Caliguiri *et al.*, 1998; Feldman and Brett, 1983; Fisher, 1985; Pinder and Schroeder, 1987). Kraimer *et al.* (2001), in particular, found positive correlations with expatriate adjustment and managerial effectiveness, thereby establishing links between spousal relationships, expatriate adjustment, and managerial effectiveness. Further research, however, is needed to determine the extent to which such findings can be applied to the context of expatriates working in China. An overview of managerial effectiveness, in terms of western expatriates in China, follows.

Effectiveness of western managers in China

The values associated with the management of workplace and home relationships differ considerably between the collectivist and Confucian styles of China and the individualistic styles of western nations. Numerous studies have explored these differences from a western perspective in recent years, while studies examining this area from a distinctly Chinese perspective are either lacking or not readily available in western-based literature (Lau, 2006; Bond, 1991; Phillips and Pearson, 1996; Zhu *et al.*, 1998; Selmer, 1998; Fan, 2000; Tung and Yeung, 1998; Luo, 2000; Tung, 1982, 1989; Hitt *et al.*, 2002; Blackman, 1998; Luo, 2002). Western expatriates working in China must navigate and contend with these vast cultural differences on a daily basis.

While knowledge of and adherence to Chinese cultural norms does not necessarily guarantee business success for expatriates in China, Tung (1982, 1989) argues that ignoring cultural differences, particularly those associated with relationships, nearly always guarantees the failure of any venture. This notion is echoed by Hitt *et al.* (2002), who found the nurturing of Confucian relationships to be necessary for the advancement of any foreign venture in China. These relationships are based on the Confucian model of placing one individual in respectful duty-based subordination to another. In descending order of import-ance, these relationships include those between sovereign and subject, father and son, husband and wife, elder and younger, and friend and friend (Fan, 2000). Each relationship is joined by a corresponding principle governing that relationship: loyalty and duty, love and obed-ience, obligation and submission, seniority and modelling subject, and trust (Fan, 2000).

Disrupting organizational harmony or causing conflict of any kind in the workplace is highly cautioned against in much of the literature, which argues that the managerial effectiveness of expatriates in China is largely dependent upon one's ability to grasp at least an introductory understanding of Chinese society (Osland and Bird, 2000; Kay and Taylor, 1997; Bond, 1991; Luo, 2000; Tung and Yeung, 1998).

Managerial effectiveness summary

Expatriate failures in China are argued to be a costly phenomenon for some multinational organizations, while the impact of such failures on smaller, locally-owned, Chinese organizations is unknown. A variety of theories have been put forth, designed to predict or support the notion of effective managers in western and cross-cultural contexts. Studies exploring the managerial effectiveness of expatriates in China, however, particularly those working in locally-owned organizations, are few. It is argued throughout the literature that western expatriates working in China need to attain at least a basic level of cultural understanding, in order to be effective in China.

To addresses the research gaps in this area, the present study is an inferential exploration into the phenomenon of managerial effectiveness, as identified through the self-reported experiences of a sample of western expatriate managers working in a private, Chinese-owned, academic college in South-east China. The aim of the study is to gain a deeper understanding of the factors which influence the managerial effectiveness of the expatriates. The study is guided by the sample-specific research question of: *What are the factors most influential to the managerial effectiveness of the western expatriate managers working in the private, Chinese-owned, academic college in South-east China?*

Interview study with expatriate managers

The interview study was comprised of six 30–60-minute semi-structured, telephone interviews with the six senior expatriate managers in the organization. The interview data were recorded electronically and transcribed immediately after each interview. Transcriptions were then reviewed multiple times until distinctly identifiable categories and themes emerged (Strauss and Corbin, 1998). At the time of the interviews, the college employed six senior expatriate managers, 22 expatriate teachers, and approximately 200 Chinese teachers, administrators, general staff, and executive managers. All of the expatriates were from western countries.

The demographic details of the interview participants are as follows: (1) Alan is a 56–65-year-old male and is the most senior-ranked expatriate in the College. He has a Bachelors degree and has lived in China with his wife and teenage son for more than ten years. Alan has also worked extensively in other developing countries and speaks Mandarin at an intermediate level; (2) Jill is a 35–40-year-old single female. She is a department head, has a Masters degree, and has lived with her adult son in China for three years. She has no other developing country experience. Jill and her son speak advanced Mandarin; (3) Larry is a 36–45-year-old male, department head, who has a Bachelors degree and has worked in China with his wife and their young son for three years. Larry has not worked in any other developing country, and has no

Chinese language skills; (4) Michael is a 70–75-year-old male. He is a senior manager in the college, has a Masters degree, and has lived alone in China for one year while his wife remains in England with their adult children. Michael worked for two years in another developing Asian country before arriving in China. He has no Chinese language skills; (5) Ned is a 46–55-year-old male and a department head. He has no formal tertiary education but has extensive business consultant experience. He and his wife have been in China for less than one year. He also worked in another developing Asian country for one year, before arriving in China. He has no Chinese language skills; (6) Sam is a 26–35-year-old male, department head, with a Masters degree. He is single and has worked in China for one year. Sam previously worked in another developing Asian country for two years. He has no Chinese language skills.

In the larger study, of which this investigation is a part, each manager was asked to respond to the following three questions: (1) *How do you define managerial effectiveness for yourself while working in China?;* (2) *What would be an effective day as a manager for you here in China?;* and (3) *How do you think your managerial effectiveness could be increased?* The present investigation focuses on the third question, which aims to identify the processes and interactions that the managers perceive as being most influential to increasing their managerial effectiveness within the organization. The participants' responses to this question consistently involved the three categories of *organizational and cultural harmony, hierarchical relationships,* and *spousal and/or familial relationships.* Each category emerged with equal importance. For the exploratory purposes of the study, these categorizations are used as organizational tools from which a body of knowledge may be constructed.

Organizational and cultural harmony

The expatriates consistently emphasized the need for maintaining organizational and cultural harmony within the college, in order to maintain and increase what they perceived to be their own managerial effectiveness. Of the six managers, only Sam expresses that he feels sufficiently effective as a manager in the college: 'It's fine', he explains, 'no problem. They [the Chinese executive] have no complaints. I don't argue. They tell me this, I do this.' Sam clearly indicates that he feels effective as long as he is able to maintain a sense of harmony within the organizational hierarchy. Alan, likewise, espouses the maintaining of hierarchical harmony within the College, while recognizing that his effectiveness could be increased:

> It could always improve, I suppose. With the Chinese [executive], you never know what they're up to. I don't figure it out. I just let it flow and it does. Just keep your head down, placate the powers at least every second day or so and always make them look good. (Alan)

Alan and Sam perceive their managerial effectiveness to be linked to the degree to which they are able to maintain organizational and cultural harmony within the college. Sustaining or improving their effectiveness, therefore, is partially dependent upon how well they can maintain a sense of harmony within the organization.

Jill's concept of effectiveness is partially based upon the extent to which she can avoid culturally offending her Chinese colleagues: 'Luck. If I'm lucky, then I won't be disrupting anyone's face. If you embarrass anyone, that's it. You're credibility for them is over. It's serious for them. Very serious.' Jill's reference to 'luck' indicates her uncertainty for how to increase her own managerial effectiveness within the College, apart from avoiding situations that may embarrass her Chinese colleagues.

Ned refers to the issue of working in China as 'the Chinese culture game of learning what offends and what doesn't'. He states that he 'won't play that game', revealing his resistance to adapting his own behaviours in order to maintain a sense of organizational or cultural harmony within the College. 'If I wanted to play the game', he says, 'I could be effective here.' Ned recognizes the need for adapting to the cultural norms of his Chinese environment in order to be effective, but consciously refuses to adapt.

Larry cites the attaining of 'Chinese language skills' as a factor that would likely increase his effectiveness as a manager in the college. This also reveals his adversarial disposition of mistrust towards his Chinese colleagues, as he says that such skills would enable him to 'understand what they are saying in front of [his] face every day'. He further explains that 'some of it, I'm told, is pretty insulting towards us [expatriates]'. Larry partially links the enhancement of his managerial effectiveness with his ability to know what his Chinese colleagues are saying in his presence every day. With Chinese language skills, he would be able to monitor and respond to what he suspects to be instances of disrespect and organizational disharmony.

Michael, perceiving that he is ineffective in the college, indicates that there is 'nothing more' he can do to increase his effectiveness, apart from trying to 'start again in another organization' elsewhere. 'I'm not effective here', he states, 'I won't be effective here. I can't be.

They need me but they don't see it.' Michael focuses on his own inef-fectiveness and his Chinese colleagues' inability to recognize what he perceives to be their need for his contributions. 'When I first arrived, they ate up my words like honey', he says, 'It was beautiful. They loved me. Now they don't even look at me in the halls. It's awful.' The apparent change in Michael's reception within the college indic-ates a dispositional movement from one of harmony to one of awkward disharmony. Michael also repeatedly mentions his wife and expresses his admiration for her: 'If she were here', he says, 'things would be better. She knows how to deal with this sort.' Besides revealing the diffi-culty that he is having being separated from his wife, this statement further confirms the troubles that he is having maintaining harmonious working relationships within the College. An analysis of the influences of spousal and/or familial relationships on the managerial effectiveness of the expatriates follows.

Spousal and/or familial relationships

Each of the managers, except for Alan, consistently refers to the importance of their spousal and/or familial relationships for helping them effectively adjust to living and working in China. Alan, for unstated reasons, made no direct mention of his wife or adult son. Michael, however, clearly states that he misses his supportive wife, who is living in England: 'I miss my wife... I haven't seen her for three months. I need her.' Michael's 'need' for his wife could be for purposes of personal consolation or to help him restore favour, as he indicates 'She knows how to deal with this sort.'

Ned, having acknowledged that his refusal to 'play the Chinese game' adversely affects his effectiveness as a manager in China, praises his supportive wife, who was with him for the first few months in China, before leaving to deal with family matters:

> That's why it was so good to have my wife here. I could tell her everything, so didn't feel the need to tell anyone else. I could stay out of trouble. You have to guard your words here. They can be used against you. Sometimes you just need someone to share with. (Ned)

Within the trust and safety of his spousal relationship, Ned was able to share his thoughts about working in the college in a manner that satis-fied his need to express himself. He clearly indicates that having such an outlet protected him from saying things in inappropriate contexts to others within the organization. Ned's spousal outlet essentially protected him from having his words re-spoken and used against him in an adversarial manner. Having someone to 'share' or 'vent' with is a core element of Ned's reflection on having his wife with him: 'If I wanted to play the culture game, I would need her to vent with at the end of each day... and maybe even find something funny in it to laugh about.' While acknowledging his ineffectiveness as a manager in China, Ned recognizes that he could be effective in the college if he attempted to honour and maintain organizational and cultural harmony. To achieve this, he says that he would need his spouse with him, in order to have a safe and trusted ally to 'vent' and 'laugh' with about the situations that they encounter on a daily basis.

Larry, likewise, acknowledging the value of his spousal relationship, perceives much of his effectiveness to be attributable to the support of his spouse:

> The first thing, the most important for my sanity... physical, emotional, intellectual, and spiritual sanity, is my wife. We've been here together, sharing the hardships and the good times. She's my comrade. I couldn't do it without her. (Larry)

Larry also values the 'sharing' component of his supportive spousal relationship. He asserts that his relationship with his wife is the 'most important' overall influencing factor for his personal well-being in China. His spousal relationship could also be a factor for his managerial effectiveness, as supportive spousal relationships have been found to be a positive predictor of expatriate adjustment and, therefore, managerial effectiveness (Adler, 2002; Kraimer *et al.*, 2001; Black *et al.*, 1991).

Although not married, Jill lives with her adult son and clearly stresses the importance of his companionship for her overall adjustment and emotional sustainability:

> If it wasn't for his company, I couldn't do it. No way. I couldn't handle it. Not alone. It's too disrupting. We talk about everything. Without that breakdown person, winding down, unwinding... getting the garbage out that happens in the day and letting each other know it's just a job. Need that. Seriously. (Jill)

Jill, as with Ned and Larry, emphasizes the importance of having someone to debrief with each day. She stresses the importance of her relationship with her son, in terms of her overall adjustment, and indicates that she 'couldn't handle it' without her son to 'unwind with' each day. Jill's connection with her son fulfils elements of the *aid, affect,* and *affirmation* that Kraimer *et al.* (2001) attribute to spousal relationships.

Sam, while firmly stating that he is sufficiently effective in the organization, admits that he misses his family:

> It's lonely here. Of course it is. I miss my whole family. Friends here are OK for a laugh but you can't trust them. If I had a wife, not Chinese, from my own culture, life would be sweet. (Sam)

Sam confesses to having personal difficulties as he misses trustworthy familial and romantic relationships with people from the western culture. Although he clearly asserts that he is 'lonely', he earlier implies that he is sufficiently effective in his job, thereby indicating that he may not perceive a connection between his overall adjustment and his managerial effectiveness. By stating that the friendships he has developed in China are 'OK for a laugh' but lack the element of 'trust' that he desires, Sam indicates an element of dissatisfaction with some aspects of his relational adjustment processes of living and working in China.

Hierarchical relationships

Besides emphasizing the importance of maintaining organizational and cultural harmony within the college and of having supportive spousal and/or familial relationships, the expatriates also emphasize the need for establishing and maintaining strategic relationships within the organization's hierarchical structure. Each of the six managers explains their approaches to hierarchical relationships and how having or not having such relationships can either help or hinder their efforts to effectively accomplish managerial tasks. Sam and Alan, for example, approach hierarchical relationships in a manner that involves regularly placating the Chinese executive in the college. Sam specifically focuses on task accomplishment and unquestioned compliance, in order to maintain his hierarchical relationships:

> They [the Chinese executive] don't have a clue about my job and they don't care... as long as it gets done. So I do it and learn the lesson of smooth relations. 'Yes' is the word for managerial effectiveness in China. Yes, yes, yes. (Sam)

Alan also stresses the need for maintaining ongoing relationships with the Chinese executive and does so by making 'little calls to the executive at night'. He contends that 'everything flows smoothly' when he does this. 'They like to know they're in control', he says, further establishing his placating approach for dealing with the executive. Sam and Alan use terms like 'flows smoothly' and 'smooth relations' as indicators of having effective hierarchical relationships. By submissively appeasing the Chinese executive without argument, Sam contends that he can maintain effective hierarchical relationships, as long as he continues to fulfill his organizational duties. Likewise, Alan says that by letting the Chinese executive 'know they're in control' by way of evening phone calls, he can let them know that he clearly understands his own position within the hierarchy. With similar approaches, Sam and Alan emphasize the recognition and appeasement of hierarchical relationships within the organization as an important means of maintaining their own effectiveness.

Larry strongly agrees with the need to establish and maintain hierarchical relationships within the college, although he is more focused on attaining methods for employee control than on honoring or placating the Chinese executive:

> There is no survival unless you are connected with a [Chinese] person in authority who has power. That is everything here. My higher-up connections are able to make things go smoothly for me as I deal with the Chinese administration... meaning that because of social pressure from [above], things go smoothly. (Larry)

Larry contends that his relationships with the Chinese executive help things 'go smoothly' for him with the Chinese administrative staff. He views 'smooth' functioning to be a product of the social pressure that can be applied on his behalf to have certain tasks accomplished. Larry, therefore, perceives his managerial effectiveness to be intimately linked to the degree to which he is able to establish and utilize hierarchical relationships within the organization.

Jill, although not specifically referring to relationships with the Chinese executive of the college, acknowledges the need to be 'good' to people at all levels in the organization. By doing so, she contends that she will likely be more able to fulfill her managerial tasks and feel more effective as a manager:

> The people who hold the power here are the people who can get things done... mainly Chinese. They're at all levels from the cleaning lady to the president himself. If you're good to them, they'll help you

get things done. If you're on their bad side, even by accident, there's no way you can be effective here... and you'll be gone in a matter of time. (Jill)

Jill indicates that the accomplishment of tasks and job security are primary reasons for nurturing hierarchical relationships within the college. Larry agrees with Jill's assessment of job security being linked to hierarchical relationships when he says that there is 'no survival unless you are connected' within the hierarchy. While Jill contends that good relationships are needed at all levels of the hierarchy, Larry emphasizes the importance of executive-level relationships. Both Larry and Jill, however, perceive managerial effectiveness and job security, in general, to be closely linked to their relationships within the organization. Jill also explains how getting on someone's 'bad side' within the hierarchy could make it difficult for her to accomplish certain tasks that require administrative assistance and how such damaged relationships could result in eventual dismissal from the organization. The importance of maintaining effective relationships within the hierarchy, therefore, is further emphasized.

Unlike the other managers, Ned and Michael clearly perceive that they are not effective managers within the organization. While Michael is uncertain about why he is no longer an effective manager in the organization, Ned offers considerable insight into his own ineffectiveness:

I do things the way I know they should be done. If they would do it my way their whole operation would be world class. Be like the Chinese and you'll be effective here. Be like me and you can't be effective. (Ned)

Although Ned contends that he could be effective in China if he were to 'be like the Chinese', he refuses to do so, thereby consciously accepting his ineffectiveness. Ned's blatant refusal to adapt to the Chinese culture within the College limits, and perhaps nullifies, his overall managerial effectiveness. The negative consequences of refusing to adapt to Chinese organizational cultural norms are emphasized throughout the literature (Hitt *et al.*, 2002; Bond, 1991; Tung, 1982, 1989). Michael, in contrast, appears unaware of the need to adapt to Chinese cultural norms in order to be effective as an expatriate manager:

It's not like the old days when a manager was a manager. You obey the manager because they are the manager. Everything's different here. They say 'yes' to your face and 'no' to your back. You look them in the eyes and they say, 'yes'. Then you turn around and it's 'no'. How could I be effective here? (Michael)

Michael takes a parochial approach to managing in China. He expects to be obeyed by all subordinates, yet appears unaware that by disregarding the Chinese cultural norms and hierarchical relationship structures, he could be greatly diminishing, or eliminating, his opportunities for being an effective manager within the college. 'This isn't China anymore', he continues, 'this is an international marketplace that needs to be run on the rules of the international culture of business.' Ned and Michael both possess egocentric and ethnocentric views on how to be an expatriate manager in China. They strongly believe that they are in China to improve the Chinese way of doing business and to introduce their Chinese hosts to the new 'rules of the international culture of business'. Such rigid views are consistent with what Van Der Zee and Van Oudenhoven (2000), through their *Multicultural Personality Questionnaire,* categorize as lacking cultural *openness* and cultural *flexibility,* which are predictors of cross-cultural managerial ineffectiveness.

Interview summary

The findings of the interview study are consistent with the literature, which contends that cultural adaptability in China is essential for expatriate managers to achieve sustainable managerial effectiveness (Kay and Taylor, 1997; Luo, 2000; Tung and Yeung, 1998; Tung, 1982, 1989; Hitt *et al.,* 2002; Bond, 1991). Although all responses consistently relate to at least one of the three categorizations of *organizational and cultural harmony, hierarchical relationships,* and *familial and/or spousal relationships,* each participant's particular view of their own managerial effectiveness differs. Alan and Sam, for example, perceive themselves to be effective when they are able to placate the Chinese executive of the college so that things 'go smoothly' for them. Jill feels effective when she has 'good' relations with the Chinese staff so that she is able to accomplish tasks and, thereby, retain her employment. Larry's concept of effectiveness involves having 'social control' over the Chinese staff, so that he can ensure the accomplishment of certain tasks. Ned perceives that he could be effective if he chose to nurture placating relationships with the college's Chinese executive. Finally, Michael perceives that his own effectiveness could be increased if his wife were with him. Each of the participants, except for Michael, perceives that their own managerial effectiveness could be enhanced in direct relation to the degree to which they *maintain organizational and cultural harmony* and *establish and maintain hierarchical relationships* with Chinese individuals throughout the organization. All responses, including those of Michael, stress the importance of having supportive *familial and/or spousal relationships*, which are also highlighted in the literature as having considerable influence on expatriate adjustment and managerial effectiveness (Adler, 2002; Black *et al.*, 1991).

Survey study of expatriate managers

The aim of the survey study is to explore the demographic, professional, and cultural factors that may influence how the college's 22 western expatriate teachers perceive their own managerial effectiveness. Each expatriate teacher was required, as a function of their employment, to manage various groups of Chinese tutors and teaching assistants. The survey for the teachers was intuitively developed from the themes that emerged from the interview study. The survey was distributed by e-mail to the 22 expatriate teachers of the college, of which 17 surveys were completed and returned. The participants were first asked ten demographic questions, followed by 16 scenario statements, which ask the participants to rate, on a five-point Likert-type scale, the degree of their agreement or disagreement with each statement. The scenarios, divided equally into four categories, were developed in accordance with the themes that emerged from the interview data as being most influential to the managerial effectiveness of the participants. These categories are: (1) *Organizational and cultural harmony*; (2) *Spousal and/or familial relationships*; and (3) *Hierarchical relationships*. A fourth category, *Managerial effectiveness*, was added in order to directly assess the degree to which the teachers felt they were effective as managers in China. While the larger study, of which this investigation is a part, examines all four categories, the present study focuses on the fourth category, *managerial effectiveness,* in accordance with the aims of this research. See Table 4.1 for a summary of the participants' demographic details.

Notably, none of the 17 expatriate teachers had been provided with any form of language or cultural training by the college prior to or during their employment. Close to 90 per cent of the participants reported having basic or no Chinese language skills, with only two participants reporting intermediate or advanced language skills. These findings are consistent with research indicating that it is common for organizations to neglect cultural training of any kind for their expatriate employees

Table 4.1 Demographic details of western expatriate teachers

Expatriate Teachers	Frequency	Per cent (%)
Gender:		
Male	15	88.2
Female	2	11.8
Relational status:		
Single	9	52.9
Spouse in China	6	35.3
Spouse outside China	2	11.8
China work experience:		
Up to 1 year	8	47.1
1 to 2 years	7	41.2
2 to 5 years	1	5.9
5 to 10 years	0	0
More than 10 years	1	5.9
Received cross-culture training	0	0
Chinese Language Skill:		
None	10	58.8
Basic	5	29.4
Intermediate	1	5.9
Advanced	1	5.9
Fluent	0	0
N	17	100

Note: All percentages are rounded to one decimal place.

(Black *et al.*, 1991; Brewster, 1995; Hutchings, 2003; Britt, 2002; Osman-Gani, 1999). Also notable is that 88.3 per cent of the managers had worked in China for less than two years and 47.1 per cent had worked in China for less than one year, indicating a potential lack of Chinese cultural experience amongst the expatriates. The indication that only 35.3 per cent of the managers have their spouses with them in China, while 52.9 per cent are single, is of interest as well, when compared to the interview finding that five of the six managers repeatedly stressed the importance of having a spousal and/or familial relationship to assist with the overall adjustments of working in China. Finally, the fact that only two of the participants are female, representing 11.8 per cent of the sample, indicates a need for further exploration into the role of expatriate women in the organization and why their representation is much less than the males. The college employed a total of three expatriate women at the time of the study. A summary of the survey findings for the category of *managerial effectiveness* follows.

Managerial effectiveness

In the category of *managerial effectiveness*, there is a clear division between the participants who agree or strongly agree with the statements and those who do not. As shown in Table 4.2, 47.1 per cent of the participants agree or strongly agree with the statement that their subordinates carry out tasks as intended, and 41.1 per cent disagree or strongly disagree with the statement.

Less than half of the participants feel as though the tasks they assign to tutors and teaching assistants are being fulfilled as directed. While this phenomenon could be due to a variety of factors, such as language issues or cultural misunderstandings, it is a clear indication of managerial ineffectiveness. It was also found, as seen in Table 4.3, that only 41.2 per cent of the participants agree or strongly agree that their managerial goals are regularly achieved in the organization, while 35.3 per cent disagree or strongly disagree with the statement and 23.5 per cent neither agree nor disagree. The majority of the western expatriate managers in the organization, 58.8 per cent, therefore, do not agree in any way that their managerial goals are regularly achieved within the college.

Table 4.4 reveals that 52.9 per cent of the participants report feeling that their positions of authority are respected within the organization. From Tables 4.3 and 4.4, it emerges that a large number of the expatriates indicate that they do not feel respected within the college and that their managerial goals are not being regularly achieved. As perceived workplace support is argued to have a positive correlation with organizational and managerial effectiveness, these findings are important for gaining a deeper understanding of the workplace support issues faced by the participant teachers (Kraimer *et al.*, 2001).

As seen in Table 4.5, only 35.3 per cent of the participants either agree or strongly agree with the statement that their colleagues ask periodically

Table 4.2 Subordinates fulfill assigned tasks

Scale	Frequency	Per cent (%)
Strongly Agree	1	5.9
Agree	7	41.2
Neither Agree nor Disagree	2	11.8
Disagree	4	23.5
Strongly Disagree	3	17.6
N	17	100

Note: All percentages are rounded to one decimal place.

Table 4.3 Managerial goals are regularly achieved

Scale	Frequency	Per cent (%)
Strongly Agree	2	11.9
Agree	5	29.4
Neither Agree nor Disagree	4	23.5
Disagree	4	23.5
Strongly Disagree	2	11.8
N	17	100

Note: All percentages are rounded to one decimal place.

Table 4.4 Managerial authority is respected

Scale	Frequency	Per cent (%)
Strongly Agree	4	23.5
Agree	5	29.4
Neither Agree nor Disagree	3	17.6
Disagree	4	23.5
Strongly Disagree	1	5.9
N	17	100

Note: All percentages are rounded to one decimal place.

Table 4.5 Professional opinions are periodically sought by colleagues

Scale	Frequency	Per cent (%)
Strongly Agree	2	11.8
Agree	4	23.5
Neither Agree nor Disagree	5	29.4
Disagree	5	29.4
Strongly Disagree	1	5.9
N	17	100

Note: All percentages are rounded to one decimal place.

for their professional opinions. This contrasts with the 35.3 per cent of the participants who disagree or strongly disagree with the statement and the 29.4 per cent who neither agree nor disagree.

As the participants of the survey are all full-time teachers in the organization, with managerial roles, it is notable that 64.7 per cent do not clearly report having their professional opinions sought. This phenomenon could be due to cultural or language communication barriers, personality conflicts, issues of managerial incompetence, or a variety of other organizational or cultural factors.

Survey summary

The findings of the survey study, while not directly indicating expatriate failure as defined in the mainstream literature, clearly reveal a high degree of perceived managerial ineffectiveness amongst the expatriate teachers. The expatriates were hired by the organization to perform as effective managers, yet fewer than half of the participants indicate that they perceive themselves to be effective. The high percentage of participants who report negatively to the statements about their own managerial effectiveness in the college resonates with the high estimates of expatriate failures documented for larger multinational organizations in China (Ralston *et al.*, 1995; Hendry, 1994; Shay and Bruce, 1997; Valner and Palmer, 2002; Tung, 1981, 1984; Garonzik *et al.*, 2000; Milkovich and Newman, 1996; Harzing, 2002; Selmer, 2002). Follow-up inquiry, four months after the survey was collected, revealed that 47 per cent of the survey participants had left or were asked to leave the college before completing their one-year contract, for various undisclosed reasons. While it is unknown if these individuals were the same who reported negatively about their own effectiveness, it does confirm that western expatriate failure rates in smaller, Chinese-owned organizations may be comparable with those reported for larger multinational organizations.

In terms of being prepared for working in China, it is notable that none of the expatriate teachers had received any form of cross-cultural or language training before or during their employment in China, despite 15 of the 17 teachers having had less than two years' working experience in China and only two of the teachers having more than basic Chinese language skills. This is particularly pertinent, as Black *et al.* (1991), although focusing on large multinational corporations, find *predeparture training* and *previous foreign experience* to be primary indicators of cross-cultural managerial effectiveness. Besides indicating a need for the expatriates and the executive of the organization to actively address expatriate effectiveness issues within the college, the survey results confirm elements of the interview study that found managerial effectiveness within the organization to be considerably difficult for some expatriates to attain. Although beyond the scope of the present study, further analysis of the expatriates' experiences underlying their survey responses would be useful for providing a more in-depth understanding of western expatriate managerial effectiveness issues in this and similar organizations.

Conclusion

The aim of this exploratory study has been to provide a deeper understanding of the phenomenon of managerial effectiveness, as it relates to a sample of western expatriates working in a private, Chinese-owned, academic college in South-east China. The study finds that the perceived managerial effectiveness of the expatriates is most positively influenced by the factors relating to the *maintaining of organizational and cultural harmony*, the *establishing and nurturing of hierarchical relationships* with Chinese individuals at all levels within the organization, and having *supportive familial and/or spousal relationships*. Through recognizing these factors of influence, expatriates and their employers, in contexts similar to those of the present study, may gain useful insights for understanding further the cultural, regional, and organization-specific dynamics associated with expatriate managerial effectiveness in China. By gaining a deeper understanding of these dynamics and how issues of effectiveness may be defined and perceived differently amongst various Chinese and western individuals, existing and potential expatriate managers may be better informed to approach the cultural challenges associated with such employment in China. Such insight is particularly pertinent, as less than half of the expatriates involved in the interview and survey studies perceive themselves to be consistently effective managers in the organization. As the survey study implies, perceived ineffectiveness may be viewed as a cautionary predictor of future failure. The term 'failure', however, needs to be re-examined in terms of what failure means for a small to medium-sized, Chinese-owned, private organization in China, as the existing literature on expatriate failure primarily focuses on large multinational organizations (Lau, 2006).

As an emergent area of research, the phenomenon of the managerial effectiveness of western expatriates working in small to medium-sized locally-owned organizations in China needs to be critically approached with a renewed cultural sensitivity to the Chinese perspective on such concepts as 'managerial effectiveness' and 'failure'. Western understandings of these concepts need to be comparatively examined in relation to the perspectives held by the individual owners of Chinese organizations, along with their leaders, general staff, and clients. Explorations of Chinese perspectives on the organizational costs associated with ineffective or failed western expatriate managers are also needed. With a deeper and more flexible understanding of how effectiveness is viewed, in various contexts and from a variety of western and Chinese perspectives, insights may be gained which could provide expatriates and their Chinese employers with a more stable and predictable employment environment. Future studies are needed which incorporate other western and non-western expatriate populations in similar, locally-owned organizations in China, in order to build upon the findings of the present study and to explore issues of generalisability and repeatability across regions and organizational contexts.

References

Adler, N.J. (2002) *From Boston to Beijing: Managing with a Worldview.* Cincinnati, OH: Thompson.
Aycan, Z. (1997) 'Acculturation of Expatriate Managers: A Process Model of Adjustment and Performance', in D.M. Saunders and Z. Aycan (eds), *New Approaches to Employee Management.* Greenwich, NY: JAI Press, pp. 1–40.
Barrett, R. (1966) 'The Influence of the Supervisor's Requirements on Rating', *Personnel Psychology,* 19: 375–87.
Black, J., Mendenhall, M., and Oddou, G. (1991) 'Toward a Comprehensive Model of International Adjustment: An Integration of Multiple Theoretical Perspectives', *Academy of Management Review,* 16(2): 291–317.
Black, J.S. (1988) 'Work Role Transitions: A Study of American Expatriate Managers in Japan', *Journal of International Business Studies,* 19: 277–94.
Black, J.S. and Gregersen, H.B. (1991) 'Antecedents to Cross-cultural Adjustment for Expatriates in Pacific Rim Assignments', *Human Relations,* 44: 497–515.
Black, J.S. and Stephens, G.K. (1989) 'The Influence of the Spouse on American Expatriate Adjustment and Intent to Stay in Pacific Rim Overseas Assignments', *Journal of Management,* 15: 529–44.
Blackman, C. (1998) 'Chinese Negotiation Strategies and Western Counter-strategies', in J. Selmer (ed.), *International Management in China – Cross-cultural Issues.* New York: Routledge, pp. 197–206.
Bond, M.H. (1991) *Beyond the Chinese Face.* New York: Oxford.
Boyatzis, R.E. (1982) *The Competent Manager: A Model for Effective Performance.* New York: John Wiley and Sons.
Brewster, C. (1995) 'The Paradox of Expatriate Adjustment', in J. Selmer (ed.), *Expatriate Management: New Ideas for International Business.* Westport: Quorum Books.
Britt, A. (2002) 'Expatriates Want More Support from Home', *HR Magazine,* 47(7): 21–2.
Caligiuri, P.M., Hyland, M.M., Joshi, A. and Boss, A.S. (1998) 'Testing a Theoretical Model for Examining the Relationship Between Family Adjustment and Expatriates' Work Adjustment', *Journal of Applied Psychology,* 83: 598–614.
Coleman, D. (1995) *Emotional Intelligence.* New York: Bantam.
Coleman, D. (1998) *Emotional Intelligence at Work.* New York: Bantam.

Coleman, D. (2000) 'Leadership that Gets Results', *Harvard Business Review*, March–April: 78–90.

Deming, W.E. (1982) *Out of the Crisis: Quality, Productivity and Competitive Position*. Cambridge: MIT Press.

Denzin, N.K. (2001) *Interpretive Interactionism*, 2nd edn. Thousand Oaks: Sage.

Drucker, P.F. (1967) *The Effective Executive*. New York: Harper and Row.

Drucker, P.F. (2001) *The Essential Drucker*. New York: Harper Collins.

Fan, Y. (2000) 'A Classification of Chinese Culture', *Cross Cultural Management: An International Journal*, 7(2): 3–10.

Feldman, D.C. and Brett, J.M. (1983) 'Coping with New Jobs: A Comparative Study of New Hires and Job Changes', *Academy of Management Journal*, 26: 258–72.

Fisher, C.D. (1985) 'Social Support and Adjustment to Work: A Longitudinal Study', *Journal of Management*, 11: 39–53.

Flores, G.N. and Utley, D.R. (2000) 'Management Concepts in Use – a 12-Year Perspective', *Engineering Management Journal*, 12(3): 11–17.

Garonzik, R., Brockner, J. and Siegel, P.A. (2000) 'Identifying International Assignees at Risk for Premature Departure: The Interactive Effect of Outcome Favourability and Procedural Fairness', *Journal of Applied Psychology*, 85 (1): 13–20.

Gillard, S. and Price, J. (2005) 'The Competencies of Effective Project Managers: A Conceptual Analysis', *International Journal of Management*, 22(1): 48–53.

Gregersen, H.B., Hite, J.M. and Black, J.S. (1996) 'Expatriate Performance Appraisal in US Multinational firms', *Journal of International Business Studies*, 27: 711–38.

Gregersen, H.B. and Black, J.S. (1992) 'Antecedents to Commitment to a Parent Company and Foreign Operation', *Academy of Management Journal*, 35(1): 65–90.

Harzing, A.W. (2002) 'On-site Adjustment Support for German Expatriates in the Republic of Ireland: An Exploratory Study', *IBAR*, 21(2): 15–38.

Hendry, C.A. (1994) *Human Resource Strategies for International Growth*. London: Routledge.

Hitt, M., Lee, H. and Yucel, E. (2002) 'The Importance of Social Capital to the Management of Multinational Enterprises: Relational Networks Among Asian and Western Firms', *Asia Pacific Journal of Management*, 19: 353–72.

Hutchings, K. (2003) 'Cross-cultural Preparation of Australian Expatriates in Organisations in China: The Need for Greater Attention to Training', *Asia Pacific Journal of Management*, 20: 375–96.

Kay, M. and Taylor, G.K. (1997) 'Expatriate Culture Shock in China', *Journal of Managerial Psychology*, 12(8): 496–514.

Kraimer, M.L., Wayne, S.J. and Jaworski, R.A. (2001) 'Sources of Support and Expatriate Performance: The Role of Expatriate Adjustment', *Personnel Psychology*, 54(1): 71–100.

Latham, G. and Wexley, K. (1994) *Increasing Productivity through Performance Appraisal*, 2nd edn. Reading: Addison-Wesley.

Lau, C.M. (2006) 'Achievements, Challenges and Research Agendas for Asian Management Research Studies', *Asian Business and Management*, 5: 53–66.

Lund, D.W. and Barker, M.C. (2004) 'Organisational Commitment of Expatriate Managers in China', *International Journal of Management and Organisational Behaviour*, 8(4): 504–24.

Luo, Y. (2000) *Guanxi and Business*. Singapore: World Scientific.

Luo, Y. (2002) 'Partnering with Foreign Firms: How do Chinese Managers View the Governance and Importance of Contracts', *Asia Pacific Journal of Management,* 19: 127–51.

Milkovich, G.T. and Newman, J.T. (1996) *Compensation,* 5th edn. Chicago: Richard Irwin.

O'Boyle, T. (1989) 'Grappling with the Expatriate Issue', *The Wall Street Journal,* 11 December.

Osman-Gani, A. M. (1999) 'Expatriate Development in the Asia-Pacific Region: A Comparative Study of Expatriates From Five Countries Across Three Continents', in K. P. Kuchinke (ed.), *Academy of Human Resource Development,* Conference Proceedings, 3–7 March 1999; Washington, USA: pp. 452–64.

Page, C., Wilson, M., Meyer, D. and Inkson, K. (2003) 'It's the Situation I'm In: The Importance of Managerial Context to Effectiveness', *Journal of Management Development,* 22 (10): 841–62.

Phillips, M.R. and Pearson, V. (1996) 'Coping in Chinese Communities: The Need for a New Research Agenda', in M.H. Bond (ed.), *The Handbook of Chinese Psychology.* New York: Oxford, pp. 429–40.

Pinder, C.C. and Schroeder, K.G. (1987) 'Time to Proficiency Following Job Transfers', *Academy of Management Journal,* 30: 336–53.

Ralston, D., Terpstra, R.H., Cunniff, M.K. and Gustafson, D.J. (1995) 'Do Expatriates Change their Behaviour to Fit a Foreign Culture?', *Management International Review,* 35(1): 109–22.

Rastogi, R. and Dave, V. (2004) 'Managerial Effectiveness: A Function of Personality Type and Organisational Components', *Singapore Management Review,* 26 (2): 79–87.

Sandholm, L. (1999) 'Quality Leadership', Proceedings of the International Quality Conference, 8–11 December, Bangkok, Thailand.

Selmer, J. (1998) 'Strategic Human Resource Management: Expatriate Managers in China', in J. Selmer (ed.), *International Management in China: Cross-cultural Issues.* New York: Routledge.

Selmer, J. (2002) 'Practice Makes Perfect? International Experiences and Expatriate Adjustment', *Management International Review,* 42(1): 71–88.

Shay, J. and Baak, S. (2004) 'Expatriate Assignment, Adjustment and Effectiveness: An Empirical Examination of the Big Picture', *Journal of International Business Studies,* 35: 216–32.

Shay, J. and Bruce, T. (1997) 'Expatriate Managers', *Cornell Hotel and Restaurant Administration Quarterly,* 38(1): 30–5.

Strauss, A. and Corbin, J. (1998) *Basics of Qualitative Research: Techniques and Procedures for Developing Grounded Theory.* Thousand Oaks: Sage.

Tung, R.L. (1981) 'Selecting and Training of Personnel for Overseas Assignments', *Columbia Journal of World Business,* 16: 68–78.

Tung, R.L. (1982) 'US–China Trade Negotiations: Practices, Procedures and Outcomes', *Journal of International Business Studies,* Fall: 25–37.

Tung, R.L. (1984) *Key to Japan's Economic Strength: Human Power.* Lexington: Lexington Books.

Tung, R.L. (1989) 'A Longitudinal Study of United States–Chinese Business Negotiations', *Chinese Economic Review,* 1(1): 57–71.

Tung, R.L. and Yeung, I. (1998) 'Confucian Connections in China', in J. Selmer (ed.), *International Management in China – Cross-cultural Issues*. New York: Routledge, pp. 197–206.

Valner, I.T. and Palmer, T.M. (2002) 'Successful Expatriation and Organizational Strategies', *Review of Business*, 23(2): 8–11.

Van Der Zee, K.I. and Van Oudenhoven, J.P. (2000) 'The Multicultural Personality Questionnaire: A Multidimensional Instrument of Multicultural Effectiveness', *European Journal of Personality*, 14: 291–309.

Wood, J., Chapman, J., Fromholtz, M., Morrison, V., Wallace, J., Zeffane, R., Schermerhorn, J. R., Hunt, J. G. and Osborn, R. N. (2004) *Organisational Behaviour: A Global Perspective*, 3rd edn. Milton, Queensland: John Wiley and Sons.

Zhu, G., Speece, M. and So, S. (1998) 'Conflicts in Sino-European Joint Ventures', in J. Selmer (ed.), *International Management in China – Cross-cultural Issues*. New York: Routledge, pp. 25–36.

Part II
Institutional and Social Issues

5
Corporate Social Responsibility in China: The Enterprise and the Environment

Robert Taylor

Introduction

China's transition from a command to a market economy has enhanced the strategic decision-making power of management and heightened the consciousness of corporate social responsibility among Chinese state, collective and private enterprises. The globalization of business and China's accession to the World Trade Organization (WTO) have intensified these trends, especially in the context of an emerging civil society, even though the latter is necessarily constrained by the Chinese government leadership's reluctance, for political reasons, to allow independent associations divorced from state control. Environmental associations fall within this category.

Accordingly, it is the purpose of this chapter to examine the extent to which Chinese enterprises are discharging these responsibilities in the field of environmental protection, for which China has a raft of laws, which are not uniformly enforced. It will be argued that in a developing economy like China's there is an inherent conflict between adherence to environmental law and the demands of market competitiveness. By reference, for example, to American environmental literature, it will be shown that such constraints impact on the execution of environmental policy in China's industries. Reference will be made to Jiutai Industrial Park in Jilin Province.

In fact, the industrial park concept will be used to illustrate measures being undertaken. It will be demonstrated, however, that there are barriers to implementation other than the issue of market competitiveness. The industrial park is designed to reduce high levels of pollution, environmental degradation and poor utilization of resources by fostering interaction within industrial groups to recycle industrial waste for productive use. That environmentally-friendly products tend to be more expensive is, however, an issue that needs to be addressed.

Attention will also be focused on high-tech industries conducive to clean production and competitiveness in world markets. Case studies relating to the Chinese steel, automobile and textile industries will be used as illustrations. Additionally, it will be emphasized that corporate responsibility extends beyond the production setting to the urban environment in general, and the contribution of enterprises to the latter area will be assessed.

Commercial survival necessitates that an enterprise should focus on consumer demand. The market economy has made Chinese enterprises customer-oriented rather than production-centred, and retailers will play a crucial role in persuading customers to buy 'green' products. Thus a prerequisite for the effective implementation of environmental policy is the engagement of a multiplicity of actors.

Nevertheless it will be concluded that, whatever the impact of global pressure and domestic consumer opinion, China's industrial enterprises will bear the major social responsibility for environmental protection.

The roles of government and enterprise

In China, as in other countries, corporate responsibility for environmental protection is to a great extent following the lead of government. Traditionally, however, developing countries have accorded sustainable development a low priority since their major concern is economic growth. The major determinant of growth in a number of Asian countries since 1945 has been the developmental state, whereby government formulates industrial policy, targeting priority sectors, a prime example being the role of a central authority in China, in the days of the command economy and, to a lesser extent, in the current market-orientated context. There is also a sense in which strong central government, like that of China, is in a position to limit environmental degradation, and yet, where the polluters are state-owned enterprises, it has been reluctant to bear social costs like closure and resulting unemployment. Thus an emerging issue for Chinese managers and for their Asian counterparts is environmental regulation, in partnership with government. For their part, since 1978, China's leaders have embarked upon a reform programme involving the restructuring of a highly polluting and increasingly technologically obsolescent state enterprise industrial sector as well as initiating greater participation by China in the global economy. Thus domestic pressures and external influences like China's World Trade Organization (WTO) membership have combined to force greater focus on environmental concerns. Recent new legislation has included the law for the Promotion of Cleaner Production. The State Environmental Protection Administration (SEPA) also has a scheme to recognise nationally environmentally-friendly enterprises (Pullam, 2006).

China's environmental crisis is a function of rapid economic growth and rising living standards. An indicator of the scope of the problem is China's energy consumption; in 2003 China's oil imports increased by 30 to 40 per cent over the equivalent total for 2002, according to a report from the International Energy Agency. China has become the world's second largest consumer of oil after the United States, accounting for one third of the annual increase in global demand (Stelzer, 2003). Such consumption, in addition to the fact that a fossil fuel – coal – still supplies most of China's energy has contributed to environmental degradation and a high cost in terms of human health. In China's main cities sulphur content in the atmosphere surpasses levels recommended by the World Health Organization (WHO) by between two and five times; the World Bank calculated in 1997 that nearly 180,000 urban inhabitants died annually as a result of atmosphere pollution (Xie *et al.*, 2002).

This level of pollution is a reflection of China's current stage of economic development. Although, as is suggested below, the pattern is changing, China's industries have been labour- rather than capital-intensive, with a low level of technology, a model of development using a high resource volume and emphasizing production quantity. This, in turn, causes the duplication of industrial plant resulting in what is often described as structural pollution. This stress on growth in the past meant that the government was slow to recognize environmental priorities. In the Seventh Five Year Plan (1986–1991) and Eighth Five Year Plan (1991–1996) periods China's national investment in environmental protection represented only 0.69 per cent and 0.73 per cent of Gross Domestic Product (GDP) respectively, even if in the Ninth Five Year Plan (1996–2001) it approached 1 per cent. (Liu *et al.*, 2003).

As a result, Chinese sources spoke of a decline in pollution after the mid-1990s (K. Chen, 2003). Meanwhile domestic industrial restructuring and the changing composition of China's exports under the impact of global competition were effecting a transition towards more value-added products. The increase in China's exports during the 1980s was heavily dependent on labour-intensive products like garments, other textiles and toys which consumed high quantities of domestically produced raw materials like cotton and wool, thereby depleting local resources. But the changing focus of China's industrial production since the 1990s, and the reduction of tariffs on agricultural imports under the terms of China's WTO accession in 2001, tend towards national resource conservation, increasing availability of land for food crops (Z.J. Wang, 2002). A further development is the import of manmade chemical fibres. (ibid; Wan and Chen, 2003). In addition, in the production process, the use of natural gas imports has the potential to curtail China's reliance on coal as an energy resource (Z.J. Wang, 2002). These trends are likely to accelerate as China accedes fully to the terms of WTO membership.

The above discussion has focused on securing raw materials and changing production processes in China's traditional industries. But more significant is the move towards high technology and value added manufacturing to meet the dynamic challenge of domestic and global markets. Since the beginning of China's transition from a command to a market economy and the emergence of a buyers' market, China's traditional smokestack and labour-intensive industries have become less competitive since they face rivals' low wage production, for instance, from the Southeast Asian countries. Moreover, economic growth and greater managerial competence are enhancing the role of the service sector. Facilitating this process is foreign direct investment, and investors have become more aware of sustainable development in their own countries. Originally, in the post-1978 context, western companies targeted China for investment in order to take advantage of the cheap labour and avoid the constraints of environmental legislation at home. Lately, however, the Chinese government has sought to promote restructuring favourable to the environment. In 1998 a directive relating to foreign ventures encouraged investors from overseas to manage energy-efficient and environmentally-friendly ventures, as China's regulations gradually converge with global standards. A barrier to implementation of this, as of other policies, is often the lack of cooperation, from provincial or local governments, which compete for foreign investment, sacrificing environmental protection for economic growth and employment (ibid.).

The restructuring of the Chinese economy, however, also necessarily responds to the pressures of 'green trade', which offer both challenge and opportunity to increase competitiveness, spurring export industries towards technological renovation and innovation, as foreign consumers demand ecologically friendly products (ibid.). Chinese sources refer to the adoption of a green trade barrier strategy on two fronts; countering green trade obstacles and justifying the use of China's own environmental non-tariff barriers. Thus in the short term the Chinese are to exploit preferential treatment accorded to developing countries and utilize conflict resolution systems in order to further the country's fair-trade opportunities, at the same time raising domestic environmental regulations to international standards. Simultaneously, green trade barriers can be used to protect China's own ecology, the health of its people, wildlife and natural resources, in addition to defending infant industries (X. Chen, 2003).

Responsibility for environmental protection and green production is incumbent upon both government and enterprise and it is to the division of labour between the two parties that attention is now turned. In the Tenth Five Year Plan (2001–2005), control and reduction of pollution, market reform and technological innovation were seen as the keys to sustainable development. It had been estimated by official Chinese sources that in order to reach the goals set in the Tenth Five Year Plan the government would need to spend US$85 billion or 1.3 per cent of GDP for the period, the bulk of this expenditure coming from central and local government. Remaining funds were to be provided by private enterprises, foreign governments and multilateral banks (Mayfield, 2003). The government is to undertake a number of tasks to assist enterprises: technical guidance to ensure that clean production does not threaten profits, financial assistance in the form of preferential loans to assist production processes and encouragement to close down polluting facilities. In addition, an increase in environmental taxes is to be introduced to curb pollution. Implementation of such measures is also undertaken by local government. In 1979 Taiyuan City promulgated the Regulations Concerning Clean Production, facilitating the provision of production equipment, skills and research and development. Local tax incentives were also being instituted in Taiyuan and national environmental tax collection was being reformed (Xia, 2001; K. Chen, 2003). To date, however, governmental environmental funds have been dispersed among a number of agencies and supervision of such investment has been inadequate, thereby constraining the effective use of such resources (ibid.). In Chinese sources the role of government is subsumed under the externalization of environmental cost; discussion of the absorption and internalization of such costs by enterprises now follows (Fu, 2002).

Enterprise internalization of cost: legal, social and commercial pressures

A number of legal, social and commercial pressures have led enterprises to internalize costs. In China environmental law has not been uniformly enforced, given the local government preferences cited above, but it does serve as a yardstick against which industrial and commercial behaviour may be judged. The formulation and influence of China's environmental law will now be outlined within a comparative global context. Chinese environmental laws have evolved in ways similar to those in western and other Asian countries, the principle being that general legislation can only be effective after laws relating to specific sectors have been operative. In the United States, for example, natural resource protection had been enacted before the National Policy Law was enforced. Japan's Basic Law was preceded by atmospheric and water pollution regulations, and Taiwan's general legislation in 2002 had been twenty years in the making. Similarly, in China twenty years of experience with specific legislation is said to have formed the basis for amendment of the trial Environmental Protection Law initiated in 1979 (J. Wang, 2003). The key to the effectiveness of law, however, is social pressure on enterprises through public awareness. In order to protect its political monopoly the Chinese Communist Party (CCP) has been reluctant to allow independent associations, focused on specific social issues, to exist as they do in the context of western civil society but in the environmental, like other areas, non-governmental organizations (NGOs) are being accepted as partners in funding and publicity. Thus co-operation between such organizations and government is intended to publicize national regulations and international agreements, thereby increasing input into business decisions (X. Chen, 2003). This role of Chinese NGOs is influenced by western practice. The Institute of Environment and Development (IED), established in the mid-1990s, is a case in point, raising public awareness of environmental issues. The Institute has been involved, in cooperation with the United Kingdom's Department of International Development, in a project to promote environmentally friendly production processes in small and medium sized enterprises in Liaoning and Sichuan. In addition, foreign partners are in a position to increase awareness of corporate responsibility for the environment in joint ventures in China (Turner, 2003).

Ultimately, however, one of the most telling pressures on enterprises to conform to environmental standards is that of consumer preference. Given the relatively recent development of the market economy in

China, environmental concern as an element of consumer choice is only just emerging. In contrast, in 1992 a European Union (EU) source found that 67 per cent of Dutch, 82 per cent of German and over half of British people considered environmental factors when buying products. In this sense environmental awareness could be seen as the highest stage of market development. There are, however, two kinds of end-user: producer goods buyers and purchasers of consumer goods. Producer goods buyers consider performance and price, and are less concerned with pollution caused by the industrial process. But for consumers environmental concern may form part of the buying decision, especially if the manufacturer internalizes costs, thereby setting a competitive price. Product differentiation, through eco-labelling, is another means of attracting consumers (Fu, 2002). In addition, consumer taste may be influenced by retailers who can pressure suppliers to stock environmentally friendly products (Liu and Zhang, 2001). Finally, implicit in the debate concerning the internalization of costs by manufacturers under legal, social and consumer pressures is the conflict between environmental protection and economic profit, and the following section addresses the processes involved in green production in specific industries.

Case studies of industries: textiles, steel and cars

This section's primary concern is the impact of industrial processes and products on China's environment. Earlier reference was made to the conflict between economic growth and environmental protection in developing countries; in China's case competitive thrust is effecting a move towards industrial restructuring and high-tech products in response to market change. As suggested earlier, China has been influenced by global environmental concerns; Chinese sources, for example, refer to the United Nations meeting concerning environment and development held in 1992. Sustainable development was then defined as respecting the needs of the present and future generations, a theme echoed at the 16th Congress of the CCP in 2002 which gave priority to an industrial strategy based on effective deployment of labour and natural resources, utilizing high levels of science and technology, thereby reducing pollution. (Luo, 2003; Wan and Chen, 2003).

Sustainable development, however, involves increased cost, although over the long term such expenditure may be recouped through greater product competitiveness. Two factors determine competitiveness: cost and differentiation. Cost internalization through green production entails higher expenditure, thereby reducing profits, but greater consumer awareness may open up new niche markets.

Thus differentiation through green products becomes the only way to ultimate profitability and market share retention. This is because, according to the principle of elasticity, consumers usually focus on prices. Unless, however, all manufacturers engage in green production, there is no scope for a normal distribution in price-based competition. There are, however, differences between large and medium-sized enterprises in their ability to sustain such costs. Sustainability depends on the ratio of environmental cost to total production expenditure; when the former is a small percentage of the latter it can be sustained. In addition, labour-intensive industries are often not profitable enough to internalize costs. Moreover large high-tech enterprises, in contrast to small labour-intensive ventures, can invest more readily in advanced production processes with long-term benefit. Finally, reduction in energy and raw material use demands higher investment in training and technical skills (Fu, 2002).

Attention is now turned to the Chinese textile and garment industries, overseas sales from which represented 20.9 per cent of China's total export value and 13 per cent of world trade in that sector. Typifying an early stage of industrialization, however, the industry is a major polluter, especially because of surplus production, which is likely to increase as both domestic and global markets become saturated in the absence of adequate market intelligence by the Chinese. This is reflected in the high and wasteful consumption of electric power, generated by fossil fuels, and water resources by the spinning and weaving sector of that industry. In this environmental context the textile and garment industry is seen as culpable on several counts. The weaving industry is notorious for noise pollution, a health hazard for the workforce and in China way above safety limits mandated by legislation. Printing and dyeing, an early stage, is a major source of water pollution in the spinning and weaving process, as it contains harmful residual fibres. In addition, the use of pesticides in cotton production, and, for example, anti-mildew preparations and agents to prevent shrinkage contribute harmful residues. Consequently, recycling of waste products after the completion of dyeing is yet to reach the standards of advanced industrial countries. There have been measures taken, however, to utilize ecologically sound raw material like the less-polluting genetically variegated cotton. Energy-saving technology for washing wool is also being introduced. Furthermore, recent research is providing new-style chemical man-made fibres which nevertheless produce sulphur residues needing treatment, as well as environmentally-friendly dyes, as aids to pollution prevention. Currently, environmental management of this kind is mainly being promoted in large rather than small and medium-sized enterprises. An ecological textile and garment industry, however, also depends on alternative printing and dyeing skills through the use of computer technology. While there is thus some evidence of corporate responsibility in the textiles and garment sector, it is nevertheless also incumbent on the government to help finance technology for recycling industrial waste (Wan and Chen, 2003).

The steel industry, like the textile sector, is being compelled to adjust both to market demand and to pressure to engage in clean production. But, in contrast with textiles, steel has been designated as a pillar industry, since it produces material necessary for the development of infrastructure and the diversification of consumer durables. Capital Steel, a major state enterprise, even in the wake of reform, continued to pursue quantitative goals and the expansion of scale, and only after 1995 increased funding for environmental protection. By the year 2000 on-site atmospheric pollution was said to have greatly declined. Subsequently, there has been greater emphasis on the ecological use of resources, recycling of waste water and, significantly for corporate responsibility, the disposal of urban refuse. These measures have been enshrined in Capital Steel's corporate strategy, related to both the environment and the market. Ecological targets include reduction in energy and water consumption per ton of steel, to result in a projected decline in discharged dust, smoke and sulphur by 2005. Pollution in Beijing, where Capital Steel's production is concentrated, has been exacerbated by the location of industries there. Thus, in addition to technological reform in the interests of clean production, some capital plant is to be relocated outside Beijing. In fact, integral to Capital Steel's strategy is social concern for the environment, which will necessarily impact on the local economy. In addition, economic demand is being addressed. In the domestic market, especially, steel supply exceeds demand, and there is now an emphasis on quality, variety and service rather than quantity. As well as this move towards high-grade steel, since 1995 diversification has begun so that eventually non-steel products are projected to constitute over 50 per cent of income from sales. As in the case of other aspects of ongoing state enterprise reform, the above objectives are only achievable through a change of managerial mindset effected through a new corporate culture encompassing social responsibility and production targets (Luo, 2003).

The focus, in relation to the textile and steel sectors discussed above, has been on the impact of production processes on the environment.

With respect to the car industry, another pillar sector, social responsibility may be seen to rest with the manufacturer and the consumer, in addition to government. In the year 2000 China had over sixteen million car users consuming about 85 per cent of the country's total oil production (Ou *et al.*, 2003). Domestically produced vehicles are more heavily polluting than foreign imports and represent a major source of pollution in China's large cities. Car ownership is also set to grow with a growing affluent middle class. A United Nations forecast suggests a tenfold increase from an average of ten to a hundred cars per 1,000 residents over the period from 1995 to 2020 (Hildebrandt, 2003; Nogales and Smith, 2004).

As a developing country China has been slow to formulate and enforce regulations relating to car-derived pollution. Nevertheless measures are currently in train at both national and local levels. In June 2000 there were moves to encourage the use of unleaded petrol through a fuel tax and in September of that year the Car Pollution Prevention Law was being implemented, with local bureaus responsible for enforcement. In June 2001 measures to recycle car scrap metal were put in motion, even though implementation is as yet inadequate. (Ou *et al.*, 2003).

Attempts to curb car use-derived pollution, however, are being hampered by the structure of the motor industry and the technological deficiencies discussed below. Currently, the industry lacks concentration and economies of scale; this is a legacy both of central planning and ironically also the decentralization undertaken as part of the post-1978 reforms. Car production is widely distributed; Beijing, Shanghai and Tianjin, for instance, all have manufacturers, led by central and local industrial bureaus. The production process is slow, innovation weak and costs high (ibid.). Management is also steeped in the seller's market values of the command economy. Chinese sources have therefore called for a change of managerial mindset and greater coordination among the country's car manufacturers, especially in terms of the establishment of national research and development centres linked to innovation for green production. Moves towards sustainable development also follow global market trends. Thus environmental concerns may be allied to economic profit. The fuel tax, briefly mentioned above, is a central government initiative to encourage energy saving technology, for example, electric batteries, and the creation of a market for low fuel consuming small vehicles. Already manufacturers of models like Santana and Red Flag have conducted research into the use of LPG and CNG. Additionally, ongoing experiments are improving the performance of batteries to further the commercial viability of electricity-powered cars.

In fact, the industry's research has been complemented by funding from the Ministry of Science and Technology which has promised to invest US$106 million to expedite the development of electric vehicles. Furthermore, there has been input from a global NGO, the International Institute for Energy Conservation (IIEC), which from 2000 to 2002 worked with the Chinese motor industry, the Ministry of Finance and other central agencies responsible for motor production to create energy efficiency standards for the Chinese car industry (ibid.; Hildebrandt, 2003; Turner, 2003). Finally, in terms of freight movement, the government has been increasing investment in waterways, through the use of which transportation is less environmentally damaging than via road or rail (Nogales and Smith, 2004).

The role of ecological industrial parks

The above discussion has focused on corporate responsibility for pollution control in selected key industries. To be effective, however, environmental protection must transcend regional and industrial boundaries. This necessitates cooperation in objective setting and goal attainment both within and between industries, as exemplified in the ecological industrial parks, the main concern of this section. Production planning must be directed towards sustainable development and effective waste disposal. But Chinese sources indicate weakness in the current application of ecological measures. It is insufficient for just a few enterprises in any given area to practice green production, since their efforts may be stymied by the activities of non-conforming companies (Liu and Zhang, 2001). In fact, however, cooperation in pollution control can be furthered by the newly created enterprise groups or national champions, designed as economies of scale and characterized by close customer–supplier relationships, in order to compete with foreign multinationals on both Chinese domestic and global markets. By virtue of such integration, enterprise groups may facilitate effective use of resources throughout the product life cycle from manufacturer to consumer, including the recycling of waste as raw material (Yang *et al.*, 2002).

This holistic approach to ecological production, increasingly advocated in Chinese sources, may be best effected through the use of the green supply chain. Prior to the reform of the command economy, Chinese state enterprise directors and managers were subject to vertical control, by central government ministries, which allocated raw materials, and there were few horizontal linkages between customers and suppliers, who might be responsible to different administrative hierarchies. With the advent of the market economy, however, from the 1980s onwards, there has been increasing choice of, say, suppliers, and middle managers have been compelled to engage in strategic decision-making in line with change in demand.

The green supply chain is an integral part of strategic management. Subsumed under that concept are the whole product life cycle and its impact on the environment through product planning, selection of raw materials, manufacturing, quality control, cost, consumption and recycling. Its operation presupposes information flow between and participation by all levels of the management hierarchy both within and between enterprises. The key players are the core enterprises, the top leadership of which sees that strategic decisions accord with the principles of the green supply chain. Middle managers and functional departmental staff disseminate environmental information to the workforce below, providing necessary training. It is the core enterprise managers who transmit requirements to suppliers. Cooperation between enterprises within a group, however, demands constant updating of technical skills to ensure that the manufacturing process for new products is low in resource and energy consumption, minimizing environmental pollution. A prerequisite is technical training, the provision of which may also be external through non-profit organizations and private consultants.

Enterprises must necessarily also be responsive to changing market demand; ecological quality may be enhanced while maintaining profitability. Here green supply chain management may confer two advantages. Firstly, by economizing on energy and raw materials, production and environmental control costs, like those for disposal of waste products, are reduced, with effects on product prices. In addition, a major source of waste derived from consumer goods is packaging, which cannot always be completely recycled. Recycling also requires energy. The green supply chain may help reduce the quantity of packaging used, which, in turn, cuts recycling costs. Secondly, while, as suggested earlier, consumer environmental awareness in China is still in its infancy, a green product brand image may enhance commercial reputation. Green production need not lower economic effectiveness. In fact, Chinese exporters are increasingly facing the green challenge in export markets. The EU, for example, has been imposing non-tariff barriers, including environmental standards like the Scrap Electrical Equipment Order, effective from August 2004, which makes Chinese manufacturers responsible for recycling fees with potential impact on the price competitiveness of such goods. In addition, an edict forbidding the use of harmful substances in electrical products is in effect from July 2006 (Tian and Wang, 2005). Awareness of trends in international environmental regulations can therefore only aid the export competitiveness of Chinese products. Thus the final stage in the product cycle is consumption after which, especially in the case of consumer durables, new are sought to replace old products. The recycling process may best be effected by manufacturers in a green supply chain. The practice of returning products for recycling, long *de rigueur* in the West, is slowly being adopted in China (Lin and Zhao, 2002).

A venue for the realization of the green supply chain concept is the Ecological Industrial Park. Like other ecological institutions, such parks were first established in the West in the 1990s and were later to develop in China. The objective is the optimum utilization of resources; enterprise waste is recycled for use by other manufacturers. In this respect, however, the Ecological Industrial Park goes beyond traditional waste recycling because it encompasses a group of enterprises and a neighbouring residential community. Waste recycling skills are shared, thereby cutting cost. This process is facilitated by the presence of different enterprise types in close proximity; for example, they may be as diverse as steel smelting, cement production, sugar and alcohol. The natural resources of a whole area are thus protected.

There are nevertheless prerequisites for establishing such parks. An ecologically favourable mindset must be inserted into corporate culture to enhance environmental awareness and technical skills throughout the enterprise. The latter is especially crucial since, while research is underway nationally regarding the creation of an ecological industrial system, specific skills are lacking. For example, comprehensive techniques to turn radioactive waste into usable raw materials are deficient. Specific skills include advanced information technology, western recycling techniques and programmes for environmental testing, the development of which is the responsibility of both government and enterprise.

In fact, a general overview of developments to date suggests that the original concept of the Ecological Industrial Park has not always been honoured in practice in China. Overseas practice indicates the need to establish industrial parks in underdeveloped areas via the introduction of advanced technologies, but in China they have so often been located in economically wealthy regions of high population concentration. Moreover seemingly clean industries like semiconductors have in fact caused toxic pollution. This is because regulations are not clear, investment is often insufficient and technical skills low; competition to establish parks for economic gain neglects the environment. The following case studies illustrate successful implementation of the Ecological Industrial Park. The first to be established in China was the Guigang Park in Guangxi. It was led by the Sugar Enterprise Group, the main industry, but the exchange and recycling of waste products and energy have facilitated the creation of an industrial network involving manufacturing, for example, paper, cement and fertilizer. Pollution is reduced, and diversification has enhanced defence against market risk. Similarly, in other parts of China enterprise groups have been pursuing a similar clean production strategy.

The second example cited, Jiutai City Ecological Industrial Park, located near the city of Zhangchun in Jilin Province, follows the model of Guigang, although it has suffered from a lack of corporate strategic direction and low levels of technology, with resulting pollution. Traditional industries include construction, drugs, processing of agricultural by-products and coal mining. The Park was started on the initiative of the Jiutai City government to promote sustainable development, and planning was entrusted to the Dong Beei Normal University Urban Planning Research Institute, the objective being to turn the traditional industries towards green production through the establishment of a unified ecological and technical network between industries, thus facilitating recycling. Thus, by-products and waste will permit the growth of new industries, producing, for instance, environmentally-friendly building materials and ecological fertilizer. In summary, the ecological industrial parks are designed to further sustainable development via cooperation between diverse industries, for example, through the industrial groups, and a key feature is the green supply chain (Liu and Zhang, 2001; Yang *et al.*, 2002; Liu *et al.*, 2003).

Environmental services: corporate social responsibility and the profit motive

The previous section has discussed sustainable development in manufacturing. Corporate social responsibility, however, may be allied to the profit motive in a service sector context, as indicated below. Post-1978 economic reform was first applied to manufacturing enterprise, but has latterly extended to the service sector, including basic urban environmental facilities. Rapid urban development has compounded the problems of managing pollution and waste disposal, and certain preconditions already exist for private sector environmental services. For example, laws have been passed to stimulate open and fair competition in this, as in other sectors. Nevertheless China's economy remains a half-reformed system, and the term 'privatization' is in a sense a misnomer when referring to the transfer of government-owned enterprise into the hands of independent operators. First, over the centuries Chinese governments have sought to control private enterprise which, in order to prosper, has developed close tributary relationships with government. This tradition continues. Secondly, in the recent reform context, crucial relational and informational networks have remained in government hands given the slow development of independent market intelligence. Nevertheless, Chinese sources indicate that criticism formerly levelled at the inefficiency and deficient cost structure of state industrial enterprises can equally well be applied to urban waste disposal and environmental facilities. Waste water treatment, for example, has not reached projected targets and, as demand increases, current government spending will be inadequate. Consequently, input of private capital is seen as a means of lowering cost through competition, simultaneously raising efficiency and service quality. The issue is how to encourage private enterprise to become involved in providing environmental amenities, given a number of existing barriers.

Currently, such facilities are owned and managed at various levels of government. This is because they are seen as a public service, a natural government monopoly, and involve high commercial risks but low rates of return for private investors. There is thus little incentive for private investment. In fact, the risks the private sector faces are political, legal and commercial. There may be future changes in government policy or new demands could be made of private operators, in disregard of contract. Legal risks concern the way in which disputes over contracts are resolved. Finally, investment may not be a sound commercial proposition, given possible inability to promptly collect charges which may in any case be set low and cannot easily be increased, with resulting uncertain profits and the inability to recoup investment costs. Moreover, service demand may not accord with forecasts.

The key to successful private involvement is state initiative, even if the aim is not complete privatization, but government–enterprise cooperation in management of environmental facilities, as outlined in the Tenth Five Year Plan. For instance, rubbish collection may be opened to market competition. Moreover, given that environmental facilities are a basic public service, the government has granted tax exemptions and low interest loans from national banks to investors – an instance being water pollution control in the Huai River Basin. Thus, in granting concessions to encourage private involvement, the Chinese authorities are following global trends, measures having been pioneered in the 1980s in Europe and the United States and later adopted in East Asian countries like Japan and Malaysia. A number of Chinese companies have entered the market for environmental protection. But, precisely because the environment is a public concern, the government has developed mechanisms to ensure that facilities are operationally effective. Such instruments include regulations regarding price setting, operational effectiveness and service standards. It is important, however, that policies concerning private involvement remain consistent, even if there are local leadership changes, lest investor confidence be reduced. Fair competition must be ensured where public bodies and private enterprises are both involved. Provincial authorities follow the lead of the central government. Fujian's promulgation of Temporary Regulations Regarding Urban Waste Water Facilities in October 2001 followed national laws. In addition, committees consisting of administrative, legal, banking, technical, financial, engineering and managerial personnel are established at various government levels. Nominally independent and designed to create a stable setting for private investors, the committees are nevertheless a control mechanism to ensure government supervision.

Within this framework private enterprise involvement in environmental facilities may take one of a number of forms, the most common of which is that whereby a government organization signs an agreement with a private company. Responsibility for financing and providing certain public services is transferred to the private concern on a contract for an extended period, usually ranging from between five and thirty years. In other forms government may elect to retain state property rights or establish a joint stock company. Thus in all cases government control is not necessarily weakened but in many respects strengthened. Private investment, however, facilitates reduction in government subsidies, once the user pay principle is adopted.

A number of successful examples have been cited in Chinese sources. In April 2002 the State Planning Commission, in conjunction with the Finance and Construction Ministries and the State Environmental Protection Bureau, issued a directive increasing the price of urban water supply and waste disposal under the market system. Public tenders for waste water disposal facilities had been advertised throughout China in November 2001, and in Shenzhen, for instance, two companies were given 15-year contracts. In the year after the operations were privatized government expenditure was reduced, while enhanced skills and improved management promise further cost effectiveness. Similarly, in Suzhou, greater efficiencies have allowed government subsidies for waste water disposal to be eliminated. Finally, in Beijing, a limited liability company has taken over the city's waste water disposal facilities, while general rubbish disposal, hitherto under the urban environment protection bureaus, is contracted to four independent enterprises. Thus, subjecting environmental protection to market forces, itself designed to reduce public expenditure, simultaneously fuses corporate responsibility and the profit motive (Xia, 2001; Xie *et al.*, 2002; K. Chen, 2003).

Summary and conclusions

Corporate social responsibility for the environment is a product both of the Chinese government's post-1978 reform programme and of China's stage of economic development. Until recently China, like other developing countries, accorded a low priority to environmental protection, but levels of pollution, industrial restructuring and international commitments like those of WTO membership have combined to stimulate growth in corporate awareness as reflected in the Tenth Five Year Plan (2001–2005). There are, however, barriers to enforcement of relevant legislation, not the least of which is the attitude of local governments intent on securing revenue from industries at the expense of environmental concerns. But in the corporate context there are, in addition, social and commercial pressures to internalize the cost of green production. Here may be cited the increasing influence of non-governmental organizations (NGOs) and greater consumer awareness, even though the conflict between sustainable development and economic profit remains. In the garment industry energy-saving technology and ecologically sound raw materials may help reduce pollution. Resource recycling now forms an integral part of Capital Steel's corporate strategy. Technological innovation, for instance in relation to cars powered by electricity, is being pioneered in the automobile industry. Pollution controls, however, transcend regional and industrial boundaries. Close relationships between suppliers and customers in a green supply chain facilitate sustainable development in ecological industrial parks, which encompass a number of industries in close proximity; one enterprise's waste through recycling becomes another's raw materials. Corporate social responsibility may also be demonstrated in the service sector.

Government-run environmental facilities like waste water disposal have proved inefficient and expensive; the input of private enterprise capital is seen as a means of raising service quality. Because private enterprise may doubt the commercial viability of managing such services, government has offered tax concessions and low interest loans as incentives.

In spite of privatization, however, there remains close government supervision of the sector. Thus environmental protection has only to a degree been subjected to market forces. Nevertheless, in the environmental sphere, corporate social responsibility is discharged in both the manufacturing and service sectors. In conclusion, partnership between government and industry in China has become crucial for environmental protection.

The evidence cited in this chapter suggests that, as China plays a growing role in the global economy, especially since its accession to the WTO, its leaders must become ever more responsive to the values and norms of international environmental regulation. Atmospheric pollution, for instance, knows no national boundaries. Additionally, debates on the respective merits of different energy sources, for example, are not confined to China, as the recent controversy in Britain concerning the nuclear option demonstrates amply. Moreover it is clear that political, economic and social issues in China have much in common with those in other Asian countries. The incidence of corruption, by which Chinese enterprises may avoid environmental responsibilities through connections with local governments, needs to be more effectively addressed. There are, nevertheless, as indicated in this chapter, trends which favour greater future environmental protection. In an era of globalization Chinese executives' greater familiarity with western commercial practices and greater environmental awareness among consumers will increase the need for the acquisition of soft skills like the marketing of green products, in turn germane to sustainable development. In addition, response to growing consumer cultures will hasten the evolution of new managerial competences throughout Asia. In examining current trends and future perspectives, however, the pitfalls of ethnocentrism are to be avoided: it is by no means a foregone conclusion that Chinese and Asian norms will necessarily replicate those in the Anglo-American tradition. In the environmental sphere, as in other managerial areas, solutions may prove to be uniquely Chinese or Asian or perhaps there is a greater likelihood of hybrids born of a blend of different cultures and practices.

References

Chen, K. (2003) 'Establishing Green Funding to Develop Environmental Protection Enterprises', *Shanghai Jingji (Shanghai Economy)* 1/2: 29–31.

Chen, X. (2003) 'Green International Trade Barriers and our Country's Response Strategy', *Jingji Tizhi Gaige* 2: 13–15.

Fu, J.Y. (2002) 'Internalization of Environmental Cost and Industrial International Competitiveness', *Zhongguo Gongye Jingji* (*China's Industrial Economy*) 6: 37–44.

Hildebrandt, T. (2003) 'Making Green in Beijing', *China Business Review* 6: 16–21.

Lin, Y.F. and Zhao, X. (2002) 'Strategic Choice of Corporations' Environmental Protection in China – Green Supply Chain Management', *Huanjing Baohu* 6: 42–4, 47.

Liu, F.X. and Zhang, X. (2001) 'Discussing the Ecology of Industry and Technology', *Gongye Jingji*, 9: 45–8.

Liu, X.F., Luo, H. and Zhang, Z. (2003) 'The Industrial Concept of Ecological Industry in the 21st Century', *Gongye Jingji* 7: 71–5.

Luo, B.S. (2003) 'Sustainable Development of the Steel Industry', *Guanli Shijie* 2: 1–3, 22.

Mayfield, J. (2003) 'Top 10 Questions on Environmental Projects', *China Business Review* 6: 10–15.

Nogales, A. and Smith, G. (2004) 'China's Evolving Transportation Sector', *China Business Review* 2: 24–9.

Ou, X.M., Zhang, X.L. and Hu, X.J. (2003) 'Enabling Green Automobile Development in China', *Huanjing Baohu* 1: 56–8.

Pullam, F. (2006) 'Corporate Responsibility as China Strategy', *China Business Review* 2: 34–7.

Stelzer, I. (2003) 'OPEC Squeeze Won't Throttle the Recovery', *Sunday Times*, 14 December.

Tian, D.W. and Wang, F.M. (2005) 'The Effects of EU Directives on China's Export Competitiveness in China's Electronic Products', *Guoji Maoyi Wenti*, 3: 51–5.

Turner, J.L. (2003) 'Cultivating Environmental NGO–business partnerships', *China Business Review* 6: 22–5.

Wan, G. and Chen, Y. (2003) 'Ecological Thinking of Sustainable Development of Textile and Garment Industry', *Huanjing Baohu* 7: 52–6.

Wang, J. (2003) 'Discussing the Current Status and Amendment of our Country's Environmental Protection Laws', *Huanjing Baohu* 6: 8–10.

Wang, Z.J. (2002) 'Entering the WTO: Challenges and Opportunities for China', *Huanjing Baohu* 3: 36–40.

Xia, G. (2001) 'Realizing the Tenth Five-Year Plan in Environmental Protection under the Market System', *Huanjing Baohu* 9: 40–2.

Xie, J., Wang, L.X., Zhou, Y., Zhou, X. and Pei, X.F. (2002) 'To Encourage Private Enterprise to Give Service to the Environment of a City', *Huanjing Baohu* 10: 33–6.

Yang, Q.S., Xu, X.P. and Wang, R.C. (2002) 'The Theory of Industrial Ecology and Eco-industrial Park Design – a Case Study of Jiutai, Jilin Province', *Gongye Jingji* 12: 63–6.

6

Managerial Perceptions of the Business Environment: Cross-national Comparison of China, Singapore and Malaysia

Yi Tan and Jeremy Cresswell

Introduction

This chapter utilizes empirical evidence to examine the dominant business environment conditions that impinge on the energy service industry in East Asia. It seeks to: (i) develop a well-defined typology for interpreting and analysing the organizational environment; (ii) provide empirical evidence on the validity of the typology; and (iii) present results on the managerial perceptions of the business environment in China, with reference to the experience in Singapore and Malaysia. The principal findings of this study show that it is possible both to conceptualize and to analyse organizational environments in terms of three dimensions. Results support our contention that the business environment in which energy service organizations operate in East Asia is perceived as uncertain, with the lowest level in China and the highest level in Singapore. Although the business environment is complex and dynamic in each country, the environmental conditions are predictable and attractive to energy service companies. Results also show significant evidence that the perceived environmental uncertainty is positively associated with perceived environmental dynamism and hostility. It is believed that this study assists senior management to gain insight into the business environment of East Asia for strategic decisions, especially in the context of the petroleum industry's upstream offshore supply chain.

This chapter seeks to provide an in-depth and contemporary understanding of the emerging business issues in East Asian countries such as China, Singapore and Malaysia. It focuses on the perceived managerial uncertainty under different geographical business conditions. The research studies executives' perceptions of the environmental characteristics in order to test, modify and develop, on an empirical basis, an environmental typology grounded in organizational and strategic management theory. The chapter also attempts to make a significant addition to existing literature in Asian strategic management by providing empirical evidence gathered in the selected countries.

Strategic management theories and practices stress that understanding the business environment is crucial. Despite most literature on organizational or strategic management theories introducing the concept of the environment, comprehensive analyses or empirical studies of the environmental characteristics in East Asia[1] are limited. Theoretical development in this field has largely been based on research into organisations that operate in a western business context. Consequently, it may have little practical application in East Asia, which is a major centre of energy industry activity.

Duncan (1972) defines a concept to distinguish the internal from the external environment. The internal environment refers to all factors existing inside an organization, including organizational culture, structure and functions. The external environment refers to all the forces outside the organization. In this study, the term environment refers to the external environment.

The features of a firm's external environment are described in numerous ways. Most strategy theories characterize environments in terms of their levels, for instance, general or macro, industry and task environment, and firm-specific variables (Duncan, 1972; Koberg, 1987; Daft *et al.*, 1988). Examples of environmental influences may include government action, economic condition, sociocultural issues, technological condition, ecology, demographics, labour market and suppliers (Johnson and Scholes, 1999). The environmental influences can refer to forces that drive the change in industry structure and competition (Porter, 1985) or critical operating factors for which firms compete. Strategies and management styles are affected by these environmental factors. Thompson (1967) suggests that the priority for an organisation is to deal with the uncertain eventualities of the environment, particularly those of the task environment (Dill, 1958).

Early in the 1950s, organizational theorists started to investigate organization–environment interaction (Tung, 1979) and they have found that the views of managers play a central role in learning about environment (Hegarty and Tihanyi, 1999). Managers are encouraged to become more responsive to the dictates of the external environment and are required to scan and assess environmental conditions when making strategic decisions (Fahey and Narayanan, 1986). Fahey and Narayanan suggest that assessment implies identifying and evaluating how and why current and projected environment changes may affect or will affect strategic management of an organization. Assessment attempts to investigate what the key issues are that are presented by the environment and what the implications of the issues are for the organization. Accurate assessment of the business environment by managers may help bring about strategies that are more effective and thereby higher performance for long-term success (Downey *et al.*, 1975; Hambrick, 1982; Daft *et al.*, 1988; Hegarty and Tihanyi, 1999).

Tung (1979) argues that a major obstruction has been how best to describe and conceptualize the organizational environment. The reliability of an instrument for measuring managerial perceptions of the business environment is still to be developed and tested. Given the importance of the perceived business environment construct to theory and research in strategic management, research on the perceived business environment remains a relevant theoretical and empirical task.

In recent years, researchers have devoted their attention to managerial perception under uncertain environmental conditions. The concept of the uncertainty of the perceived environment advanced by many researchers (Tung, 1979; Hrebiniak and Snow, 1980; Koberg, 1987; Daft *et al.*, 1988) has been a key aspect or a central component of a number of strategy theories (Miles and Snow, 1978; Lawrance and Lorsch, 1967; Mintzberg, Ahlstrand and Lampel, 1998; Miller, 1993). Research (Ireland *et al.*, 1987; Kotha and Nair, 1995; Sutcliffe and Huber, 1998; Sutcliffe and Zaheer, 1998; Elenkov, 1997; Simerly and Li, 2000) integrating the perspectives on organizational uncertainties has been developed. As Miller (1993) finds out, 'a major obstacle to empirical research on perceived environmental uncertainties is the lack of well-established measurement instruments. Existing measures from organisation theory suffer from conceptual problems and inadequate reliability and validity'. That difficulty still exists.

For different industries in different geographical regions, the nature of the business environment can mean different things. Some of the macro-environmental influences are commonly seen as important to organizations. On the other hand, Johnson and Scholes (1999) argue that environmental forces that are especially important for one organization may not be the same for another; and, over time, their importance may change. A multinational corporation might be especially concerned with government relations and understanding the policies of local governments, since it may be operating plants or subsidiaries within many different countries with different political systems. A retailer, on the other hand, may be primarily concerned with cultural related issues such as local customer tastes and behaviour. An oil- and gas-related company is likely to be concerned with its technological environment which leads to product or service differentiations. In this sense, environmental analysis involves efforts to identify key issues.

Here, we address some of the above concerns by examining the relative effects of the business environment on the offshore oil and gas service sector in East Asia. Based on previous research (Simerly and Li, 2000; Sutcliffe and Zaheer, 1998; Elenkov, 1997) and preliminary investigation (Tan, 2001), this study focuses on six major sectors, namely, economic, regulatory, technological, customers, suppliers and competitions. Although the examination of other environmental influences was not highlighted in this study, the authors remained aware of the significance of these issues in the geographical area under review. As Johnson and Scholes (1999) have said that none of the environmental forces will remain constant and managers need to be aware of their changing impact, other macroenvironmental factors that have not been covered in this study can be investigated in future work.

The principal country chosen to locate the research was China, but we also included comparisons from two other nations – Singapore and Malaysia – as these three countries are considered politically stable and in favour of profitable business opportunities. The presence of domestic-based manufacturing plants and service organizations, professional high-tech service companies from North America and Europe as well as other foreign companies indicates that the selected countries are fertile investigation areas.

It has been argued that it is very challenging for any researchers, especially those who are familiar with western theories and contexts, to conduct empirical work in East Asia. This chapter provides a useful methodological solution to collecting and analysing primary data in an East Asian context. The chapter also presents a conceptual framework to assess the environmental uncertainty. The generated theoretical typology is deemed useful for academics and practitioners in doing similar research in other industrial or geographical arenas.

The rest of this chapter is organized as follows: firstly, the definition and characteristics of the energy service industry are introduced and the reason why this particular industry was selected for the empirical studies. Then the national contexts of the environmental conditions in China, Singapore and Malaysia are introduced. A theoretical literature review discusses the problems with existing environmental typology and develops an alternative approach. Research methods utilized in the study are outlined. The chapter then presents the results of the research and examines the validity of the developed typology; the final section presents discussions and conclusion, including the implication of empirical findings for theory and business practice.

The energy service industry

The supply chain of the oil and gas industry extends upstream through the suppliers and manufacturers, and downstream through distributors and other suppliers to the final consumer. It is a complex and dynamic network of facilities and organizations with different and conflicting objectives. The upstream petroleum industry supply chain consists of many sub-industrial sectors that comprise mainly contracting and construction companies, service companies and vendors. Within each of the sub-sectors, firms usually have their own specialized (focused) area and they rarely become involved with other activities apart from their advanced ones.

Phillips (1998) suggests that, within the oil and gas industry, a group of professional companies often engage in highly specialized supply and service work. Integrated contractors offer a portfolio of interlinked services and products, all geared towards client oil companies or other oil and gas service companies. Service organizations form a clear embodiment of the supply chain within the oil and gas industry, which comprises upstream, covering exploration and production; midstream, covering oil and gas transportation pipelines and tankers; and downstream, covering refining marketing and sales. Halliburton, for example, a technologically focused oilfield service company, covers the complete supply chain from exploration, via field development to production.

Service businesses cover a broad range such as: the drilling of wells by drilling contractors; services associated with drilling and evaluating wells, including casing, cementing, logging and testing; specialist technical services in support of the platform operations, including instrumentation, helicopter and ship operations as well as completion, 'fishing' and workover solutions. Service organizations design, manufacture and own specialist equipment to enable them to serve their niche markets. In addition, general services such as catering and cleaning, deck labour and crews are also included in the supply chain. Normally, a service company in one sub-sector might have no knowledge or interest in any other service activities.

Service companies serve the needs of not only the oil and gas industry but also other economically important energy sub-sets, such as nuclear energy, coal, power generation and petrochemicals (Simmons and Company International, 1999). Many are even involved in business outside energy. Hence, in this study, the energy service industry is classified as entities engaged in the business of providing products or services to oil organizations such as operators, other oil service and supply companies, or to organizations in another energy sub-sector.

Previous research examining the relative impacts of the business environment in the energy service industry is rare. Evidence from existing literature shows that the offshore service sector in East Asia is at a developing stage, and that there is ample space for conducting empirical studies. Consequently, the energy service sector in China, Singapore and Malaysia is treated as the essential background for this study.

Regional business contexts

Among East Asian countries, China has become the regional economic driving engine in the past decade and will potentially dwarf the US and the European Union to become the third global economy (Wolf, 2003). The country is also the regional leader in terms of oil and gas exploration and production (E&P). As power rests with the Chinese Communist Party (CCP) of 60 million members, its impact on the business environment could be expected to be very strong. Within the energy sector, all industry regulation is government controlled (Scottish Enterprise, 2002). The substantial Chinese exploration and production industry has been generated by the ministries and state-owned enterprises (SOEs). However, continuing reform of the Chinese petroleum industry has created more room for service sector development by allowing indigenous firms to have greater control of resources and more freedom to manage their own affairs (Chen, 2000). This also represents a considerable opportunity for foreign service companies to compete in the marketplace.

Malaysia ranks as an attractive emerging E&P market and a significant regional player in terms of offshore activity (BP, 1998; Mackay and Adam, 1998). Like China, there are initiatives that promote indigenous suppliers. All companies supporting the upstream sector must be licensed by Petronas, the state oil and gas company, which was established in 1974, and those supplying the downstream sector must be registered. Companies wishing to supply equipment, services or materials to the upstream sector must collaborate with a local firm run by Bumiputras (Bumiputra means 'Son of the Soil' and refers to the indigenous Malays). The Bumiputra policy is designed to encourage participation of indigenous Malays in the Malaysian economy which, at the time, was dominated by Malaysian Chinese, and foreign business people (DTI, 1996). Many Malaysian companies are now developing their domestic base and seeking to become involved in playing an important role in the region of South East Asia and beyond.

The island state Singapore has no oil and gas reserves nor has there been any offshore activity. Like Japan, this country is a substantial importer of oil and gas (DTI, 1996). Nevertheless, it is unquestionably Asia's leading petroleum industry centre. Refining, bunkering, petrochemical production, oil trading, and drilling and floating production unit manufacturing are all important components of the industry. Appreciating its strategic location and attractiveness to foreign investors, Singapore established itself as the region's leading oil-refining and petrochemicals centre. It is also regarded as an important logistics support base from which international service firms deliver their services to the region, mainly South East Asian E&P countries (DTI, 1996; Abraham, 1999). It is well known that Singapore offers environmental advantages in terms of good financial and economic stability as well as advanced information technology. Although it is encountering increasing competition from others in the region in refining and petrochemical production, Singapore remains the preferred regional hub for numerous international service and supply companies.

With respect to the remaining East Asian nations or regions, with the exception of Japan, they were neither significant energy players in the region nor were they financially, economically and politically stable. The language barrier is another factor applied when selecting countries for this study. In short, the combination of the above points rendered China, Singapore and Malaysia very suitable sites for empirical research concerning the assessment of the regional business environment.

Theoretical review

Environmental typology

In the past, researchers have made a distinction between the composition of an organizational environment and environmental characteristics or dimensions (Tung, 1979). The composition of the environment refers to the factors or sectors encompassing the crucial environment, for example, economic, regulatory, technological, social, customers, competitors and suppliers (Koberg, 1987; Daft *et al.*, 1988; Ireland *et al.*, 1987; Hegarty and Tiahnyi, 1999; Luo and Park, 2001). For environmental characteristics or dimensions, it refers to the aspects of the environment confronting the organization, for example, complexity, dynamism and hostility (Daft *et al.*, 1988; Tung, 1979; Hrebiniak and Snow 1980; Miles and Snow, 1978). The organizational environment can be static or dynamic, complex or simple, hostile or favourable (Mintzberg *et al.*, 1998).

Managers operating in the external environment context confront a variety of uncertain factors. Most commonly, general environmental uncertainty includes the uncertainty of politics, economics, sociocultural influence and technology (PEST). Industrial or task environmental uncertainty encompasses suppliers, buyers, potential entrants, substitute products or services and rivalry among competitors. Researchers in international business studies have focused primarily on the assessment of political government policy and macroeconomic uncertainties and appropriate organizational responses. Miller (1993) argues that uncertainties are related to market demand for products or services, product and process technologies, the availability of critical inputs, and strategic actions by competitors and potential entrants.

Previous researchers (Miles and Snow, 1978; Tan and Litschert, 1994) have developed a number of sectors or categories to measure the three dimensions of environmental uncertainty in general and also in the task environment. However, the limitation of the validity of their environmental components is that the scope of the concept on each of the environmental factors is still too broad for managers to understand the meaning perfectly. Very recently, several studies (Hegarty and Tihanyi, 1999; Luo and Park, 2001) were conducted to measure the perceived business environment through quantitative analysis, but few considered how to combine the degree and scope of determinant environmental sectors and environmental dimensions to gain a comprehensive perception of the business environment. As such, it is indeed necessary to develop a well-defined typology for interpreting and analysing the three environmental dimensions.

In order to portray a picture of the perceived environmental uncertainty, three environmental dimensions investigated in this study were complexity, dynamism and hostility. Using the identified six environmental sectors as a basis, we established a scale that categorizes the environment and provides a rating for its degree of uncertainty. The three dimensions were developed as the typology presented in Table 6.1.

Table 6.1 Environmental typology: dimensions versus sectors

Dimensions	Sectors	7-point Bipolar Scale		
(I)	Homogeneity			Heterogeneity
Complexity	Economics	1 2 3 4 5 6 7		
	Technology	1 2 3 4 5 6 7		
	Regulatory	1 2 3 4 5 6 7		
	Customers	1 2 3 4 5 6 7		
	Competitions	1 2 3 4 5 6 7		
	Suppliers	1 2 3 4 5 6 7		
(II)	Stability			Instability
Dynamism	Economics	1 2 3 4 5 6 7		
	Technology	1 2 3 4 5 6 7		
	Regulatory	1 2 3 4 5 6 7		
	Customers	1 2 3 4 5 6 7		
	Competitions	1 2 3 4 5 6 7		
	Suppliers	1 2 3 4 5 6 7		
(III)	Friendliness			Hostility
Hostility	Economics	1 2 3 4 5 6 7		
	Technology	1 2 3 4 5 6 7		
	Regulatory	1 2 3 4 5 6 7		
	Customers	1 2 3 4 5 6 7		
	Competitions	1 2 3 4 5 6 7		
	Suppliers	1 2 3 4 5 6 7		
Uncertainty level	Very High			Very Low

Environmental complexity, dynamism and hostility

Fahey and Narayanan (1986) note that complexity refers to the degree of similarity or differentiation between elements or entities within and across environmental factors or components. It pertains to the number and heterogeneity or diversity of factors and components in the external environment. Tung (1979) explains that the heterogeneity or diversity included two arrays of variables: the number of factors and components in external environments, and the relative differentiation or variety of these factors and components.

Previous works (Lawrence and Lorsch, 1967; Duncan, 1972; Tung, 1979; Dess and Beard, 1984) have directed attention to managerial perceptions under changing environmental conditions and suggested that dynamism is an important dimension. Industry dynamics have been viewed as giving rise to managerial uncertainties. They suggest that environmental dynamism is the product of several forces operating at one time, including the growth of the size and number of organizations within an industry, and the growth of the rate of technological change and its dispersion throughout the industry. Dess and Beard (1984) define environmental dynamism as the rate and the degree of instability of environmental change. The Change rate refers to the frequency and enormity of turbulence of environmental factors and components. Instability may increase the complexity of environmental factors and require prompt organizational action (Hegarty and Tihanyi, 1999). Miles and Snow (1978) emphasize that uncertainty refers to the unpredictability of environmental or organizational variables that have an impact on corporate performance. An effect of increasing levels of environmental dynamism is to reduce access to knowledge needed to make strategic decisions. This, in turn, reduces the stability and predictability perceived by executives regarding environmental factors or components (Tung, 1979).

Research has shown that there are two aspects to hostility (Luo and Park, 2001). First, it points out how critical resources are controlled by each environmental sector and, secondly, it refers to the deterrence factor, in other words, the extent to which each environmental sector becomes a threat to the growth of an organization. In the first case, hostility shows the extent to which resources required by the organization are available in its environment and describes the capacity of the environment to support organizations in the marketplace (Fahey and Narayanan, 1986). In the second case, Pfeffer and Salancik's (1978) resource dependency theory proposes that organizations arrange their external relationships in response to the uncertainty rising from dependence on components of the environment. Using the Tan and Litschert (1994) approach and drawing from the resource dependence perspective, hostility focuses on the degree of the organisation's dependence on others for resources.

Research assumptions

Historically, the service industry is highly uncertain and is very dynamic due to the instability of oil prices. Bankruptcies, mergers, and acquisitions, organizational restructuring, and changed ownership structures have substantially reduced the number of companies of all sizes and types active in the industry (Pearce and Smith, 1997). Looking at Petromin's Oil and Gas Directory (2000), industry consolidation had changed the number of service firms in East Asia. The market for the energy service industry is also changing. In China and Malaysia, state-owned companies used to be the key buyers from the service industry.

In recent years, with international oil firms stepping into exploration and production (E&P) activities in the East Asian domestic markets, the buyer structure has widened. Buyers of service companies from the wider energy or marine industries are becoming one of the market segments. Based on these facts, Assumption 1 is generated below for the investigation of the empirical study.

Assumption 1: For energy service organizations in East Asian countries like China, Singapore and Malaysia, the nature of the business environment will be perceived to be uncertain.

The service sector used to be simple but is becoming more sophisticated as it has taken more and more responsibilities from petroleum companies. In their study, Tan and Litschert (1994) have provided empirical evidence that the environment in China is dynamic, complex and hostile. In order to make a comparison with Singapore and Malaysia, Assumption 2 emerges.

Assumption 2: For energy service organizations in China, Singapore and Malaysia, executives perceive that the business environment in which they operate will be dynamic, complex and hostile.

It was intended to explore some of the relationships between two variables amongst environmental characteristics or dimensions. Early work (Lawrence and Lorsch, 1967; Duncan, 1972; Tung, 1979; Downey *et al.*, 1975; Dess and Beard, 1984; Luo and Park, 2001) found that if the number and diversity of environmental factors or components increase, the executives' cognitive abilities to figure out the significances are increasingly limited. As a result, the level of perceived environmental uncertainty increases.

Tung (1979) defines that the concept of dynamism pertains to change rate, which includes frequency and magnitude of change; and the stability of change or predictability of the change pattern. If the change is more or less random rather than following a trend, the change may be too sudden and completely unpredictable for organizations to possess the capabilities to deal with the change. It was hypothesized that this sort of change would greatly increase the degree of environment uncertainty perceived by executives (Tung, 1979). When it is difficult or impossible for an organization to predict the latest changes and grasp their implications of operations and activities, the dynamism dimension thus has an impact on the degree of uncertainty perceived by executives (Thompson, 1967; Duncan, 1972; Downey *et al.*, 1975; Simerly and Li, 2000). Simerly and Li (2000) propose that greater environmental uncertainty is associated with greater environmental dynamism.

What is more, the level of perceived environmental hostility depends not only on resource availability, but also on relationships with environmental agencies and competition within the same industry (Mintzberg *et al.*, 1998). As the environment becomes less favourable or more hostile, firms are subjected to greater uncertainty (Tan and Litschert, 1994; Luo and Park, 2001; Kotha and Nair, 1995). As such, Assumption 3 is developed for exploiting the empirical evidence.

Assumption 3: For the energy service industry in China, Singapore and Malaysia, the perceived environmental uncertainty will be associated with the perceived environmental complexity, dynamism and hostility.

Research methods

The empirical research was progressed by employing a multi-method approach. Joint methods of data collection, coding and analysis of data are the fundamental operations of this study. Data collection involved a formal questionnaire survey addressed to senior management. The data obtained represent the problems to be investigated and highlight the critical issues that form an important part of research findings. The findings revealed by the survey are discussed in order to portray a comprehensive picture of the content of the questionnaire results. This is crucial to understanding the implications behind some of the data gathered in questionnaires.

Research instrument

The survey questionnaire was arranged to begin with easy or general questions before moving into more difficult or sensitive and specific areas. Participants were told there was no such thing as right or wrong, nor were there good or bad answers, what mattered was their thoughts. The subjects were therefore encouraged simply to respond by justifying from their own experience, how they felt about each topic. A Chinese version questionnaire was also prepared for collecting data from China.

A multidimensional construct (Elenkov, 1997; Luo and Park, 2001) is used to conceptualize environment. Three environmental dimensions, viz. complexity, dynamism and hostility, were defined as the measures for assessing the environmental sectors at a task environment level. The senior executives' views of and attitudes towards the environmental factors were measured by using a 45-item scale. The questions were arranged as multi-item scales corresponding to the six environmental sectors. Each of the environmental items indicates the degree of environmental complexity, hostility and dynamism, and in turn, the level of the environmental uncertainty. The respondents were asked to rate the degree to which they agreed on various characteristics of the environmental sectors.

The answers on the perceived complexity and hostility were measured by a series of seven-point bipolar rating scales (Zikmund, 2000). Bipolar adjectives anchor the right and left of the scale, with 1 indicating that the respondent most strongly agrees with the left assessment; 7 indicating that the respondent most strongly agrees with the right assessment; and 4 showing that the respondent feels that, for his organization, the situation lies midway between both. Environmental dynamism was similarly measured, but with 1 indicating very predictable, 7 indicating very unpredictable and 4 indicating a neutral situation. For instance, to measure the attitude towards perceived dynamism, from left to right, the scale intervals were interpreted as very static, static, tend to be static, neutral, tend to be dynamic, dynamic and very dynamic. As such, a question may ask:

The business environment in which you operate is

very static 1 2 3 4 5 6 7 *very dynamic*

Should '5' be selected by a respondent, it indicates that the respondent 'agrees with the assessment as stated on the right'. Hence, in each measuring situation, a score has been assigned for the perceived business environment.

Data collection

The collected primary data were based on a questionnaire survey sent to the senior managers of oil and gas service organizations operating in China, Singapore and Malaysia. Between late 2001 and early 2002, 500 questionnaires were distributed via post (mainly), e-mail and fax; then follow-up phone calls and e-mails were made in an attempt to achieve the proposed response target. Each of the packets mailed contained a covering letter with the correspondent's photograph on it, the questionnaire and a self-addressed envelope for return. As a result, by August 2002, 108 completed questionnaires had been returned by managers involved in operating businesses in China, Singapore and Malaysia, with a response rate of 21.6 per cent (the response rates from China, Singapore and Malaysia are approximately 18, 23 and 14 per cent respectively). Among those, 98 completed questionnaires were usable for the final primary data analysis. For reasons of confidentiality, the names of respondents and companies were classified in a code term. The associated details of these companies can therefore not be identified by anyone except the correspondent.

Analytical techniques

Different statistical techniques are used in this analysis. The collected data are summarized using frequencies and histograms. Various descriptive statistics are calculated in terms of means, which are adopted to provide hypothetical connotations (Field, 2000) of the data. This is done for each of the environmental variables. Further statistical analysis is carried out to evaluate the relationship of the perceived environmental characteristics. In order to distinguish the organizations in China from those in Singapore and Malaysia, cross-tabulation statistics are utilised for comparative analysis.

In short, frequency distributions are used to analyse the background information on company profiles. The Spearman correlation and chi-square tests are used to test cognitive coherence between the perceived business environment uncertainty and the perceived dynamism, hostility and complexity. To evaluate the relationship between the two variables among the three dimensions of the perceived business environment, the Spearman correlation and Crosstabs with two-way contingency table analysis and chi-square tests are employed. To test the differences of the perceived environmental uncertainty by country groups, the Mann-Whitney and Kruskal-Wallis tests are applied. A number of Boxplot graphs and Scatter diagrams are also applied to highlight the pattern of differences or correlations.

Research results

Of the 98 participating organizations, 31 were situated in China, 39 in Singapore, 21 in Malaysia and 7 in other countries such as Thailand, Indonesia and the UK. Those companies located outside China, Singapore and Malaysia operated businesses in these three countries, but their business strategic decisions were made at the headquarters elsewhere. A large majority (93.9 per cent) of the organizations had operated for five or more years since their existing businesses were formed. Most (61.2 per cent) of the respondent organizations are wholly foreign-owned or joint ventures and a considerable proportion (38.8 per cent) are domestic organizations, including wholly domestic state owned, wholly domestic private or individual owned and domestic share holding or public limited companies.

Perceived environmental factors

Because of the exploratory nature of preliminary analysis, the mean is employed as a hypothetical value (Field, 2000) for the measure of central tendency. For instance, in order to gain an assessment of the perceived complexity, if the mean is above 4, hypothetically, the perception is associated with the right statement showing the level of complexity; if below 4, it is associated with the left statement showing the extent of simplification. By doing this, the observed results emerge as below.

Complexity assessment

Five environmental influences hint at the levels of complexity (Table 6.2). The knowledge required to understand the economic situation in the region where they operated was complicated ($M = 4.77$). The government regulations, legislation and policies tended to be sophisticated ($M = 4.34$). The level of technology involved in the oil and gas service sector was high ($M = 5.09$). The number of oil and gas customers they served tended to be large ($M = 4.30$). The scope of companies within the service sector in which they operated was extensive as they came from all over the world ($M = 5.03$).

In contrast to complexity, five other issues appear to show the simplification of the environmental influences. The observed results show that the needs and preferences of the oil and gas clients whom they served

Table 6.2 Perceived complexity, dynamism and hostility ($N = 98$)

(i) Complexity Assessment

Variables	Measurement	Minimum	Maximum	Mean
Economics Knowledge Required	Simple/Sophisticated	1.00	7.00	4.77
Technological Level	Low/High	2.00	7.00	5.09
Industrial Products/Services	Similar/Different	1.00	7.00	3.51
Government Regulations, Legislation and Policies	Simple/Complicated	1.00	7.00	4.34
Number of Oil and Gas Clients	Small/Large	1.00	7.00	4.30

Needs and Preferences of Oil and Gas Clients	Similar/Different	1.00	7.00	3.22
Number of Suppliers	Small/Large	1.00	7.00	3.92
Supply Conditions by Suppliers	Similar/Different	1.00	7.00	3.80
Number of Firms within the Industry Sector	Small/Large	1.00	7.00	3.26
Scope of Firms within the Industry Sector	Narrow/Extensive	1.00	7.00	5.03

(ii) Hostility Assessment

Variables	Measurement	Minimum	Maximum	Mean
Size of Market Demand	Big/Small	1.00	7.00	3.32
Changing of Market Demand	Increase/Decrease	1.00	6.00	3.34
Access to Available Technologies	Easy/Difficult	1.00	7.00	3.73
National Government Regulations and Legislation	Benefit/Limit	1.00	7.00	4.03
Local Government Policies	Positive/Negative	1.00	7.00	4.14
Relationship with Government	Close/Distant	1.00	7.00	4.13
Levels of Key Customers Switching to Competitors	Difficult/Easy	1.00	7.00	4.66
Relationship with Customers	Good/Poor	1.00	6.00	2.29
Access to Suppliers for Materials or Goods	Easy/Difficult	1.00	7.00	3.01
Relationship with Suppliers	Supportive/ Unhelpful	1.00	5.00	2.70
Entry Barriers	High/Low	1.00	6.00	3.14
Rivalry among Competitors	Orderly/Turbulent	1.00	7.00	4.54
Competitive Actions	Reasonable/ Unreasonable	1.00	7.00	4.29
Relationship with Competitors	Collaborative/ Un-collaborative	1.00	7.00	4.17

Table 6.2 (Continued)

(iii) Dynamism Assessment

Variable	Measurement	Minimum	Maximum	Mean
Customer Demand for Existing Products/Services	Predictable/ Unpredictable	1.00	7.00	3.01
Customer Demand for New Products/Services		1.00	6.00	3.50
Customer Demand for Higher Quality or More Service		1.00	7.00	2.93
Customer Preference for Lower Prices		1.00	7.00	2.31
Changes in Competitive Price		1.00	7.00	4.04
Competitors' Quality Improvement		1.00	7.00	3.51
Competitors' Introduction of New Products/Services		1.00	7.00	3.69
Suppliers Rising Prices		1.00	7.00	3.43
Suppliers Quality Reduction		1.00	7.00	3.85
Suppliers Introduction of New Materials or Standard Products		1.00	7.00	3.69
Changes in Oil and Gas E&P Level		1.00	7.00	3.76
Changes in Well Counts		1.00	7.00	3.47
Changes in Rig Counts		1.00	7.00	3.64
Technological Changes		1.00	6.00	3.26
Rate of Technological Diffusion		1.00	6.00	3.52
Changes in National Regulations and Legislation		1.00	7.00	3.76
Changes in Local Government Policies		1.00	7.00	3.80

were similar ($M = 3.51$). Both the number of firms within the industry sector and the number of suppliers tended to be small ($M = 3.26$ and 3.92), suggesting that the niche market was shared or dominated mainly by a few firms. Supply conditions (for example price, quality, speed or service) provided by their suppliers tended to be similar ($M = 3.80$).

Hostility assessment

Three environmental influences made the environment unfavourable and therefore hostile to the energy service organizations. From Table 6.2, the respondent executives perceived that it was easy for their key customers to switch to another competitor's products or services ($M = 4.67$). Competitive actions adopted by firms within the service sector might tend to be unreasonable ($M = 4.29$), indicating that some firms imitated the changes or innovations created by leading companies that could in turn become very concerned about being followed closely by their competitors. The rivalry among the competitors within the service sector in which they operate was turbulent ($M = 4.54$) and competitions were largely based on price.

Seven environmental influences were discovered in favour of operating businesses in the region. The favourable scenarios include the big market demand within the oil and gas industry that they serve ($M = 3.32$), an easy access to available technologies ($M = 3.73$), or high entry barriers to the oil and gas service sector in which they operate ($M = 3.14$). In the last circumstance, the situation discourages new competitors from entering into existing industrial sectors. Remaining environmental influences are interpreted as having a neutral impact on the service organizations.

Dynamism assessment

Apart from the fact that the influence of changes in competitive price appeared to be at a neutral point between predictable and unpredictable ($M = 4.04$), most of the factors in the six environmental sectors stayed about the same from year to year. This indicates that organizations within the energy service industry were able to predict environmental changes. From Table 6.2, clients' demand and changes of industry economic conditions such as the level of exploration and production or well counts were predictable ($M = 3.76$ and 3.47). The service firms were also able to forecast technological changes in their niche sectors ($M = 3.27$).

Nature of business environment

On average, the participating executives perceived that the business environment in which they operated in East Asia was uncertain ($M = 4.1$), complicated ($M = 5.0$) and dynamic ($M = 5.2$). However, for the perceived environmental hostility, the environment tended to be benign ($M = 3.8$) for service organizations conducting their businesses in the region (Figure 6.1). At this stage, the intention (Assumption 1)

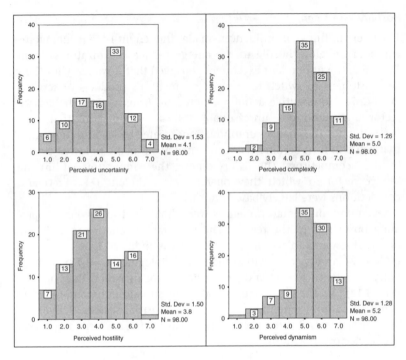

Figure 6.1 Making sense of the nature of the business environment

that the nature of the business environment is perceived to be uncertain is supported preliminarily. However, Assumption 2 has gained only limited support from the preliminary results.

The graphs displayed in Figure 6.1 represent various scenarios. First, it looks as if the uncertainty score is somewhat normally distributed. In this sense, a few (4) respondents perceived the business environment as very uncertain and a few (4) perceived it as very certain, but half of the respondents' (49) perceptions on the environment turned out to be uncertain. Secondly, the hostility scores are distinctive because this distribution is fairly clearly not normal and there are two peaks indicative of two modes. This suggests that the respondents' opinion towards the environmental hostility was divided: most respondents perceived that the environment was pleasant (41.8 per cent); 26.5 per cent of the respondents felt it was at a middle situation between pleasant and unpleasant; whereas 21.6 per cent perceived that it was an unpleasant environment. Finally, complexity and dynamism tests produced very negatively skewed data, indicating that the majority of the respondents perceived the business environment as complex and dynamic whereas the minority perceived the environment as simple and static.

Cross-national comparison: China, Singapore and Malaysia

In order to emphasize the differences and similarities pictorially among the items, Figure 6.2 shows the bar charts of the environmental dimensions' variables split according to the country where the service organizations were located. It is observed that the perceived uncertainty in China is the lowest (mean = 3.6) whereas in Singapore, the managerial perception on the degree of environmental uncertainty is the highest (mean = 4.7). The Malaysia organizations' executives have a neutral view on the environmental uncertainty (mean = 4) indicating that the business environment in which they operate cannot be identified as either certain or uncertain.

For the perceived environmental complexity scores, the distribution is negatively skewed in the China group (there is a larger concentration at the higher end of scores) whereas the organizations based in Singapore and Malaysia are normally distributed around a mean of 5.1 and 4.7 respectively. Therefore, the overall negatively skew observed earlier is due to the mixture of countries (the China organizations affect the normally distributed scores of Singapore and Malaysia). The results indicate that in each country, the business environment is perceived to be complex.

Nevertheless, for the perceived environmental dynamism, the distribution is negatively skewed in both the China and Malaysia groups yet the Singapore organizations are normally distributed around a mean of 5.2. Hence, the organizations based in China and Malaysia contribute the overall negative skew observed previously. It is observed that, in each country, the business environment is perceived to be dynamic.

When looking at the distribution of perceived environmental hostility scores, all the distributions are bimodal (that is, there are two peaks indicative of two modes). It seems that regardless of the country, there is always a split between organizations' executives: they are either pleased (one mode at 2 or 3 indicating pleasant conditions) or displeased (one mode at 6 indicating unpleasant conditions) with the business environment in which they operate. Though it is perceived that the business environment is pleasant for operating businesses in East Asia, in each of the three countries, there is a split between organizations' executives: they are either pleased or displeased with the business environment in which they operate. In particular, for Singapore and Malaysia, there is a great concentration of executives' perceptions around the higher mode

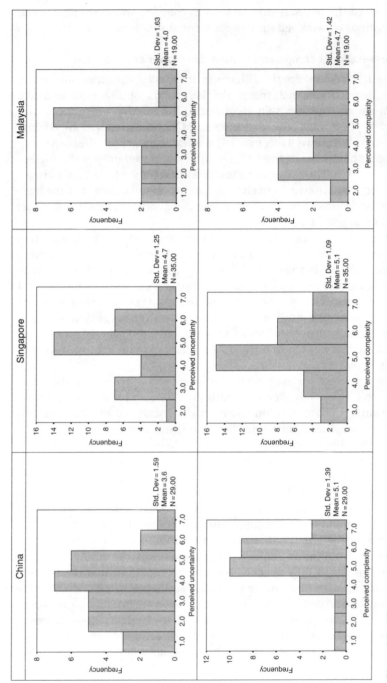

Figure 6.2 The perceived business environment for the energy service organizations in China, Singapore and Malaysia

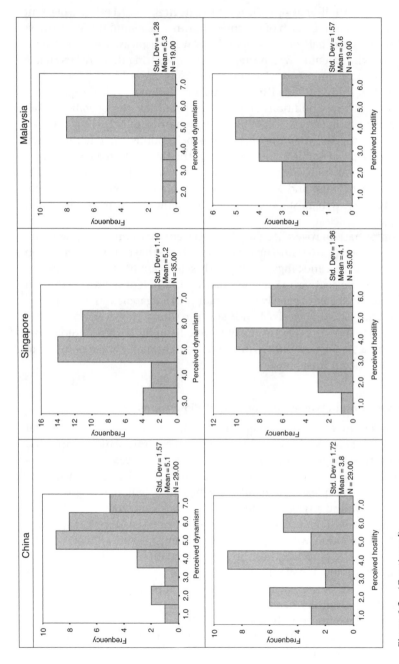

Figure 6.2 (Continued)

(the peak is taller) at 4, indicating the neutral point between pleasant and unpleasant. In each of the three countries, a common feature shows that less than half of the respondents were displeased with the business environment in which they operate, suggesting they are favourable places for oil and gas service businesses.

As the study intended to compare the differences of the perceived environmental conditions across three countries, the overall Kruskal-Wallis tests and the Mann-Whitney were carried out. There is no evidence to suggest that the managerial perceptions on environmental complexity, dynamism and hostility in the three selected countries are dissimilar. As such, the observed results may indicate that executives in China, Singapore and Malaysia share similar views on environmental complexity, dynamism and hostility. Nonetheless, to prove similarity, bigger samples are needed.

In contrast, the overall test for the perceived environmental uncertainty is significant ($p = 0.030$). Further analysis shows that only the comparison between China and Singapore is greatly significant (0.004). This suggests that senior executives in Singapore had rather different views from those in China: the degree of perceived uncertainty in Singapore was much higher than the degree of perceived uncertainty in China. However, no evidence is given to show the views in Malaysia were dissimilar to those in Singapore or China. As such, executives in Malaysia might share similar opinions to those either in Singapore or China.

Association between environmental dimensions

In order to examine further whether the perceived environmental uncertainty is associated with the perceived environmental complexity, hostility and dynamism, Spearman's rho (r) values were computed. The prediction is that the perceived uncertainty would correlate with the perceived complexity, dynamism or hostility. This hypothesis is not directed and so a two-tailed test was selected (Field, 2000).

The results (Table 6.3) show that the perceived uncertainty has a 0.209 correlation with the perceived dynamism, and a 0.269 correlation with the perceived hostility. The correlation coefficients in these samples are low but significant ($p = 0.039$ and 0.007). The correlation between the perceived uncertainty and complexity is not significant ($p = 0.157$). Hence, when the perceived hostility and dynamism are high, the perceived uncertainty also tends to be high.

The result proves the assumption that the higher the degree of the perceived environmental dynamism and hostility, the greater the degree

Table 6.3 The association of environmental dimensions

		Correlations			
		Perceived complexity	*Perceived dynamism*	*Perceived hostility*	*Perceived uncertainty*
Spearman's rho	Percived Complexity				
	Correlation Coefficient	1.000	.236*	.064	-.144
	Sig. (2-tailed)	–	.019	.530	.157
	N	98	98	98	98
	Perceived Dynamism				
	Correlation Coefficient	.236*	1.000	.234*	.209*
	Sig. (2-tailed)	.019	–	.020	.039
	N	98	98	98	98
	Perceived Hostility				
	Correlation Coefficient	.064	.234*	1.000	.269**
	Sig. (2-tailed)	.530	.020	–	.007
	N	98	98	98	98
	Perceived Uncertainty				
	Correlation Coefficient	-.144	.209*	.269**	1.000
	Sig. (2-tailed)	.157	.039	.007	–
	N	98	98	98	98

Note: * Correlation is significant at the .05 level (2-tailed).
** Correlation is significant at the .01 level (2-tailed).

of perceived uncertainty. However, findings do not support the assumption that there is a relationship between the perceived complexity and the perceived uncertainty. In the context of this study, not enough evidence can be given to prove that only the three environmental dimensions (perceived complexity, dynamism and hostility) alone can reflect the perceived uncertainty. Consequently, the research results give limited support to Assumption 3.

Discussions and conclusion

This chapter has portrayed a picture of the environmental uncertainty by evaluating factors of the six-task environmental sector – namely, customers, suppliers, competitors, regulatory, technology and economics – from the three dimensions of complexity, dynamism and hostility. The research results support Assumption 1 that the nature of the business environment for service organizations is perceived as slightly uncertain in East Asia. Amongst the three countries, the perceived uncertainty is supported by the Singapore groups. The perceived environmental uncertainty in China is the lowest and the business environment is perceived to be certain in that country. Generally, Malaysian organizations' executives have a neutral view on the environmental uncertainty.

Assumption 2 that executives in East Asia perceive the business environment in which they operate as complex, dynamic and hostile is supported in part by the research. Significant statistical evidence proved that the business environment for the oil and gas service sector is complex and dynamic. The perceived complexity and dynamism are supported by the results that emerged from each of the three countries. However, managerial perceptions on environmental hostility tend to be benign when conducting their businesses in the region.

The research results give limited support to Assumption 3 that the perceived environmental uncertainty is associated with the three environmental dimensions of perceived complexity, dynamism and hostility. It has been proven that the perceived uncertainty is positively related to the perceived dynamism and hostility: the higher the degree of the perceived environmental dynamism and hostility, the higher the degree of the perceived uncertainty. The results do not support the initial assumption that there is a relationship between the perceived complexity and the perceived uncertainty.

Having gathered empirical evidence from the questionnaire survey of both indigenous and foreign executives operating businesses in China,

Singapore and Malaysia, this research will have made a significant addition to existing literature on Asian strategic management. This claim must, however, be substantiated by analysis of both the theoretical and methodological contribution together with a brief account on practical implications for the industry in East Asia.

First, in strategic management literature pertaining to the business environment, most writings have addressed issues such as the industry driving forces, key success factors or major environmental indicators. Through this study, these themes can be evaluated quantitatively by using available models illustrated in this chapter. Furthermore, the applications of relevant environmental theories have been examined and evaluated in the context of the energy service industry in East Asia. This achievement enables the authors to fill in the existing theoretical gap in this field.

The principal findings of this study in China, Singapore and Malaysia show that it is possible both to conceptualize and to assess environmental uncertainty through analysing organizational environmental influences in terms of three dimensions. The environmental dynamism and hostility are shown to be significant interpreters of the degree of the perceived environmental uncertainty. It is also believed that the results of this study provide a significant improvement for measuring three environmental dimensions. A better-defined environmental typology can assist organizational and strategy theorists and researchers to identify more clearly the problems confronting organizations in each of the different environmental sectors.

Secondly, the methodological contribution derived from this study is deemed important. The research methodology designed for this study contains both qualitative and quantitative attributes and this methodology can be applied generally to business and management studies. It is considered challenging for any researcher channelled into western thinking to conduct empirical work in East Asia. This study provided a methodological solution for data collection in China, Singapore and Malaysia. Particularly, the generated analytical techniques for cross-national comparisons can be applied by academics and practitioners who wish to conduct similar work. The comparative environmental analysis employed in this study can also be adopted by multinational corporations to gain a comprehensive understanding of any geographical or industrial conditions.

Thirdly, the practical implication of this study is the contribution of knowledge to the industry. As the firms under investigation operate in East Asia, the findings from this research can enrich knowledge of the petroleum and wider energy industries and the service sector in particular. Conclusions drawn from this study can be practically useful for industrial experts and management to tackle environmental issues when formulating strategic options. The means used in this study for the assessment of environmental uncertainty help senior executives to identify the environmental situations. Strategic approaches such as scenario planning or forecasting for strategy formulation can be utilized after making accurate appraisal of the business environment.

Because of limited responses, this study was unable to deploy other statistical tests such as association analysis for each of the selected countries. Therefore, a future study can explore relationships amongst environmental dimensions in individual countries. One debate could be that the degree of dependency on environmental components affects or restricts the executives' management capabilities for carrying out business activities. Hence, a research orientation emerges to examine the proposition pertaining to how dependency on resources (Pfeffer and Salancik, 1978) is associated with the environmental uncertainty. In addition, as mentioned in the Introduction section, other macroenvironmental factors, which have not been highlighted in this study, can be investigated in future work. One possible study can, for instance, devote attention to how cultural factors affect managerial style and the applications of strategy in a business environment.

In conclusion, the merit of this chapter is that the empirical research results should prove valuable to both business strategists (or those responsible for formulating strategy for business) and to researchers in academic, industrial and government spheres. The environmental typology generated in this chapter provides a useful tool in assisting managers to gain insight into the business environment in which they operate. We recommend that when initiating businesses in an immature or a non-Western standardized business environment, senior executives should devote attention to significant environmental indicators and be confident in coping with that business environment. For any organization, not only should environmental dimensions be considered carefully, but also individual environmental influences, in order to obtain an accurate interpretation of the business environment.

Acknowledgement

We would like to thank Douglas Gourlay and Alex Wilson at the Robert Gordon University for their supervision and guidance throughout this research study. Special thanks go to all survey participants and those who provided support and assistance.

Note

1. In this study, East Asia refers to the countries or regions including China, Hong Kong, Taiwan, Vietnam, Indonesia, Malaysia, Thailand, the Philippines, Singapore, South Korea and Japan.

References

Abraham, K.S. (1999) 'Upstream Climate Brightening in Southeast Asia: A World of Oil', *World Oil*, December: 29.

BP (The British Petroleum Company plc) (1998) *BP Statistical Review of World Energy*. London: BP.

Chen, G., (2000) 'The Development and Reform of the Chinese Oil and Gas Industry in the 21st Century', *International Petroleum Economics*, 8 (1): 5.

Daft, R., Sornumen L J. and Parks, D. (1988) 'Chief Executive Scanning, Environmental Characteristics, and Company Performance: an Empirical Study', *Strategic Management Journal*, 9: 123–39.

Dess, G.G. and Beard, D.W. (1984) 'Dimensions of Organisational Task Environments', *Administrative Science Quarterly*, 29: 52–73.

Dill, W.R. (1958) 'Environment as an influence on managerial autonomy', *Administrative Science Quarterly*, 2: 409–43.

Downey, H.K., Hellriegel, D. and Slocum, J.W., Jr. (1975) 'Environmental Uncertainty: the Construct and its Application', *Administrative Science Quarterly*, 20: 613–29.

DTI (Department of Trade and Industry) (1996) *Report on the Oil, Gas, and Petrochemical Sectors in South East Asian Markets*. Singapore: British Embassies and High Commissions in South East Asia.

Duncan, R.B. (1972) 'Characteristics of Organisational Environments and Perceived Environmental Uncertainties', *Administrative Science Quarterly*, 17: 313–27.

Elenkov, D.S. (1997) 'Strategic Uncertainty and Environmental Scanning: the Case for Institutional Influences on Scanning Behaviour', *Strategic Management Journal*, 18(4): 287–302.

Fahey, L. and Narayanan, V.K. (1986) *Macroenvironmental Analysis for Strategic Management*. St Paul: West Publishing Company.

Field, A. (2000) *Discovering Statistics: using SPSS for Windows*. London: Sage.

Hambrick, D.C. (1982) 'Environmental Scanning and Organisational Strategy', *Strategic Management Journal*, 3: 159–74.

Hegarty, W.H. and Tihanyi, L. (1999) 'Surviving the Transition: Central European Bank Executives' View of Environmental Changes', *Journal of World Business*, 34(4): 409–22.

Hrebiniak, L.G. and Snow, C.C. (1980) 'Industry Differences in Environmental Uncertainty and Organisational Characteristics Related to Uncertainty', *Academy of Management Journal*, 23, 750–9.

Ireland, R.D., Hitt, M.A., Bettis, R.A. and Porras, D.A.D. (1987) 'Strategy Formulation Processes: Differences in Perceptions of Strength and Weaknesses Indicators and Environmental Uncertainty by Managerial Level', *Strategic Management Journal*, 8: 469–85.

Johnson, G. and Scholes, K. (1999) *Exploring Corporate Strategy: Text and Cases*, 5th edn. London: Prentice Hall.

Koberg, C.S. (1987) 'Resource Scarcity, Environmental Uncertainty, and Adaptive Organisational Behaviour', *Academic of Management Journal*, 30: 798–807.

Kotha, S. and Nair, A. (1995) 'Strategy and Environment as Determinants of Performance: Evidence from the Japanese Machine Tool Industry', *Strategic Management Journal*, 16: 496–518.

Lawrence, P. and Lorsch, J.W. (1967) 'Differentiation and Integration in Complex Organisations', *Administrative Science Quarterly*, 12: 1–47.

Luo, Y. and Park, S.H. (2001) 'Strategic alignment and performance of market-seeking MNCs in China', *Strategic Management Journal*, 22: 141–55.

Mackay, T. and Adam, J. (1998) *Prospects for the World Offshore Oil and Gas Industry 1998–2000*, industrial report. Scotland: Mackay Consultants Limited.

Miles, R.E. and Snow, C.C. (1978) *Organisational Strategy, Structure and Process*. New York: McGraw-Hill.

Miller, K.D. (1993) 'Industry and Country Effects on Managers' Perception of Environmental Uncertainties', *Journal of International Business Studies*, 24: 693–714.

Mintzberg, H., Ahlstrand, B. and Lampel, J. (1998) *Strategy Safari: A Guided Tour Through the Wilds of Strategic Management*. London: Prentice Hall.

Pearce II, J. and Smith, G., (*1997*) 'Note On the Oil and Gas Exploration and Production Industry', in J.A. Pearce, and R.B. Robison, (eds), *Strategic Management: Formulation, Implementation and Control*, 6th edn. London: Irwin.

PetroMin Magazine (2000) *Oil & Gas Directory*, 15th edn. Singapore.

Pfeffer, J. and Salancik, G.R. (1978) *The External Control of Organisations*. New York: Harper & Row.

Phillips, A., (1998) 'Offshore Management', MBA course handout, Aberdeen Business School, The Robert Gordon University, Scotland.

Porter, M. (1985) *Competitive Advantage*. New York: The Free Press.

Scottish Enterprise (2002) *The People's Republic of China – A Profile of the Energy Industry*, unpublished report, Scotland.

Simerly, R.L. and Li, M. (2000) 'Environmental Dynamism, Capital Structure and Performance: A Theoretical Integration and an Empirical Test', *Strategic Management Journal*, 21: 38–41.

Simmons and Company International (1999) *Company Profile*. Houston.

Sutcliffe, K.M. and Huber, G.P. (1998) 'Firm and Industry as Determinants of Executive Perceptions of the Environment', *Strategic Management Journal*, 19: 793–801.

Sutcliffe, K.M. and Zaheer, A. (1998) 'Uncertainty in the Transaction Environment: An Empirical Test', *Strategic Management Journal*, 19: 1–23.

Tan, J.J. and Litschert, R.J. (1994) 'Environment–strategy Relationship and its Performance Implications: An Empirical Study of the Chinese Electronics Industry', *Strategic Management Journal*, 15: 1–20.

Tan, Y. (2001) *Managerial Perceptions of the Business Environment: An Empirical Pilot Test in China.* Proceedings of the American Society of Business and Behavioural Sciences conference, London.

Thompson, J.D. (1967) *Organisations in Action.* New York: McGraw-Hill.

Tung, R.L. (1979) 'Dimensions of Organisational Environments: an Exploratory Study of Their Impact on Organisation Structure', *Academy of Management Journal*, 22(4): 672–93.

Wolf, M., (2003) 'The World Must Learn to Live with a Wide-awake China', *Financial Times*, 12 November.

Zikmund, W.G. (2000) *Business Research Methods*, 6th edn. London: Harcourt College Publishers.

7
Appropriation of EMS Standards in Thailand

Erik Hagelskjær Lauridsen and Ulrik Jørgensen

EMS as a means to enter global markets

Global standards for environmental management like the ISO14001 follow the globalization traces of industrial activities and trade and are thus introduced in changing cultural and political settings. This phenomenon is evident in the high speed of implementation of environmental management standards (EMS) in the recently industrialized countries in Southeast Asia – as in the case of Thailand. The environmental management systems are commonly introduced based on either demands from transnational corporations' headquarters or a response to demands from major customers and markets throughout the product and distribution chain. A third important mentioned reason for implementing EMS is as a preparation for exports to European countries based on the anticipated demand from these markets and the product standards to be met (Hansen, 1999). The importance of building accountable export industries has also led to massive support programmes for the introduction of EMS.

EMS has the role of ensuring commitment and sustain trust (Deegan, 2002). The success of EMS in this regard seems to be unquestionable in the European setting to the extent that many studies even take this as a normative outset. Especially in the recently industrialized countries of Southeast Asia, in-depth studies of the actual performance of implemented EMS are quite scarce (see, for example, Lynn, 2006). EMS' are a possibility for the local industry to become more thoroughly embedded in the globalized market, but they do not necessarily lead to the environmental improvements they are believed to lead to in Europe or the USA (Gallagher, 2005).

The ISO14000 standards have been based on experiences from industrialized countries in Europe and their management cultures and environmental regulation. They are often seen as an extension of protective measures beyond compliance with governments' legal requirements. However, the ISO14001 standard leaves quite an open agenda for the choice of environmental objectives and performance criteria. Previous examples of the introduction of environmental management suggest that EMS play only a minor role in developing the actual environmental objectives and, following this, also in setting the agenda for companies' specific environmental focus (Lauridsen *et al.*, 2003; Hertin *et al.*, 2003; Gouldson and Murphy, 1998). The mere introduction of EMS, however, may lead to more conscious search activities in relation to environmental knowledge and innovative potentials as EMS has often been seen as a tool for improving the resource efficiency of production facilities.

The acceptance and influence of EMS in the business community relies on the performance of the management system and how it contributes to develop environmental issues and to translate them into concrete problems and solutions in specific settings. The implementation of EMS in Southeast Asia has been highly successful taken by numbers. Outside Europe and Japan these countries have the third largest concentration of for example ISO14000 certified systems [http://www.iso.org/iso/en/iso9000-14000/pdf/survey12thcycle.pdf]. However, taking a more qualitative approach, the management system's ability to support the enactment of environmentally favourable policies is crucial – and it is still unclear what preconditions are necessary in the local context in order to support this result in Southeast Asia and avoid EMS being reduced to merely documentation practices.

The following case studies carried out in Thailand demonstrate different roles and impacts of EMS in a number of contextual settings. The research has been undertaken through four years of studies based partly on local case studies and partly on interviews carried out during longer field studies every year. Some of the companies have been revisited to follow their improvements and responses to EMS during the years while others only have been interviewed once or twice. The overall development of the policy context concerning environmental legislation, support programs and competence building has been followed for a longer period of time

EMS as a travelling concept

When an EMS is transferred and implemented in new settings it is much more than just a management technology which has to be adopted. As the management technology is implemented, it becomes a key element of the embedding of the environment in company practices. It becomes a part of the local interaction with involved institutions and stakeholders and constitutes what counts as environment in the company (Georg *et al.*, 2002). Making environmental problems concrete requires that they are enacted and thereby given meaning in local settings (Georg and Füssel, 2000). Perspectives from science and technology studies provide us with a framework to conceive the regulatory elements that have appropriated from their western origins as artefacts which are constituted and used in a specific context (Sørensen, 2000). These perspectives also provide the more general understanding that these enactment processes involve the construction and attachment of social meaning and representations for negotiation and mediation (Latour, 1999). The intentions and impacts delegated to the working of these artefacts are complex and not based on consensus among all involved actors, although certain impacts on industrial behaviour and impacts on environmental performance are supposed to be the outcome. This identification of the role of ISO14000 underlines previous understandings of environmental management systems as human constructs that are developed in relation to and intertwined with other human constructs like science and politics (Roome, 1992). And, more importantly, what we understand as nature and environment is shaped in these interactions (Braun and Castree, 1998).

EMS are shaped along with the implementation and the creation of linkages to the existing technological and strategic set-up. The standard itself (that is, the written text) has almost no specific reference to the topics to be accounted for, but is building on the presumed existence of a number of knowledge networks circulating and aligning sociomaterial entities in the context in which the standard is being used (Jørgensen 2003). These entities form the base used to identify what counts as environment and what can be used as problem-solving technologies and organizational procedures. A number of issues in the ISO14001 standard have previously been identified concerning the standard's openness and interpretative flexibility. The standard leaves a number of what have been termed 'hot spots' open for local interpretation and adaptation, to be defined during the implementation process (Behrndt 2002). Through the continued creation of routines in the daily practices of managing the standard, the EMS is embedded in a local context where different environmental objectives are identified in the constitution of what counts as environmental problems to be handled.

The interpretation of the 'hot spots', and as such the performance of environmental management has been shown in specific cases to be dependent on a number of other aspects of environmental activity relating to for example regulatory regimes and available technologies (Jørgensen 2001). In the case of EMS implementation in Thailand the focus is on the Thai context as a combination of recent industrialization, newly established democratic institutions and ongoing decentralization of government institutions as a distinctive feature. The competence of the networks of environmental professionals that work in the environmental organization, in consulting and regulatory enforcement (Simmons and Wynne, 1993) and dominating business and management cultures are also of significant importance. The performance of the EMS is sensitive to the context where it is implemented. This may be less evident in many European cases where EMS operate under relatively comparable and homogenous regulatory conditions and standardized constitutions of the environment as object. These elements may exist as such in the Thai context but have not been through the same process of alignment and coordination commonly referred to as 'modernization' in a western European context. New conceptions of the environment piggy-back (Sørensen, 2000) onto a number of the different initiatives that are introduced in order to facilitate the development of local environmental strategies; legislative norms, the Cleaner Production promotion programmes and EMS.

Introducing the Thai context

For almost a decade, and especially after the Asian economic crisis in 1997, Thai government and industrial organizations as well as foreign donors have been involved in the promotion of EMS throughout Thai industry. Many of the promotion programmes have built on the implicit assumption that Thailand is undergoing a co-development of industry and environmental awareness comparable to the experiences of western industrialized countries. In this sense, Thailand current development is comparable to Denmark 20 years ago for example, producing support programmes that aim to help local industry and government regulation to 'catch up' with the more developed industrialized countries. Developmental activities are consequently aimed at achieving transfers that will speed up this process. However, many technology transfer programmes have been unable to sustain these technology initiatives in the new context once the project organization ended their implementation activities. Technology studies explains this by arguing that it is not only technology which has to be transferred, but also the configuration of users, maintenance programmes, organization and so on. All these interdependent elements are to be transferred into the new setting, where it must be re-negotiated and realigned in order to function (Edwards, 2000; Kuada, 2003). The view of the transfer as a 'catch up' has undoubtedly contributed to shape the Thai cleaner production (CP) programmes as dissemination efforts with focus on the introduction of already existing knowledge of technology and production to selected industries in prioritized sectors using foreign experts. In contrast to this, for example, the Danish cleaner technology (CT) programmes of the 1990s both included elements on knowledge dissemination, development of technological alternatives and the development of local networks of professionals with innovative competences (Andersen and Jørgensen, 1995).

The transfer of technologies and regulatory instruments including such management technologies as EMS is based on a linear theory of history giving development aid the role to boost progress in order to move more quickly through the earlier stages of this development path. This concept of linearity is also prevailing in the field of environmental regulation. Newly industrialized countries in Southeast Asia are considered to be 'lagging' behind in environmental protection and should be brought up to common western legal institutions, standards, and enforcement practices.

The most radical objective – at least in the view of the standards' authors – of the ISO14001 standard is to create the means for continuous improvements in the environment performance of the organization in which it is implemented. Even in the European context the outcome of the objective of continued improvements can be questioned (Hertin *et al.*, 2003), and looking to the mapping of ISO14001 implementations in Thailand the perspective of continued improvements seem to be overshadowed by more short-term concerns about the first impacts from the implementation phase (Lauridsen *et al.*, 2003). One of the primary reasons for Thai companies to implement ISO14001 standards was its associated symbolic value, in demonstrating that new, accountable, and rational management procedures were introduced in the wake of the economic crisis in 1997 (Kolloff, 2002).

In Europe EMS were developed as 'voluntary supplements and extensions to existing legislation', while EMS in the recently industrialized countries such as Korea, Thailand and Malaysia appear to have a different function as a 'creator of awareness and transparency in legislation enforcement' (Lauridsen *et al.*, 2003). As a result, EMS may over time produce contributions to the performance of companies in these countries, but this is as much the result of the improved enforcement of the regulatory measures and outside demands on the companies as the result of the independent working of the ISO14001 standard. Radical environmental improvements should not be expected from the implementation of EMS (Gallagher, 2005).

Searching for patterns of coherence

In order to further understand the conditions of appropriation of EMS, we take the established divisions between company management, government regulation, environmental objects, standards, technologies, and professional knowledge networks as the starting point without anticipating specific conditions for how they are constituted or how they are working. Both the boundaries between and the workings of these elements are as influenced by the process of change as are their inter-relations and inter-actions.

We have used the concept of coherence to analyse interactions between different institutionalized domains such as networks, practices, technologies, and professional knowledge. The concept is closely linked to actor–network theory, where it is used to describe processes of alignment (Lauridsen, 2003; Latour, 1999). The concept of coherence is used to describe processes where domains interact to develop common references and understandings in order to conceptualize the complexity of socio-material interactions that are involved in the creation of the environment as a shared reference for societal activities and as a measure for company performance.

Instead of delegating the outcome of environmental activities to single instruments such as management procedures, policies and so on relating to and centred around specific institutions such as the enforcement of legislation or the introduction of certified EMS, we see the results of environmental efforts as produced through and from day-to-day processes creating certain forms of coherence between the involved institutions – or in some cases reducing the coherence between them. The involved institutionalized domains describe the context in which environmental management is implemented, and are taken from the dominant actors involved in environmental policy and business management. The involved actors are constituted in part by the ongoing process of working with the environment, even though their presence is not only related to the specific local conditions concerning the environmental efforts in companies but also relate to other activities and policies. The domains comprise of institutional elements including *regulatory and policy measures, business and management cultures, competences of environmental professionals, technological processes and innovation.* Market relations and the common, public interest could also be examined. It is worth noting that the working of the process of coherence building is not dependent on the details and boundaries of the involved elements, but gains its potential as an analytic concept from the focus on coordination and interaction between the involved domains.

The process of building coherence is not a determined and one-way road of development; rather, it is a continuous process of constructing, sustaining, and building on the environmental objects. The stabilization of these objects involves interaction and contribution from several of the involved domains whether they are in cooperation, in conflict, or even relate to each other through proxies represented in standards, environmental measures, or general normative demands. The process of building or destructing coherence introduces concepts that counter the tendency of compartmentalization and institutional reductionism at stake in most policy analysis.

Case introductions and observations

The following introduces sketches of three characteristic cases on the uptake and implementation of EMS in Thailand. The cases provide a picture of the working and the impact of the systems as the daily routines of the companies are changed and new arenas for the environmental agenda-setting are established. The chapter then returns to address how elements of the coherence process contribute to the (re)construction of environmental objects. The (re)construction of the environment is a highly political process. Some elements are forgotten while others are brought forward as important. These processes are ongoing transformations in heterogeneous networks that in some instances may lead to a redistribution of agency (that is power) – in many cases though, the result reflects earlier power relations. In this process some stakeholders are or remain forgotten, while others become or are reconfirmed to be at the centre of translations.

The Shoe Manufacturer

The Shoe Manufacturing (SM) company was set up in 1993 as a production plant by a Danish-based multinational with it own brand.

It is located in an industrial estate owned by a very large Thai shoe manufacturing group, which is also a minor shareholder in the company. The company considers itself to be a world leader on sole casting. About 50 local suppliers are involved in the manufacturing of one type of shoe including materials as moles, lasts and rubber and specialized production machinery including mechanical- and robot-technology typically used in the car industry. SM implemented ISO14001 as a demand from the Danish HQ, and the system has adopted the Danish legislative norms for environmental emissions. The plant appears very clean and well managed. The environmental aspects identified by the EMS appear to be relevant, and the action taken involves relevant parts of the organization and external partners as consultants and suppliers. For example, the major impact from the production is identified to be waste leather, which, due to the chromium content from the tanning process, cannot be burned. This problem is addressed at strategic level in the mother company.

The Battery Manufacturer

The Battery Manufacturer (BM) was originally a part of a large Thai industrial conglomerate. As a result of the economic crisis of 1997 the company today is Japanese owned. The local Thai management, however, remains and the physical location of the factory is also at one of the industrial estates of the Thai industrial conglomerate. ISO14001 was implemented at BM because close friends of the production manager were involved in the early Thai ISO14000 promotion programme. The Japanese HQ is not involved in establishing the local environmental norms and policies of BM. BM produces mainly 'dry' batteries for trucks, cars and motorcycles. The batteries are sold to the retailers without battery acid, and therefore the factory has to dispose of the acid initially used for pre-charging the batteries in production. Neutralization of the acid causes a high amount of dispensed solids in the waste water, which has been recognised as an important problem by the company. Throughout the period of the case study (four years) the framing of the problem has changed radically: initially, the problem was 'solved' by using some of the waste water for irrigation within factory grounds and diluting the rest with other types of waste water from the industrial estate in order to reduce the concentration. Later, the problem was transformed into an issue of developing a product where the fluid can be sold together with the batteries, 'wet' batteries. At the final visit the problem was described as a question of how to mature the local market to adopt a version of the dominant international product standard which is sealed batteries (where there is no extra fluid from pre-charging). In the BM case one relevant aspect is brought to the centre of strategic business development while others such as the high amounts of lead dusts in the factory are ignored.

The Automobile Parts Manufacturer

The Automobile Parts Manufacturer (AP) was established two genera-tions ago as a family business and today it is still remains owned and managed by the same family. It employs through gradual expansion approximately 1,500 people in production and manufacturing of auto-mobile parts: suspension and doors, frame chairs and upholstery. A share of the production (mainly chairs and upholstery) is subcontracting for foreign automobile brands. Another important activity is the rebuilding of pick-up trucks (Isuzu, Nissan) as SUVs for the domestic market. The company's ISO14001-based management system was implemented with help from a national consultant company and economic support from a national promotion programme. AP describes ISO14001 as a natural element in the portfolio of standards of modern car manufacturing, and as such it is an attempt to increase the share of subcontracted products for export. The environmental aspects of AP are identified as too much noise, too much degreasing agent in the waste water and too much waste. But all three are framed in a superficial manner: The machinery and processes causing the noise are not changed nor are they shielded – rather they are moved further into the centre of the factory grounds in order to abide with limits on noise emissions to neighbours. The process of degreasing is not identified in relation to the waste water – rather the waste water treatment facility is increased in capacity. Production processes are not analysed in order to identify the origins of the amount and mixed composition of the waste – rather the employees are (with only limited success) instructed to perform waste separation.

Coherence in regulatory and policy measures

Thailand has demanding environmental regulations as expressed in words and legislation, but there is still very weak and uneven enforce-ment. As such, there is an obvious lack of coherence in this domain, where misalignments include: legislation versus enforcement, the requirements of the standard versus enforcement practice and the normative programme of environmental improvement versus the promotion programmes cost reduction argument.

It is common for large and respectable companies to have obvious problems in complying with the legislative standards in some areas. This was the case in respect of metal dusts at both the BM and AP companies. Interviews with environmental auditors and consultants revealed that this is due to a widespread practice among auditors of accepting strategies to achieve regulatory compliance rather than demanding this as a prerequisite of acquiring a certificate: 'We got our certificate for having good intentions'.

There appears to be an obvious parallel between these auditors' lack of pursuing the norms of the ISO14001 standard and the government authorities' weak enforcement of the emission standards set up in accordance with the environmental legislation. In both the BM and AP companies the implementation of an ISO 14001 system is the first time the environmental legislation is applied to a company's activities in a systematic way, but regulatory compliance does not appear to be the original aim of the companies. Nevertheless EMS implementation evidently supports an increased coherence as a means of self-enforcement.

At BM the EMS was initially implemented as the result of personal connections between the plant manager and a senior consultant at a state EMS promotion initiative, SM got EMS as a part of HQ policy and AP wanted the accreditation for export marketing. After four years of accredited ISO 14001 operations at AP, the company still does not abide by legislation, but uses the environment for the purposes of window dressing: Brooms have been decorated with ribbons in honour of the birthday of HM. the King, and the workers sweep the floors of the factory to show their commitment to protect the environment.

The EMS helps to establish a continuous focus on the environmental problems, as, for example, the dispensed solids in the waste water of BM company. However, in order for a problem to be documented and monitored it must already be well described as, for example, a common regulatory and internationally standardised object of legislation. At BM a continuous focus on the acid waste stream was established with the monitoring of the concentration of dispensed solids in the waste water. This problem was eventually solved through technological and market development. But other issues were never formulated as environmental problems. The high amount of lead in the blood of some workers is, for example, defined as a problem for the working environment, and workers have been transferred to less exposed functions, and ordered to exercise (which helps the body to expel the lead from the blood). While noticeable lead fumes and large quantities of dust remain in the production today, the most recent audit report focuses on more scarce lighting for areas, where sunlight may be sufficient, as an area for improvement. The exposure of certain issues that are labelled 'environmental aspects' contrasts with other issues that are labelled as 'working environment' and not part of the standard, thereby not subject to international attention to the same extent as the environment.

The AP company focuses its efforts on waste water treatment and waste separation. Given the current problems of the institutional waste handling in Thailand this appears to be a very relevant issue. However when visiting the company, the waste separation process does not appear to be an issue which is related to the main activity of the company, i.e. the manufacturing of parts for automobiles and automobile assembly. No waste separation activities are identified on the shopfloor. Rather, different coloured bins placed outside the administration are described in a company leaflet about environmental management as:

Waste management:

1. Yellow bins are for common waste such as food, fruit peels, dust, paper scrap and used diskettes.
2. Green bins are for reusable waste such as plastic bottles, cardboard boxes, steel wire scrap, soda cans and newspapers.
3. Red bins are for hazardous waste such as all kinds of batteries, printer ink, chemical markers, correction markers and glue.

Waste management is thus locally appropriated to be a concern related to the office waste from the administration: paper, cardboard boxes and printer cartridges. The coloured bins for sorting office waste show a kind of visible beauty (though also a superficial understanding of the environmental agenda) at the same time as it shows a visible and for company management easy example of environmental response.

In some ways, the strict but not enforced legislation performs very well. The strict norms produce legitimacy for the formal environmental regulation created by government. From the government's perspective it is thus better to have a strict legislation, which lacks enforcement, than a less strict, but enforced legislation which reflects the actual conditions of industry. The strict norms may also function as a basis for bringing up environmental problems as scandals in the press or as issues for NGOs and thereby shape a ground for public environmental enquiries without the need of government and state authorities to secure and enforce the policies in detail. A change in this situation would be helped by improving the competencies of regulatory officials, but there is resistance from industry towards empowering officials with improved environmental knowledge, as this may function as one more opportunity for corruption with such officials becoming critical counterparts to the companies.

The EMSs of the cases have all been set up in relation to one of the different programmes on cleaner technology, efficient production and environmental management that have been promoted in Thailand.[1] These programmes have been part of actions trying to make companies go beyond regulatory requirements using similar arguments to those used when such activities were introduced in Northern Europe. Both government agencies and foreign donor organizations have promoted separate programmes in order to initiate companies' environmental activities on a business opportunity basis emphasizing the competitive advantages and cost reductions often resulting from these schemes. In their internal motivation the introduction of EMS is often even solely motivated by the potential economic gains, while improved environmental performance is seen as a secondary outcome. These programmes also typically operate with only brief knowledge of the existence of other similar initiatives. Whereas these programmes in Europe have typically had a strong element of technological innovation and process improvements, in Thailand they are primarily promoted as technology transfer actions.

Coherence in business and management culture

In Thailand it is typically the larger companies that first introduce EMS (Hansen, 1999). The implementation of management systems such as ISO14001, and particularly ISO9001 can be seen as a sign of emerging change in the paternal management strategy. The successful introduction of ISO14001 in Southeast Asia comes just after the economic crisis of 1997 where the personal networks of the paternal business culture were seen to be insufficient to secure economic reliability. The general status of reconfiguration was also a 'window of opportunity' for transforming business by EMS implementation (Dauvergne, 1999). The organizational set-up of EMS is related to contemporary European management tradition, and the widespread introduction of EMS can be seen as an attempt to build new mechanisms of trust by using 'modern' management.

Especially the AP case demonstrates how the business culture in Thailand often reflects the traditional paternal family structure of ownership and control. Knowledge on diverse matters such as the economy, organization, technical equipment and environment is the privilege of central management. While managerial professionalism is part of the promotion of EMS in Europe, supporting the involvement of employees and the spreading of knowledge in the organization, the paternal structure of management is very dependent on centralized decision-making and may not be in favour of an EMS supported spreading and development of knowledge. Whilst European companies see their EMS as a way to integrate environmental management in the overall management of the company and demonstrate that they are environmentally reliable to a large number of stakeholders, companies introducing EMS in Southeast Asia are oriented towards exports for the international, that is, European market, and see EMS as a way to gain trust and acceptance by their major industrial customers in these markets. Seeing employees as a resource for new knowledge and ideas has been taken up in many companies, but only as far as it does not question the paternal authority of management and often as an inconsistent response to the impact of these prevailing structures. At the same time poor knowledge on environmental issues in general and viewing the environment issue as a 'luxury' problem that is predominantly taken up by the 'rich' countries and that should only be dealt with when more basic necessities have been taken care of does still play a major role in the priorities and practices of companies in the newly industrialized countries.

BM suffers from the global distribution of work, where the newly industrialized countries are 'left' to use yesterday's technology for products that can no longer be exported to the industrialized countries. The Japanese mother company of BM has no other production of 'dry' batteries. These are no longer used in European, American and Japanese markets, but they are used nationally and exported for countries in Southeast Asia and the Middle East, where more modern wet-sealed batteries are traditionally believed to be problematic due to heat and humidity. This market is shrinking now as, for example, Japanese car manufacturers have begun to use wet batteries for the cars they sell in the region. Comparing the BM with the SM company demonstrates how foreign ownership can have very different implications for the environmental strategy of a company. The Thai branch of BM is left with an unfavourable niche production, but the SM factory is fully integrated into the multinational mother company, with equal production machinery and a group of senior management who share experience through rotation between factories in different countries as an aspect of career strategy. Affiliated with the Danish mother company (which is actually also family owned) the SM company presents a business culture of the delegation of competences, which also helps to facilitate the vertical integration of knowledge in the multinational through exchanging staff between factories. In this perspective BM appears to function more like a subcontractor than as a part of the Japanese multinational mother company.

Coherence in competences of professionals

The competence of the professionals in Thai industry have been developed by previous promotion programmes of cleaner technology, cleaner production and other programmes in relation to the environmental agendas of industry, and through the distribution of EMS through business and management networks. But these projects are reported to have had limited lasting effect (Zatz, 2003). In addition, consultants are not widely used as they are conceived by business management to be too expensive. This leaves the certifying companies with a rather difficult task, as they often become involved as part-time consultants for the companies they certify. The strict division between consultants and certifying companies prescribed as a third-party relationship and often also found in Europe is therefore less obvious in Thailand. Many of the certifying companies offer a range of different management certificates, especially different varieties of quality management, and health and safety management systems. Their knowledge of the specific environmental issues needed to control the environmental performance of their clients may therefore be limited.

The environmental competences at the AP company are only weakly integrated into a very hierarchical family business. The environmental manager is also the quality manager, and is actually in charge of documentation rather than the function of technical processes such as exhaust and filtering equipment. Knowledge on specific technologies and processes lie with the technicians in different departments of the company, and is thus neither vertically nor horizontally integrated into the organization. When EMS implementation is carried out by in-house technicians, or, more frequently, quality assurance managers, they only have a general knowledge of current environmental issues and discussions. This gives the certifying companies an opportunity to focus their advice on management issues and to limit their demands to the companies' environmental competence or their use of environmental consultants. There is no trace of environmental issues in the company's development strategies.

Environmental management at the BM company is the responsibility of the very experienced senior plant manager who has developed a personal environmental concern. He recognised at an early stage that the problem of dispensed solids was linked to the inevitable surplus acid of the dry-battery production, and that the move to wet-sealed batteries would require a change of technology as well as of customer demands. He discusses these issues in a group of metal manufacturing companies within the Thai industrial conglomerate. Eventually a technology/product shift is brought about by local ad hoc competences rather than being the result of strategic development strategies established in connection to the company's EMS or the aid of the Japanese mother company.

At SM the priorities of the EMS reflect the different competences in the context of the plant. General waste management is dealt with through an internal project group with participants from the industrial estate. The industrial estate receives the waste from the factory as part of its services to the companies located on the estate. Energy is dealt with by a local Thai consulting company that has competences in compressed air, lighting and ventilation. Water is dealt with by help of a German company which has previously delivered and installed the plant's waste water treatment facility. The main waste water problem comes from the tanning process, which is treated in accordance with a German GIN standard for the tanning industry. Chemical control is a 'good house-keeping' project, where possibilities for substitution are investigated in cooperation between the SM plants in different countries under supervision from the HQ.

None of the environmental professionals at the companies considered in our case study had received specific training in industrial environmental management and regulation. The weak environmental competences can be seen as a side-effect of the weak legislative enforcement. The lack of effective enforcement in the everyday activities of the environmental authorities has been counterproductive to building competencies on the environmental problems of industry among the staff of the authorities. This tendency is further supported by the lack of use of environmental consultants as a way of distributing a common interpretation and practice concerning the criteria for enforcing the general requirements in the legislation.

Coherence in technological processes and innovation

If environmental management is to achieve the continuous improvements prescribed in the ISO14001 standard, environmental management cannot be limited to changes in behaviour or organization, but must also be embedded in the innovation of new technology and processes. A general problem for many Thai production companies is that they operate foreign off-the-shelf production machinery, which they have had no part in developing. They may have acquired good skills in operating and maintaining the machinery, but they most often have limited knowledge concerning the design and eventual innovation of these machines. A number of different promotion programmes on CP and environmental management have been aimed at promoting improved knowledge of environmental issues related to production technologies and specific strategies for environmental improvements, including business concerns of pay back times and costs. The tendency, however, has been that the examples of initial implementation have not spread to other comparable companies, nor has it initiated a process promoting subsequent environmental initiatives in the original company (Zatz, 2003). Even when installing new equipment for, e.g. waste water treatment or improved production processes, most often foreign suppliers and specialists are setting up the machinery which is then operated in parallel to older production lines and facilities.

A change in this situation can, however, be observed, in some companies at least on a smaller scale. At the BM company the development of the new wet batteries and production technology appear to be initiated, or at least influenced, by the EMS. Some of the greatest challenges from the production of wet batteries are overcome by the company with the development of a low-tech technology for condensation of acid fumes from the charging batteries as an alternative to the mother company's rather complex and expensive equipment for exhausts, monitoring and refilling of pre-charging batteries. However, it also appears that the EMS-induced focus on abiding to the legislation demands, to some extent, has hindered technological innovation, as the necessary investments in cleaning technology in order to live up to legislation has taken resources from product development. An expensive

waste water treatment facility or heavy investment in filtering technologies bought as turn-key facilities from the outside may function as
sunk costs in relation to the existing production technology, and as a
barrier to the further implementation of cleaner production elements.
For some years BM had actually invested heavily in reducing emissions
from the production of second-grade batteries that could no longer be
exported, and this promoted a continued technological dependency on
less clean production processes and thus slowed down an updating of
production facilities.

Whereas a co-development of environmental management and technology development can be observed in the BM company, there is
no noteworthy development regarding production technologies and
products at the AP company. The sale of SUVs from rebuilt pick-
ups on the domestic market has suffered from the prolonged effects
of the economic crisis. Only the cheaper models are produced at a
significant volume, and the production uses old-fashioned technologies: manual lathe pressing, manual welding, angle grinding and so
on. The focus of environmental management is on separating waste,
reduced energy consumption and treating waste water, all of which
already are in the focus of environmental legislation – and this is not
specific for car factories alone. The company is not using environmental management as an opportunity to be challenged and recon-
sider existing production and products. Other environmental initiatives typically relevant for an automobile parts manufacturing company
such as for example substituting specific organic solvents by alternate
processes to reduce air pollution and improve health and safety conditions including change of processes and the use of alternative materials,
were typically recognized by the employees working with environmental
topics in the company, but at the same time seen as very complicated,
as a change of practices would demand very specific, new production
knowledge.

The SM company is a remarkable example of how the transfer of seemingly quite advanced and specialized technology such as sole casting
machinery can be successful. SM company has now begun to take on
independent development projects, where environmental concerns can
be integrated into the product design. We suggest that this is due to the
organizational context of the plant, i.e. the close involvement with the
Tai shoe manufacturing group and the resulting access to knowledge
and raw materials. This has made it possible for SM company to take the
standardized manufacturing technology which is also used in the other

factories of the mother company and use it. All of the brand's new golfing shoes are now developed and produced in Thailand.

It can be observed in all three cases that much of the production technology of Thai companies has been imported or transferred and is not developed locally. The situation of the AP and BM companies demonstrates how this often leaves the Thai companies with a poor basic knowledge of the technical principles of production and little capacity for product development and improvements. Product requirements and standards are typically defined in the industrialized countries, leaving only a small space for local improvements and local competence building in the supplying company. This lack of local knowledge on specific details in the production process also makes it difficult to establish specific environmental initiatives that are closely related to the actual production. From the perspective of coherence the isolation of the domain of technologies focusing on environmental improvements has to become integrated into the activities of the company at both the managerial and the professional levels. The SM case demonstrates that capacity building through local networking can make it possible to acquire 'ownership' of the company's own manufacturing technology and products.

Concluding discussion

Our attempt in this chapter has been to go beyond the first judgements and impressions based on rather simplified characteristics concerning the role of EMS and its relation to and interplay with other aspects of how the environment is constructed and handled in different societies and societal settings. The circulation of knowledge in relation to defining the environmental aspects, establishing consistent standards and practices for regulation and bringing environmental competence into the core of companies' innovative activities is seen as the crucial and needed outcome of the implementation of EMS if these should have a lasting and developing impact on industry and the environment.

Accounting for environmental performance

It is not evident what measures should be used to evaluate the success of EMS implementation. Counting the number of implemented systems is not in itself representative of environmental achievements. But also more qualitative assessments of for example, the environmental priorities of the implemented systems can be misleading without relating these to the regulatory and societal context. Our empirical studies indicate that the key issue is not whether environmental management actually enhances environmental performance measured by emission standards (as, for example, the DIW waste water standards), but to identify the core processes that constitute a well-performing environmental management process and under what conditions these processes take place.

The description of the embedding of EMS suggests that the potential of EMS lies in achieving better relations and as such more coherence among the different stakeholders and domains of knowledge. A well-performing environmental effort requires the involved actors to be able to transfer knowledge elements and have some common references for good performance, and to share visions of environmental improvements and the routines and everyday practice of engineering and management. The individual elements of environmental regulation (policies, legal procedures, standards, control officers and so on) may all be present, but they will not accomplish a self sustained basis for enforcement nor for more ambitious goals like continuous improvements. As a way of providing an analytical understanding and evaluation of the success of EMS in new settings, we see 'processes building' and 'obstructing coherence' as key elements to an understanding of environmental management. EMS have a potential to catalyse alignment processes that produce coherence among the different elements involved in societal and industrial environmental awareness and improvements. However, this will not be achieved without additional efforts.

Conceptually, 'coherence' addresses the gap where there may appear to be a high level of awareness of individual environmental problems, but these are still not interconnected in a manner that could accommodate future developments to address the problems. In a situation with coherent environmental problems these will function as a frame for the discussions. This does not imply that the different interested parties necessarily agree about the state of the environment, but that there is a limit to how far the conflict may spread, as the different actors are engaged to keep these representations at the centre of their discussions. The potential for industrial transformation through environmental management is linked to an improved alignment of interests and understanding. This implies a reshaping of the company to become an element in a network with distributed competences where there are less clear-cut boundaries between the company, the consultants, the authorities and the customers. And this is somewhat in conflict with a business tradition of complete hierarchical control.

The diversity of environmental management and regulation

The question of coherence is not only a question of bringing different environmental issues together, but also a way of analysing whether different interested parties are committed to maintain a discussion of environmental problems in relation to specific issues. As different parties are engaged, enrolled and committed the network gradually gains strength and translates environmental issues from matters of potential uncontrolled conflict to more transparent dispute. Heterogeneous elements such as legislative norms, regulatory practice (for example, enforced legislation, corruption practices), production facilities, workers practice, individual concerns, management practice, environmental management standards, customer demands, supplier capacity, the competence of consultants, and sector structures are combined to contribute to new and more transparent entities of environment. Coherent environmental issues are 'good' – that is, manageable environmental problems that are recognized by a wide group of actors and transparent through association with commonly accepted practices of representation.

The lack of coherence between the different domains of the Thai context reflects how the different elements in some instances have been developed in parallel as separate entities that are otherwise not related. The coherence that may have existed between the separate elements in their western origins is often lacking after the implementation and transformation to the Thai context. The transformation to newly industrialized countries demonstrates that these relations, and the coherence they constitute, is not necessarily present in countries that have different histories. EMS dissemination in Thailand should therefore not be seen as an isolated measure that can in itself be expected to support a development towards continuous improvements beyond the definitions of the existing legislation. It seems to be important to further understand the mutual connections between individual elements including legislative norms and management programs. Improved environmental management is shaped as part of a mutual process with increased professional competences, performance regulation, technological ownership and changing business culture. International trade and multinationals are important, but not unambiguous elements that contribute to shape these processes.

Dependency and innovative capability

In order for EMS to contribute to the alignment of heterogeneous elements in coherent networks that can transform companies' environmental efforts, environmental concerns must be integrated into companies' design strategies for products and services, as this will ensure continued improvements in environmental performance. However, this is not easy to achieve. Thirty years of experience has shown that neither environmental legislation nor technology promotion programmes such as Cleaner Production programmes or environmental management standards such as ISO14000 have by themselves necessarily led to the integration of proactive design strategies for the environment in companies. Rather, new strategies are developed as a result of a multiplicity of heterogeneous factors that makes it possible for the company to integrate such pressures as legislation and customer demands into innovative strategic design processes. The innovative capacity of the company with regards to design processes is related to new products and services but also to the re-conceptualization and shaping of the context of the company. The ability to use 'internal' factors such as in-house competences and technologies as well as trans-company professional knowledge networks while playing an active role in the re-configuration of 'external' factors such as users and markets is crucial for companies' innovative potential.

The challenge for Thai industry is to realize that the new demands from, for example, electronics and food regulations in Europe are challenges that do require innovative rather than reactive responses. This also implies a need for re-thinking the traditional paternal structure in business management and the lack of involvement of professionals in in-house innovative activities. In this respect the environmental activities will serve as a promoter of change and improve the circulation of knowledge.

Notes

1. These include:

   - The Industrial Environmental Management Project 1990–1995 (Federation of Thai Industries, FTI/Institute of Environmental Management, IEM-supported by USAID).
   - The CDG project on Industrial Pollution Control for SME's in Thailand 1992–1994 (AIT/CU/CMU/DIW).
   - Promotion of Cleaner Technology in Thai Industries 1996–1998 (FTI/Thai Environment Institute, TEI – supported by DANCED).
   - The Cleaner Technology Unit at TEI.

- First Asia Pacific Roundtable on Cleaner Production 1997 (Pollution Control Department, PCD).
- CP in municipalities 2000–2001 (PCD/TEI).
- Cleaner Production for Industrial Efficiency, CPIE (PCD/Environment of the Royal Thai Government).
- Cleaner Technology Capacity Building at DIW 1998–2003 (Department of Industrial Works – supported by DANCED).

References

Andersen, M.S. and Jørgensen, U. (1995) *Evaluering af indsatsen for renere teknologi 1987–1992* (Assessment of the Cleaner Technology program 1987–1992). (Copenhagen: Orientering fra Miljøstyrelsen 5).

Behrndt, K. (2002) 'Hot Spots in the Interpretation of the ISO 14001 Standard to Ensure Continual Improvements', in *Corporate Social Responsibility & Governance for Sustainability*, Proceedings of the 2002 Greening of Industry Network Conference, 23–6 June. Gothenburg, Sweden.

Braun, B. and Castree, N. (eds) (1998) *Remaking Reality: Nature at The Millennium*. London: Routledge.

Dauvergne, P. (1999) 'The Environmental Implications of Asia's 1997 Financial Crisis', *IDS Bulletin*, 30(3): 31–42.

Deegan, C. (2002) 'The Legitimising Effect of Social and Environmental Disclosures – a Theoretical Foundation', *Accounting, Auditing & Accountability Journal*, 15(3): 282–311.

Edwards, T. (2000) *The Sociology of Translation: Technology Transfer & The Teaching Company Scheme*, Aston Business School Research Paper RP 0005.

Gallagher, D. (2005) 'Environmental Management Systems in the US and Thailand', *Greener Management International*, 46: 41–56.

Georg, S. and Füssel, L. (2000) 'Making Sense of Greening and Organizational Change', *Business Strategy and the Environment* 9(3): 175–85.

Georg, S., Lauridsen, E.H. and Jørgensen, U. (2002) *Environmental Management Perspectives: a Study of How Environmental Management Systems Travel*, DUCED Research Network Program paper, Copenhagen.

Gouldson, A. and Murphy, J. (1998) *Regulatory Realities: The Implementation and Impact of Industrial Environmental Regulations*, Earthscan Publications.

Hansen, M.W. (1999) 'Environmental Management in Transnational Corporations in Asia: Does Foreign Ownership Make a Difference?', *Occasional paper no. 11*. Department of Intercultural Communication and Management, Copenhagen Business School.

Hertin J. et al. (2003) 'Are Soft Policy Instruments Effective? Establishing the Link between Environmental Management Systems and the Environmental Performance of Companies', in K. Jakob and S. Lindemann (eds), *Governance for Industrial Transformation*, Proceedings of the Berlin Conference on the Human Dimensions of Global Environmental Change, 5–6 December, Germany.

In-na, Y. et al. (2003) 'CP in Municipalities: A Demonstration Project in Thailand', paper presented at *The 4th Asian Pacific Roundtable on Cleaner Production*, 20–2, January, Chiang Mai, Thailand.

Jørgensen, U. (2003) 'The Hidden Networks of Practice in ISO 14000' in *Innovating for Sustainability*, Proceedings of the 2003 Greening of Industry Network conference; San Francisco, USA, 12–15 October.

Jørgensen, U. (2005) 'Cleaner Technology in Denmark – Support Measures and Regulatory Efforts', in T. de Bruijn and V. Norbert-Bohm (eds), *Shared Responsibilities and Reinvention: New Roles for Industry in European and US Environmental Policy*. Cambridge, MA: MIT Press.

Kollof, N.B. (2002) *Environmental Management in Thailand*, Masters Thesis, Lyngby, Dept. of Manufacturing Engineering and Management, Technical University of Denmark.

Kuada, J. (ed.) (2003) *Culture and Technological Transformation in the South – Transfer or Local Innovation*. Copenhagen: Samfundslitteratur.

Latour, B. (1999) *Pandora's Hope: Essays on the Reality of Science Studies*. London: Harvard University Press.

Lauridsen, E.H. (2003) 'Coherence and the Continuous Development of the environment'. Paper presented at *Environmental Management Perspectives: The challenges of certification research workshop*, 17–19 March, Bangkok, Thailand.

Lauridsen, E.H. *et al.* (2003) 'Changing Settings – Changing Roles: the Different Conditions of EMS in Thailand and Europe', in *Innovating for Sustainability*, Proceedings of the 2003 Greening of Industry Network conference, San Francisco, USA, 12–15 October.

Lynn, L.H. (2006) 'US Research on Asian Business: A Flawed Model', *Asian Business and Management* 5: 37–51.

Rojanapaiwong, S. (ed) (2000) *State of the Thai Environment 1997–1998*. The Green World Foundation, Bangkok: Amarin Printing and Publishing Company.

Roome, N. (1992) 'Developing Environmental Management Systems', *Business Strategy and the Environment* 1(1): 11–24.

Simmons, P. and Wynne, B. (1993) 'State, Market and Mutual Regulation? Socio-economic Dimensions of the Environmental Regulation of Business', in *The Fifth Annual International Conference of the Society for the Advancement of Socio-Economics*, New York, USA, 26–8 March.

Sluijs, J.P. van der, *et al.* (1998) 'Anchoring Devices in Science for Policy: The Case of Consensus around Climate Sensitivity', *Social Studies of Science* 28(2): 291–323.

Sørensen, K. *et al.* (2000) 'Against Linearity', in M. Dirkes and C. von Grote, (eds), *Between Understanding and Trust – The Public, Science and Technology*, Amsterdam: Harwood Academic Publishers, pp. 237–57.

Zatz, Mike (2003) 'From Technology to Management: The Evolution of CP Technical Assistance Programs', paper presented at *The 4th Asian Pacific Roundtable on Cleaner Production*; Chiang Mai, Thailand, 20–2 January.

8
Financial Management and Accounting in State Islamic Religious Councils in Malaysia: A Grounded Theory

A.R. Abdul Rahman and A.R. Goddard

Introduction

In order to understand Asian management, we must first study the management processes that are embedded in its cultural and social context. This chapter reports in-depth case studies of financial management and accounting practices in two Islamic organizations in Malaysia, using a grounded theory methodology. The chapter has two main purposes. The first is to contribute to the understanding of financial management and accounting in religious organizations in general and in Islamic organizations in particular. The dominant theme which emerged from the research concerned the sacred/secular divide which prior studies had identified as an important aspect of Christian organizations. The study of the Malaysian organizations showed that this divide was not evident in the Muslim context. Rather, the Islamic *verstehen* is characterized by Islamic values and beliefs concerning the all-encompassing nature of Islam and also by the *Taklif* notion of personal accountability to God. The study also showed that important differences in accounting practices occur between organizations within the same religious denomination. These differences are due to the different accounting *verstehen* in each organization which emerge from the differences in the complex contexts of power and other cultural influences within which the organizations are located.

The second purpose of the chapter is to provide an example of how a grounded theory study is undertaken in practice and to encourage its use in similar and different settings. The methodology used was a combination of Strauss and Corbin (1990, 1998) and Glaser (1978). The grounded theory which emerged used Weber's (1947, 1949, 1968) concept of *verstehen* to explain the differences in accounting practice. The study showed that the broader social, historical and religious contexts in which organizations are embedded, together with the power relationships within them, resulted in unique accounting *verstehen* and also therefore in unique accounting practices.

This chapter contributes to an understanding of Asian management in two ways. The first is a contribution to the use and development of interpretive methodology in such research in general, and grounded theory in particular. Humphrey and Scapens (1996) were concerned that the growth in case study research had failed to realize the potential of 'explanatory' case studies in providing more challenging reflections on the nature of accounting knowledge and practice and also that prior case studies had not generated much 'new theory'. They argued that for accounting research to become more explanatory of accounting as a social practice, case-based researchers have to recognise that theory both informs, and is developed by observation. Such research needed to be more directly involved in conversations concerning theories of the organizational and social functioning of accounting. However, by avoiding recommendations as to the adoption of any particular methods, their chapter did not provide guidance as to how such theories might be constructed. This chapter argues for the use of grounded theory as one such method and applies the method in practice to develop an 'accounting theory'.

Grounded theory, developed in the 1960s by two sociologists, Glaser and Strauss, is defined as 'a general methodology of analysis linked with data collection that uses a systematically applied set of methods to generate an inductive theory about a substantive area' (Glaser 1978). The number of studies using grounded theory has grown steadily since the original treatise and it has attracted a number of management researchers (for example, Turner, 1983; Gummeson, 1991). Its use in accounting research has been limited. Parker and Roffey (1997) point out the dearth of studies in accounting using grounded theory despite its years of development and its potential to make a significant contribution to interpretive research. They advocate using the theory to examine its potential utility in the accounting domain and to inform the contemporary methodological debate in accounting research. They conclude that rigorous grounded theory research, which has methodological discussion firmly embedded in its procedures, would improve the quality of management accounting and control field research and that it offers itself as an under-utilized and potentially valuable addition to future accounting theory development.

The second contribution of this chapter is to extend our knowledge of financial management and accounting to religious organizations in general and to Muslim organizations in particular. This is achieved by describing two case studies of accounting practices as embedded in two religious, public service organizations in Malaysia. Malaysia is a federation of 14 Malay states. It has about 18 million inhabitants, with 60 per cent being Muslims. As a federal structure, the Malaysian Constitution clearly stipulates the division of power between the federal and the state governments. In the Malaysian Constitution, religion has been identified as within the jurisdiction of the state. The State King is also the Head of the religion of Islam in his state. In every state, the State Islamic Religious Council (SRC) was established to administer Islamic affairs. The primary duty of SRCs is the management of Islamic Taxes (*Zakat*). This raises issues of both financial and religious accountability, as *Zakat* is one of the pillars of Islamic faith. *Zakat* is essentially a wealth tax and those eligible to receive benefits from *Zakat* are laid down by Islam and include the poor and destitute, and those in the path of God. Today this is taken to include the establishment of hospitals and schools, and a wide range of social security schemes so that the SRCs are very significant public service providers.

There is a limited literature directly concerned with accounting in such organizations. This literature is mainly concerned with accounting in churches and focuses on prescribing 'good' accounting practices. Very few of these studies try to explain accounting practices in use (Booth, 1993). Laughlin (1988, 1990) is an exception who provides insight into accountability and accounting practices in a western Christian church environment and more recently Irvine (1996) and Parker (2001, 2002) have provided more interpretive studies of accounting practices in religious organizations. Karim and Ali (1989) and Karim (1990, 1995) have studied financial reporting and auditing in Islamic Banks. However, there has been no extensive and systematic study of accounting as a situated social practice in Islamic religious settings.

Two main themes emerge from the existing literature. First, there has been a concern with the inadequacies of accounting practices in churches. The solution advocated for these problems are generally for churches to follow 'good commercial practices' (for example, Rowe and Giroux, 1986; Zietlow, 1989; Faircloth, 1988). Secondly, there has been an emphasis on the differences between the 'spiritual' and 'non-spiritual' or the 'sacred' and 'secular' aspects that need to be taken into account in the study of accounting systems and in their design and implementation (Booth 1993; Laughlin, 1988, 1990).

Studies of western Christian churches indicate that accounting practices may interact with the spiritual dimension of a church. Accounting usage may be linked to management issues that are involved with the survival of the Church, and to be implicated in the process of the centralization of control (Booth, 1993, 1995). Laughlin (1988, 1990) provides an insight into the nature of accounting systems at various levels in the Church of England. In his understanding of the uses of accounting, specific attention was paid to the issue of historical context and unique features of the organization. An understanding of this variety in the accounting systems had to be related to an understanding of the social dynamics of the Church. Laughlin's use of the sacred and secular metaphor emphasizes the role of belief systems of religious organizations in explaining the use of accounting. The sacred/secular divide, therefore, separates the 'legitimate' part of a church from its profane support activities which include accounting systems (Booth, 1993). Accounting is regarded as an irrelevancy in the life of the organization and only tolerated to the extent that it supports the sacred.

Parker's (1998, 2001, 2002) study developed a grounded theory of the financial management strategy of a community welfare organization in Australia, founded by Christian religious denominations. This study found that the organization was coping with a dynamic, complex and at times inhospitable environment. Yet its strategic financial orientation emerged as a key proactive response to that environment. In this case, the issue of sacred/secular was not found to be important. Irvine (1996), however, found that the notion of a sacred/secular division would be a useful starting point for a study of any religious organization. In her study of a local church in Australia she revealed that accounting was not generally portrayed as being contrary to the spiritual aims of the church. This may be partly due to the greater uniformity in beliefs within a local church, and the church's responsibility for its own resourcing. Within this church an interest was displayed in the accounting system. The past and present treasurers and churchwardens displayed a keen awareness of the spiritual emphasis of the church, but they saw no inconsistency or division between the operations of those aspects and church accounting. Although there was resistance to the notion that accounting might dominate spiritual concerns, there was little evidence of resistance to the use of accounting in principle; in fact, accounting was used on various occasions to objectify goals, and also to justify opinions on various financial matters.

Methodology

The methodology adopted by this study combines a general model of interpretive research based on that developed by Russell (1996) and grounded theory methods of data analysis and theory construction developed by Strauss and Corbin (1990) and Glaser (1978). It commenced with a broad description of the phenomenon to be studied following Glaser's approach whereby the research problem should emerge rather than be forced by the methodology. For instance, in this study, although the initial phenomenon to be studied was the accounting practices in the case studies, it emerged that the core phenomenon was the accounting *verstehen* of the organization, as explained in more detail below. The empirical work followed and the researchers emerged themselves in the data by interviews, document searches and participant observation. This was undertaken in two stages of data collection and analysis and development of theory. The first stage was predominantly concerned with obtaining an understanding of the organizations and of the pertinent phenomena. Following analysis of the data from the first field study a period of theoretical reflection was undertaken and an emerging theory constructed. The second stage entailed detailed testing and further development of this emerging theory resulting in a validated grounded theory of accounting in the two organizations, which is reported in this chapter.

This methodology views the research process as being iterative, involving ongoing analysis and reflection through stages of exploration of an initial phenomenon. The researcher gradually discovers the issues and questions of centrality to the informants, then develops an emergent theoretical perspective. Through further reflection and data analysis the researcher eventually develops a theoretical understanding of the phenomenon being studied.

The empirical analysis and theory construction was undertaken using Strauss and Corbin's (1990) grounded theory procedures. They described grounded theory as 'a method that uses a systematic set of procedures to inductively derive a grounded theory about a phenomenon'. The central aim is to construct a theory by grounding it in a rigorous observation of the phenomenon, 'in interplay with data and developed through the course of actual research' (Strauss and Corbin, 1998). The theory will often be complex, formulated through iterative analysis of data, and through the development of core concepts whose relationships are investigated in order to generate an explanatory theoretical framework which emerges from the data collected (Strauss 1987). Therefore, the task is to interpret the varied perceptions of the participants in the research process in order to construct a 'theory that is conceptually dense' (Strauss and Corbin, 1990). Analysis of the data is itself an emergent process and the researcher seeks gradually to develop an empathy with the data. The aim is to understand what the data tells of the participants' realities and the process through which they unfold. The researcher needs to constantly construct alternative interpretations until they are satisfied that the representation is a faithful account.

The procedures comprise three interrelated aspects: theoretical reflections, coding and theory generation. Theoretical reflection of prior theories of accounting studies serves to generate the theoretical frameworks to be used by the study. This approach, as asserted by Clifford (1994), provides a powerful theoretical framework informed by prior literature to serve as a guide for the process of data analysis. This is considered appropriate since the grounded theory researcher cannot profess neutrality and distance from the research subject in the way that the positivist researcher attempts. Nonetheless, Strauss (1987) specifically delineates the importance of the researcher's academic and professional experience in coding, categorizing and verifying data in grounded theory research. Prior theories and the researcher's experience serve as guides for interpreting the emerging concepts through the close scrutiny of field notes, interview transcripts and other documents.

Coding is the process of analysing the data and proceeds through several stages (Strauss and Corbin, 1990, 1998). *Open coding* is the process of breaking down, examining, comparing, conceptualizing, and categorizing data collected by the researcher's observation/interview/reflection notes as well as interview transcripts. These categories are discovered when concepts are compared one against the other and appear to pertain to a similar phenomenon. Thus concepts are grouped together under a higher order, this being a more abstract concept called a category.

Axial Coding follows open coding. Once initial open coding has been conducted, the researcher then recombines the data by making connections between categories. The grounded theory researcher describes the properties of initial categories by the use of theoretical memos. *Theoretical memos* are written theoretical questions, coding summaries, and hypotheses, used to monitor and stimulate coding, and as a basis for theory integration. They are used to reflect upon and explain meanings ascribed to phenomena by actors and researchers; to identify relationships between codes; to clarify, sort and extend ideas; and to record crucial quotations or phrases.

The final stage of coding is *selective coding* which requires the selection of the focal core category, that is, the central phenomenon which has emerged from the axial coding process. All other categories derived from that axial coding process must be related in some way to this focal core code, either directly or indirectly (Parker and Roffey, 1997).

The final grounded theory can be explained in accordance with the 'paradigm model' as developed by Strauss and Corbin (1990) and used illustratively by Parker (1998). The 'paradigm model' is a process of connecting categories or conceptual data developed from the process of open and axial coding, by relating, restructuring and rebuilding the data into various patterns with the intention of revealing links and relationships.

The *central phenomenon* is the central idea or central event that is considered to be the most significant and which becomes an inherent part of the organizational properties. The *causal conditions* are the events or incidents that lead to the occurrence or development of a phenomenon. The *context* refers to the specific set of properties that pertain to a phenomenon. The *intervening conditions* are the conditions which describe the environment in which the individual examples of phenomenon occur. They are not part of the phenomenon or the causal conditions, but they also contribute to the particular phenomenon or to the causal conditions. The *action/interactional strategies* are the processes of managing, handling, carrying out, or responding to a phenomenon. The action/interactional strategies are processual, and evolving in nature. They are also purposeful, goal-oriented, undertaken for some reason and in response to or to manage a phenomenon. The *consequences* are the result of action and interaction strategies. They may be actual or potential, and happen in the present or the future.

Study methods

The primary objective of this study was to explain accounting as a social practice and to develop an explanation of accounting in religious organizations located in different cultures to those found in the West. Culture, values and religion have been argued by many to be important in shaping the role of accounting (for example, Rosenberg *et al.*, 1982; Laughlin, 1990; Dent, 1991). Based on the preliminary review of literature relating to the study of accounting in its organizational and social contexts and also by focusing upon Booth's (1993) framework for research on accounting practices in religious organizations, three initial research questions were formulated to serve as a guide to the data collection process.

1. What is the perceived role of accounting practices in Islamic State Religious Councils (SRCs)?
2. How and to what extent do cultures, religious values and sociopolitical environments influence the way accounting is being practised in the SRCs?
3. Does a conflict between 'secular' and 'sacred' activities in the organization exist and how do the participants perceive the role of accounting in relation to this?

In order to examine these questions, two State Religious Councils (SRC) organizations, namely, ASRC and BSRC, were selected. For the purpose of confidentiality the real name of each state is concealed. These were chosen to provide a range of cultural settings. There were two stages of data collection.

Field Study 1

The first stage of data collection took place over a period of one month. This stage involved, firstly, semi-structured interviews with the staff of ASRC and BSRC. Semi-structured interviews were adopted in order to allow the interviewees a degree of freedom to explain their thoughts and to highlight any areas of particular interest that they had, as well as to enable certain responses to be questioned in greater depth – for example, to bring out and resolve any apparent contradictions (Horton *et al.*, 1996). This form of interviewing also revealed certain aspects which had not previously been identified and which were able to be followed up in further questioning as well as in later interviews and/or investigated empirically. Ten personnel in ASRC and fourteen in BSRC were interviewed over a period of one month. These included the chief executives, senior management, accounting staff and religious officers.

Secondly, at this stage, documents such as annual reports, proposal papers, newspaper cuttings, minutes of meetings were also collected and compiled. This enabled a more detailed analysis of the functioning of individual units and members of the organizations to be made. This documentation also helped in the identification of issues facing the organizations and its members. This method enabled interview findings to be studied in context and provided a triangulation process whereby the reliability of interview data and of the documents collected could be ensured.

The initial field study was reported in Abdul Rahman and Goddard (1998). The aim of the second field study was to test the emergent theories and to develop new relationships and concepts.

Field Study 2

The second stage commenced some six months after the first and comprised three months of data collection, involving follow-up semi-structured interviews, participant observation, and document collection. In the semi-structured interviews, open-ended questions were constructed based on the theories that had emerged during the first stage. This allowed participants to give feedback on the preliminary theories and gave them adequate opportunity to explain in more detail.

Participant observation was adopted primarily 'to get a good feel for what it's like out there' (Nahapiet, 1988). However, due to the practical restrictions set by both organizations, only the 'observer as participant' method of data collection could be adopted for the current study (Adler and Adler, 1987; Denzin, 1970, 1978). The researcher was not permitted to participate actively in the organizations' activities, but was granted permission to discuss matters with any members of the organizations. In addition, the researcher was given permission to be present at a number of meetings. This method was found to serve the purpose of exposing the meanings, perceptions and interactions from an insider's perspective and to shed light on the phenomenon under investigation in an everyday life situation or setting (Jorgensen, 1989).

Grounded theory

This section briefly outlines the coding analysis undertaken using the grounded theory methodology, commencing with the open and axial coding procedure, before arriving at the final stage of selective coding.

Open and axial coding

Open coding of interview, document and observational data commenced with the identification of provisional categories, which are 'the early conceptual names assigned to data fragments' (Locke 2001). The provisional categories were next examined and compared with each other to identify any natural groupings that existed. The groupings which were derived solely from immersion in the data and captured substantive aspects of the research situation are termed substantive categories. They represented another level of conceptual generality in the data and were allocated appropriate labels. Other groupings were derived from the researchers' own disciplinary sensibilities and introduced sociological and organizational meaning to the data. These are termed theoretical categories. The process of axial coding followed, whereby the relationships between substantive and theoretical categories were explored using theoretical memos, as described above.

The whole process is illustrated in Table 8.1. This provides brief descriptions of the original 32 provisional categories and shows how they were grouped into 11 substantive and theoretical categories.

Selective coding and theory generation

The final procedure involved using the grounded theory methodology to perform the process of *selective coding*. This requires the selection of the focal core category – that is, the central phenomenon which has emerged from the axial coding process. All other categories derived from axial coding process must be related in some way, either directly or indirectly, to these focal core codes. This was achieved using a simplified version of Strauss and Corbin's paradigm model. In this way a theoretical framework of interrelated concepts was developed which showed posited relationships between the central concept (the focal core category which represents the central phenomenon), its conditioning (or influencing) concepts, the action/interaction strategies in response to, or managing the core, and their consequences. The whole social process discovered in the research is summarized in Figure 8.1.

The central phenomenon: values and perceptions of accountability

The central phenomenon to emerge from this study is the understanding that organizational members share concerning the meaning of accountability and accounting. This understanding, or 'accounting *verstehen*', underpinned the way in which accountability processes in general, and accounting practices in particular, were undertaken and perceived. Weber (1949) considered persons to be 'cultural beings endowed with the capacity and will to take a deliberate stand toward the world and to lend it meaning'. He conceived that the social action of individuals includes both a social and a subjective meaning and *verstehen* is a method of obtaining an 'interpretive understanding' of such social action (Kalberg, 1994). Moreover, he conceptualized social action as involving one of four types of meaningful action: means–end rational, value rational, affectual or traditional. It is the concept of value rational action (*wertrational*) that most informs this research, when action is 'determined by a conscious belief in the value for its own sake of some ethical, aesthetic, religious or other form of behaviour' (Weber, 1968). However, Weber uses the individual as a unit of social analysis as a means

Table 8.1 Summary of coding process

Substantive and theoretical category	Provisional category
(1) Influence of power structures on organizational decision-making processes	1. The existence of power elite groups 2. Power and decision-making process 3. Authority in the decision-making process 4. Organizational control by coercion or consent
(2) Managerialist culture and values	5. Level of involvement of accounting staff in organizational management 6. Staffing levels 7. Professional training and exposure to contemporary accounting techniques 8. Interdepartmental conflicts and tensions. 9. Professionalism and authoritative leadership
(3) Islamic culture and values	10. Relationships between the 'Ulama' (clergy) and management. 11. Centrality of religious activities: religious vs commercial activities
(4) Traditional Malay culture and values	12. Organization change and increase in power of Sultan in ASRC.
(5) Accounting values	13. Ex-post reporting. 14. Accounting information and probity of expenditure.
(6) Centrality of accountability	15. Coercive and consensual use of authority in decision-making process. 16. Formality of accountability relationships. 17. Power elite and accountability 18. Personal vs managerial accountability. 19. Accountability and fraud.
(7) Financial control practices and processes.	20. Financial regulation procedures 21. Budgetary processes and the usage of budgetary data for control purposes. 22. Emergence of use of performance measures and Zakat collection in BSRC.
(8) Financial decision-making processes	23. Financial decision-making processes
(9) Financial reporting process	24. Accounting and the external auditing requirement. 25. Accounting and the community
(10) Role of accounting and authority of the accountant	26. The role of accounting practices 27. Adequacy of financial information. 28. Accounting perceived as a routine process. 29. The authority of the accountant

Table 8.1   (Continued)

Substantive and theoretical category	Provisional category
(11) Relationship between accounting practices and the mainstream religious activities	30. Existence of distinct religious and non-religious occupational groupings with different attitudes. 31. Centrality of religious activities: religious vs commercial activities. 32. Acceptance of accounting as a valid organizational practice.

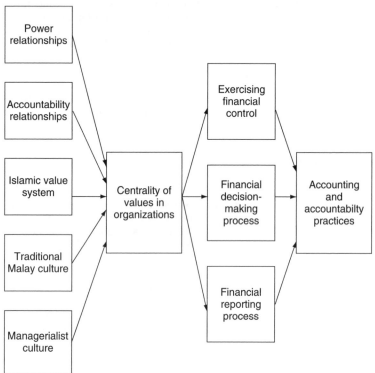

Figure 8.1   Accounting and accountability process in KSRC and FTSRC

of understanding how individuals act in concert. Indeed he defines the concern of the sociological enterprise in terms of action by individuals in delimited groups and the identification of patterned regularities of action (Kalberg 1994). Accounting practices can be viewed as one such patterned action in an organization comprising individual actors. Parker and Roffey (1997) note that grounded theory (and ethnomethodogy) has *verstehen* (understanding) as a goal in a phenomenological sense. The usefulness of the concept of *verstehen* in this study is that it provides a link between culture and action. It can therefore explain the process by which culture, a social phenomenon, interrelates with accounting practice, the product of individuals' actions. This process is usually omitted from studies investigating culture and accounting. The accounting *verstehen* phenomenon that emerged in this study refers to the set of values and beliefs held by individuals that causes them to develop particular accounting practices. It comprised a set of values influenced by Islam, Malay society and western managerialism combined with a perception of individual and organizational account-ability. The value mix held by organizational members, and therefore also the accounting *verstehen*, was different in ASRC and BSRC.

The Islamic value system is derived from the original source which is Revelation, confirmed by religion and affirmed by intellectual and intuitive principles (e.g. Al-Attas, 1995; Abu-Sulayman, 1994; Al-Faruqi, 1992). Muslims consider humans to be vicegerents of God. Thus, whatever worldly possessions a Muslim has are to be held in a steward-ship capacity – that is simply in trust from God (Abu-Sulayman, 1943). Islam does not concede to the dichotomy of the sacred and the profane (Al-Attas, 1995; Al-Faruqi, 1992). The world view of Islam encompasses both the worldly aspect and the religious aspect, in which the worldly aspect must be related in a profound and inseparable way to the reli-gious aspect (Al-Attas, 1995). Islam has also developed its own concept of accountability (*Taklif*) which means that everyone is accountable for his/her actions or inaction's on the day of judgment (Al-Safi, 1992).

Both organizations reflected the presence of the Islamic value system. The objectives and the mission of both organizations clearly stipulate that the aim of the organizations is to serve the Muslim public. The characteristics and the activities of the organizations are, in general, reflective of Islamic beliefs and principles. All employees as well as the management were Muslims and they also shared a belief in the stated objectives of the organizations. The main activities of the organizations were centred around Islamic activities such as managing Islamic funds and carrying out welfare activities.

Another important value system, which may also explain the kind of power relationships in ASRC, was that of Malay culture, with its tradi-tional class system. The line of power is vertical, from top to bottom. At the apex of the triangle stands the ruling monarch, followed by those belonging to the royal class with the titles *raja* or *tengku*, ascribed by birth. Below the royal class are the nobility or the titled gentry. Below the nobility are the 'free men' (*orang merdeka*) and at the bottom of the social scale were the 'debt-bondsmen' and the slaves (Osman, 1985). The study of ASRC reveals the strong influence of the traditional social class system. Even though it may not reflect such a highly structured system as shown above, it does suggest that the concept of Kingship still binds the fabric of the power relationships and the culture of ASRC could be described as traditional Malay. The power elite of the royal family was a significant factor in the way the staff exercised their authority in organizational management and decision-making. This was associated with the passive involvement of staff in managerial decision-making and their lack of authority. In addition, the role of accounting and the authority of accountants were very limited in that organization. It was observed that most staff in ASRC shared a concern about their lack of authority and they felt that they did not play much role in decision-making processes, in the organizational activities and policy-making. Most of them also shared a concern over managerial problems and the limitations of the organization but felt that they could not change the situation.

The influence of the traditional Malay culture in BSRC, although present, was found to be limited. A managerialist culture was found to be more predominant. This emergent culture seemed to stem partly from its location in a city where the organization was more exposed to commercial and modern life. Thus, the organizational culture was more influenced by managerialist values from the outside world. There was consequently more active involvement in managerial decision-making among the staff of BSRC and accounting practices also seemed to be more meaningful. The accountant also had more authority in financial decision making and accounting as a professional activity was held in more esteem.

The issue of accountability also emerged as central to understanding accounting in the two organizations. In particular, the organization members' perceptions of what constituted accountability in their workplaces was most important. There were many facets to these perceptions, including to whom accountability was due and to what extent, and by what means accountability should be demonstrated. Moreover, these perceptions were highly interrelated with their values. However, the aspect of accountability that emerged as being most important was the dichotomy between personal and organizational accountability. Personal accountability seemed to be at the core of most actors and was rooted in the Islamic concept of *taklif*, according to which each person is directly accountability for their deeds and will answer directly to God on the day of judgement. Organizational accountability, although acknowledged, was far less influential. There would appear to be little room for practices concerned with organizational accountability, such as accounting, to contribute to achieving *taklif* and this may explain why such practices are not held in high esteem, but were still accepted. In ASRC the traditional Malay culture combined with deeply held Islamic beliefs resulted in an almost complete marginalization of accounting. In BSRC, the Malay influence was far less strong than the emerging managerialist culture and accounting was deemed to be more important. However, the importance of accounting did not approach that found in western organizations in either BSRC or ASRC. This was almost certainly explained by the different cultural, social and historical context. The combination of values and perceptions of accountability provides a powerful conceptual framework, or *verstehen*, for organizational members to undertake accounting.

Conditioning context

From the above discussion it can be seen that there were at least four conditioning contexts (power, Islamic, Malay and managerialist values and cultures) that influence the nature of the central phenomenon in each organization.

Power relationships have contributed to the accounting *verstehen* and to the way organizational processes were conducted. This is especially evident from the way power was exercised in both organizations. Weber viewed power as ubiquitous in social life and developed his own taxonomy of power and domination (Weber, 1947). He makes a basic distinction between power and authority. Power involves forces or coercion and is an important factor as an internal process in organizations. Authority, on the other hand, is a form of power that does not imply force. Rather, it involves a 'suspension of judgement' on the part of its recipients. Directives or orders are followed because it is believed that they ought to be followed. Compliance is voluntary, thus it requires a common value system among organizational members. This study found Weber's typology of the types of power in social organization to be the most useful for explaining the power relationship in both organizations. Weber (1947) distinguishes between types of authority, developing his well-known typology of traditional, charismatic and legal authority. *Traditional* authority is based on belief in the established traditional order and is best exemplified by operating monarchies. Vestiges of this form can be found in organizations in which the founder or a dominant figure is still present. *Charismatic* authority stems from devotion to a particular power holder and is based on his or her personal characteristics. This type is certainly found in modern organizations, for which it can be either a threat or a benefit. The third form is *legal* authority and this type of power is evident in most modern organisations. It is based on belief in the right of those in higher office to have power over subordinates.

Weber's classification of power in social organizations is useful as an approach to explaining accounting practices in the context of power relationships in both organizations under study in the present context. Using Weber's schema, ASRC can be considered a 'traditional' organization. However, the exercise of power was mainly coercive, as one group of participants, the staff, were relatively powerless in comparison with the power elite comprising top management and the *Sultan*. BSRC, in contrast, can be viewed as a 'utilitarian' organization in which relationships are generally based on 'legal' or 'formal' relationships.

The second conditional context, and closely related to power, is the underlying influence of traditional Malay culture. ASRC was much more influenced by traditional Malay culture than BSRC, as demonstrated by the way the Sultan, representing the power elite group, played a very dominant role in organizational activities. Organizational accountability was closely associated with meeting the needs of the Sultan, who was not concerned with accounting information. The combination of both personal and organizational accountability having little regard for accounting led to its marginalization. However, the third conditioning context, emerging managerialist cultures, was found to be more influential in BSRC. Unlike in ASRC, BSRC staff were more active in, and felt more part of, the decision-making process. Managerial professionalism had also became part of the organization's culture and organizational accountability had a higher profile. Fourthly, the Islamic value system was one of the major underlying influences on the central phenomenon, particularly with respect to influencing the core perceptions of personal accountability. The predominance of personal accountability, itself characterized by *taklif*, over organizational accountability may well have been the source of the relatively low esteem that accounting was held in inside both organizations.

Action/interactional processes

Interactional processes are processual and evolving in nature and comprise major activities which are directed at managing, handling and carrying out or responding to a phenomenon. Three interactional processes were identified in the current study concerned with accounting practices: namely, the way financial control was exercised; the financial decision-making process; and the financial reporting process. The way in which accounting practices were carried out was a response to the accounting *verstehen* in each organization.

Financial control was exercised through budgeting practices, the use of financial regulations and the use of performance measures. ASRC was characterized by very routine budgeting practices and limited use of budgeting; there were no formal financial regulations and no formal target performance measures. BSRC was also characterized by routine budgeting practices, but budgeting information was used to aid planning. BSRC also adopted formal financial regulatory procedures that were reviewed regularly and made some effective use of performance measures. Financial decision-making processes in both organizations were found to be underdeveloped. The lack of sophisticated accounting and management techniques to either evaluate alternative courses of action or as a means of financial analysis may be partly attributable to the lack of necessary expertise and to a shortage of staff, but certainly reflected the low regard for accounting in both organizations. However, with regard to financial reporting processes, there was a contrasting picture in ASRC and BSRC. In ASRC, annual financial reports were not produced regularly and nor were they up to date, whereas in BSRC, the financial information system was well organized, financial statements were produced regularly and were up to date. The members of the organization also considered the system to represent the main mechanism for achieving financial accountability.

It therefore appears that the accounting practices in each organization were a response to the accounting *verstehen* in each organisation. In ASRC, where the accounting *verstehen* was characterized by a traditional Malay culture and marginalized accounting, the accounting practices were extremely limited. In BSRC, where the accounting *verstehen* was characterized by an emerging managerialist culture which valued organizational accountability practices, accounting practices were more developed though still limited.

Consequences

The consequences of the accounting *verstehen* as the central phenomenon in both organizations were evident in two areas – namely, the role of accounting and authority of the accountant and the relationship between accounting and religious activities. Staff in both organizations perceived accounting to be an important tool for the organizations. However, the role of accounting and the authority of the accountant was found to be very restricted. Accounting was regarded as little more than a technology to record financial transactions and information and the authority of the accountants, especially in financial decision-making processes, was found to be minimal. In the case of ASRC, the accountant was not actively involved in the decision-making process. The production of external annual financial statements was not considered to be an important process, nor were the reports themselves considered important documents. They were not kept up to date and little emphasis was placed on them by the management.

The role of accounting and the accountant in BSRC seemed to be more important, though still very limited. The accountant was encouraged to take part in decision-making, and although financial reporting was directed towards meeting the external auditing requirements, it was considered to be the main mechanism for achieving financial accountability.

However, the low standing of accounting practices in both organizations appeared not to be due to them being located in the secular domain for there was no evidence to suggest that there was a dichotomy between secular and sacred activities in either organization. There appeared to be no strong resistance to the use of accounting or other management practices per se. On the contrary, as a result of more involvement in commercial activities especially by BSRC, the need for accounting tools and practices was seen as necessary support techniques for performing core religious organizational activities. The low esteem for accounting practices appears not to be due to an antipathy towards the secular, but rather to the accounting *verstehen* and particularly the predominance of personal, *taklif* accountability. If each person is personally responsible to God, then organizational accountability is attributed much less importance. Consequently, processes which are designed to achieve organizational accountability such as accounting are also attributed less importance.

To summarize, there are three main interacting aspects of the phenomenon studied. First, at the core is the accounting *verstehen* comprising a set of values and perceptions of accountability and accounting held in common by organizational members. The *verstehen* is socially constructed and conditioned by a context comprising a set of power structures and relationships and a set of values derived from the religious, national and managerial setting. These conditioning contexts not only influence the social construction of the accounting *verstehen*, but are also influenced by it. Finally accounting practices are an outcome of the *verstehen* which influences the actions of organizational members and results in differing practices. However, these phenomena are not static but in a constant state of flux.

Theoretical discussion

The theoretical contributions of this study can be woven together with prior theories and theoretical frameworks developed by earlier studies. As argued by Strauss and Corbin (1990), literature and prior theories stimulate theoretical sensitivity by providing concepts and relationships that can be checked against actual data. In addition, prior theories and frameworks will also act as a form of supplementary validation. Moreover, the theoretical discussion will enable a more generalized theory of accounting practices in religious organizations to be posited. For ease of exposition the theoretical discussion will be divided into three interrelated areas that encompass the paradigm model. These are accounting *verstehen* and culture, accounting *verstehen* and power, and accounting *verstehen* and accountability.

Accounting *verstehen* and culture

Many prior interpretive studies have noted the influence of culture on accounting (Berry *et al.*, 1985; Dent, 1991; Covaleski and Dirsmith, 1988). This study also observed the influence of contrasting cultural factors with respect to the organizations and found clear evidence that the accounting practices were constructed by the cultural contexts within which they existed. The findings support the view of Bourn and Ezzamel (1986a, 1986b) that the technical issue of accounting is firmly rooted in the context of the issue of culture.

Within interpretive accounting literature accounting is considered both constitutive and reflexive of organizational reality and culture (Chua, 1988). Hopwood (1987), Hines (1988), Miller and O'Leary (1987) and others have argued for its constitutive role in the construction of organizational life. Boland and Pondy (1983), Covaleski and Dirsmith (1986), Preston (1986) and Dent (1991) have all observed how the meanings of accounting practices are constructed by the social contexts within which they exist. However, these studies do not examine the processes by which these interactions are enacted. In general the way in which accounting *verstehen* informs accounting practice is explained by Weber's concept of social action as outlined above. The process by which the paradigm model in grounded theory is constructed embodies the interactional nature of the core phenomenon and the interactional strategies. The identification of accounting *verstehen* as the core phenomenon and acccounting practices as interactional strategies confirms the constitutive and reflexive nature of accounting.

Accounting and Islamic values

As outlined above, only a limited amount of accounting research has been conducted in religious organizations. The most noteworthy studies in Christian organizations have been undertaken by Laughlin (1988, 1990), Booth (1992, 1993), Irvine (1996) and Parker (1998). The dominant theme of this research has concerned the sacred/secular divide. Laughlin (1988, 1990) uses the 'sacred' and 'secular' metaphor to emphasize the role of the particular belief systems of religious organizations in explaining the uses to which accounting is put. The sacred and secular divide was asserted to be the underlying social dynamic of all churches, and perhaps of all religious organizations. Laughlin's starting point in considering accounting systems in the Church of England was to give some insight into the underlying nature, or 'central dynamic' of religious organizations (Laughlin, 1988). The 'sacred' and 'secular' divide separates the 'legitimate' part of a church's activities from profane support activities. Booth (1993) asserts that accounting, as a support activity, is profane and is an irrelevancy to the life of the organization which is only tolerated if it supports the sacred. There is a necessary interaction between secular and sacred, particularly in organizational terms through various support activities around the 'sacred core'. This means that the tension between them will be a fundamental aspect of organizational life (Booth, 1993). In Parker's study the issue of sacred vs. secular did not emerge as a key issue. Irvine (1996), however, found that the notion of a sacred/secular division was a useful starting point, but accounting was not generally portrayed as being contrary to the spiritual aims of the church. Although there was resistance to the notion that accounting might dominate spiritual concerns, there was little evidence of resistance to the use of accounting in principle.

In our study, in both organizations the resistance to 'secular management solutions and methods', evident in Laughlin (1990) and Booth's (1993) studies was not generally found. Accounting practices in both organizations were, however, less developed and there was low esteem for accounting practices. Nevertheless, this phenomenon does not appear to stem from the existence of a sacred/secular divide. The difference between the findings can be explained in terms of the different accounting *verstehen* in each organization. The Islamic *verstehen* is characterized by Islamic values and beliefs concerning the all-encompassing nature of Islam and also by the *Taklif* notion of personal accountability to God. This may marginalize accounting compared to Christian organizations because such practices are not perceived as central to individual's achievement of personal accountability which is at the core of their beliefs.

This different conception of the sacred and the secular and of *Taklif* may be difficult for non-Muslims to comprehend and this is a problem of *verstehen* itself. As Weber himself stated, 'many... values towards which experience shows that human action may be oriented, often cannot be understood completely... The more radically they differ from our own ultimate values... the more difficult it is for us to understand them empathically' (Weber, 1968).

Accounting and managerialist values

In organizations, the operation of work technologies is not a purely technical-rational affair. Rather, it is embedded in a cultural system of ideas (beliefs, knowledge) and sentiments (values), in which actions and artifacts are vested with symbolic qualities of meanings (Dent, 1991). Accounting practices are a common feature of most work organizations. Inevitably therefore, accounting will be implicated in organizations' cultures. In public sector accounting research there has been a great deal of interest in concepts such as 'managerialist culture', 'managerialism' or 'economic rationalism'. Managerialist culture and managerialism are concepts associated with values that can influence and change the character of organizing, management, accounting, auditing and accountability in an organization (Guthrie, 1990). These values are also associated with the advocacy of formal rational management, emphasising the necessity for clear goals, corporate plans and, above all, internal and external accounting systems with clear responsibility lines for output performance measurement. Broadbent and Guthrie (1992) argue that there is currently an emphasis, in the western public sector, on changing organizational discourses and technologies to promote managerialism. The emergence of the concept of 'new public management' in the public sector sphere can also be attributed to the increasing need and use of managerialist values and technologies (Lapsley, 1997).

A number of empirical studies have been undertaken to investigate the emergence of managerialist values in organizations. There is, however, a diversity of approaches in investigating this issue and of the results emanating from such research. Dent's study (1991) acknowledged the centrality of a professional culture and managerialist values. Dent documents how the new business culture in British Rail transformed and rose above the engineering/railway culture which had existed previously. Bourn and Ezzamel (1986a, 1986b) examine the construction of costing information in the National Health Service in the UK and consider the role of culture in change. They conclude that the technical issues of costing and budgeting are firmly rooted in the context of the issue of culture.

An emerging managerialism, similar to that identified by Dent (1991), was evident in BSRC. Staff were more actively involved in managerial decision-making and accounting practices appeared to serve the organization by providing financial information to assist in economic decision-making. As has already been noted, the accountant also had more authority in financial decision-making and accounting as a professional activity was held in more esteem. Moreover, there was some tentative use of managerialist accounting techniques such as performance measures. It was the emerging managerialism that was the most striking difference between the two organizations and its effect on accounting practices can be explained by the differences in the accounting *verstehen*.

Accounting *verstehen* and power

In the accounting literature, several approaches to understanding power structures in organizations have been used. A political economy approach insists that accounting systems are often a mechanism through which power is exercised (Cooper and Sherer, 1984). Covaleski and Dirsmith (1986) argue that budgeting systems are an integral part of the politics and power at work in any organization's activity, and are used to legitimize actions. More specifically, budgets may represent vested interests in political bargaining processes, and may contribute to the maintenance of existing power relationships. Participants in the accounting system may therefore find it necessary to communicate in terms acceptable to powerful interest groups in order to obtain and preserve access to resources. In this way, accounting may be employed as a means of suppressing sub-unit objectives not approved by powerful interests and of quelling any potential social conflicts. Roberts (1996) asserted that accounting has established itself as the most powerful and legitimate instrument for realizing the visibility of action and it is also effective through generating an apparently inescapable and indisputable image of the results of organized activity. Hopwood (1987) sees accounting as wholly implicated in the creation of structures of surveillance and power that permit modern management to function at a distance from the work process itself. Miller and O'Leary (1987) argue that accounting changes cannot simply be seen as a rational development for improving the accuracy and for the refinement of managerial information but rather, they are just one part of a wide-ranging extension of the apparatus of power.

This study builds upon this prior research and the findings suggest that the more unequal the power distribution (*traditional* and *charismatic* type of authority) and the more dysfunctional the relationships among organizational participants (*coercive* type of organization), the more likely it is that accounting practices will be used as legitimizing mechanisms to justify actions, and the less authority accounting technology will have over managerial decision-making. The existence of the power elite of the royal family in ASRC seemed to limit the potential role of accounting technology and marginalized accounting as a professional activity. Accounting was only considered to be a recording tool to verify financial and management information. Even though the accounting personnel realized that the importance of accounting went beyond the accounting practices actually undertaken they were subservient to whatever decisions were made by the power elite. Rather than accounting serving as a tool to institutionalize organizational practices in ASRC it served only as a tool to ensure organizational practices were in accordance with what had been decided by the organizations' higher authorities. Accounting as a technology in this sense will be shaped in whatever way the power elites find necessary to suit their own objectives. Indeed, accounting seems to be reflective of this organizational reality in the main. BSRC was not characterized by a power elite but might be summarized as representing an emergent managerialist culture. There was a more active involvement in managerial decision-making among the staff of BSRC. Accounting practices seemed to serve the organization by providing financial information to assist in economic decision-making. The accountant also had more authority in financial decision-making, and accounting as a professional activity was held in more esteem.

The study also found evidence of the accounting and management practices representing vested interests in political bargaining processes, and contributing to the maintenance of existing power relationships. Staff in the accounting section of ASRC found it necessary to communicate in terms of what was acceptable to the power elite group in order to obtain and preserve access to resources. In this way, accounting technology may be employed as a means of suppressing sub-unit objectives not approved by powerful interests and of quelling any potential social conflicts. In this case, accounting systems are reflective of organizational reality or mirrors of the societies or organization in which they are implicated (Burchell *et al.*, 1980). In the case of BSRC, in the absence of a power elite, accounting more often served the function of rationalizing managerial actions by the use of accounting tools such as target performance measures and financial reporting.

However, the accounting *verstehen* is the mechanism through which power is enacted by individuals and is an important, though subtle, way in which power influences accounting practice. It is implicated in structuring which values and beliefs inform individuals' *verstehen*. In the case of ASRC the power elite ensured the values associated with the Malay culture were dominant whereas in BSRC the legal-rational mode of domination allowed managerialism to emerge more prominently.

Accounting *verstehen* and accountability

There was a clear emphasis in the case studies on personal rather than organizational accountability. Personal accountability was rooted in the religious and moral concept of *taklif*, and practices concerned with organizational accountability, such as accounting, made a relatively small contribution to achieving *taklif*. Several prior researchers have identified a distinction between organization and personal accountability. Of particular relevance to this study is that of Sinclair (1995) undertook a study of accountability as perceived by chief executives in Australian public sector organizations. She found accountability to be subjectively constructed with two discourses; structural and personal and that, 'accountability is multiple and fragmented: being accountable in one form often requires compromises of other sorts of accountability'. Although similar to the findings in the Islamic organizations, the overriding importance of personal accountability, rooted in religious beliefs and values, does suggest that Sinclair's schema needs to be extended in order to incorporate the cultural context.

Similarly, Roberts, drawing upon the work of Merleau-Ponty and Mead, develops a concept of an individualizing form of accountability and links this to organizational accountability. Roberts' approach was used by Broadbent *et al.* (1999) to investigate accounting in the public sector. These approaches, however, concentrate on the way in which accounting contributes to individual accountability and the detrimental consequences. Our research was more concerned with the moral construction of personal accountability. Moreover, Roberts concedes that his arguments apply specifically to Anglo-American organizations, where perhaps all-pervading religious values are not as common. Our research suggests that personal accountability influences accounting more than vice versa in such organizations, thus reducing the power of accounting practices to create a distance between individuals.

However, there is a real possibility that accountability perceptions were changing in BSRC where the influence of western managerialism was already evident. Over time, this may well lead to more emphasis on organizational accountability. Indeed, it is becoming clear that NPM, with its emphasis on organizational accountability, is becoming more prevalent across the whole world. Several studies have discussed accountability in light of New Public Management (Humphrey, Miller and Scapens, 1993; Ezzamel and Willmott, 1993; Gray and Jenkins, 1993; Cochrane, 1993; Gendron, Cooper and Townley, 2001). However, many of these studies have been sceptical of the success of NPM in achieving accountability. There is also an extensive literature on the relationship between accounting and NPM (Osborne and Gaebler, 1993; Olsen *et al.* 1998; Meyer 1998; Lapsley 1999). This literature is more diverse in its findings. Most stress the importance of accounting to NPM, though whether this is deleterious or beneficial is less clear (Lapsley, 1999). The research reported in this chapter suggests an even more uncertain future for accountability in Islamic organizations as new, unproven concepts of accountability become more dominant and perhaps push personal and moral conceptions into the background.

Conclusions

The main methodological contribution of this chapter is that it provides researchers with an example of how a grounded theory study is undertaken in practice. An interpretive, grounded theory methodology was found to be appropriate for studying accounting practices in the complex environment of religious organizations. The strength of this methodology lies in its ability to reveal the complexity of human values and culture and their integration with aspects of organizational practice. The method which informed this research required an iterative approach to theory development whereby initial theoretical perspectives were tested by reference back to the research site. In this way a deep theoretical understanding, or grounded theory, of the phenomenon was constructed. The theories that emerged were grounded in context and arrived at through continuous interaction and interpretation with the data in a rigorous and structured way. This was achieved by using coding procedures to analyse data and identify concepts and a paradigm model to explain how these concepts related with other. Without prior hypotheses being determined, but with some theoretical insights obtained from a literature review, the study discovered the meanings and applications of accounting practices in the organizations concerned. These were interpreted and used to develop an emergent theory in the first stage which was further developed and tested in the second stage before being discussed within the broader context of prior research and theory.

The chapter also contributes to the understanding of Asian management, particularly financial management and accounting, in the context of religious organizations in Malaysia. As outlined above, only limited financial management and accounting research has been conducted in religious organizations. The dominant theme of this research has concerned the sacred/secular divide. The study of the SRCs showed that this divide was not evident in these Muslim organizations. Rather, the Islamic *verstehen* is characterized by Islamic values and beliefs concerning the all-encompassing nature of Islam and also by the *taklif* notion of personal accountability to God. The study also showed that important differences in accounting practices occur between organizations within the same religious denomination. These differences are due to the different accounting *verstehen* in each organization which emerge from the differences in the complex contexts of power and other cultural influences within which the organizations are located.

The theoretical framework developed in this research provides an approach to the understanding of the nature of accounting and management practices in religious organizations. This may encourage future researchers to further test and develop the framework in a variety of empirical settings including similar types of Islamic organizations in other Muslim countries and similar organizations in different religious environments, as well as public service organizations generally.

References

Abdul Rahman A.R. and Goddard A.R. (1998) 'An Interpretive Inquiry of Accounting Practices in Religious Organisations in Malaysia – Emergent Theoretical Perspectives', *Financial Accountability and Management*, 14(3): 183–202.
Abu-Sulayman, A. (1994) *Crisis in the Muslim Mind*. Herndon, USA: International Institute of Islamic Thought.

Adler, P.A. and Adler, P. (1987) *Membership Roles in Field Research*. Newbury Park, CA: Sage Publications.

Al-Attas, S.N. (1995) *Prolegomena to the Metaphysics of Islam*. Kuala Lumpur: International Institute of Islamic Thought and Civilization.

Al-Faruqi, I.R. (1992) *Al-Tawhid: Its Implications for Thought and Life, International Institute of Islamic Thought*. Herndon: International Institute of Islamic Thought.

Al-Safi, A.K. (1992) *Accountability: Islam versus the Man-made Doctrines*. Kuala Lumpur: Darulfikr.

Berry, A.J., Capps, T., Cooper, D., Ferguson, P., Hopper, T. amd Lowe, E.A. (1985) 'Management Control in An Area of the NCB; Rationales of Accounting Practice in a Public Enterprises', *Accounting, Organizations and Society*, 10(1): 3–28.

Booth, P. (1993) 'Accounting in Churches: A Research Framework and Agenda', *Accounting, Auditing and Accountability*, 6(4): 37–67.

Booth, P. (1995), *Management Control in a Voluntary Organisation – Accountants in Organizational Context*. New York: Garland Publishing Inc.

Bourn, M. and Ezzamel, M. (1986a) 'Costing and Budgeting in the NHS', *Financial Accountability and Management*, 2(1): 53–71.

Bourn, M. and Ezzamel, M. (1986b) 'Organisational Culture in Hospitals in the NHS', *Financial Accountability and Management*, 2(3): 203–25.

Broadbent, J. and Guthrie, J. (1992) 'Changes in Public Sector: A Review of Recent "Alternative" Accounting Research', *Accounting, Auditing and Accountability*, 5(2): 3–31.

Broadbent, J., Jacobs, K. and Laughlin, R. (1999) 'Comparing Schools in the UK and New Zealand: Individualising and Socializing Accountabilities and Some Implications for Management Control', *Management Accounting Research*, 10(4): 339–61.

Chua, W.F. (1988) 'Interpretive Sociology and Management Accounting Research – A Critical Review', *Accounting, Auditing and Accountability*, 2: 59–79.

Clifford, J. (1994) *The Predicament of Culture: Twentieth-Century Ethnography, Literature and Art*; Cambridge, MA: Harvard University Press.

Cochrane, A. (1993) 'From Financial Control to Strategic Management: the Changing Faces of Accountability in British Local Government', *Accounting, Auditing & Accountability Journal*, 3: 30–51.

Covaleski, M.A. and Dirsmith M.W. (1986) 'The Budgetary Process of Power and Politics', *Accounting, Organizations and Society*, 11: 193–214.

Covaleski, M.A. and Dirsmith, M.W. (1988) 'The Use of Budgetary Symbols in the Political Arena: An Historically Informed Field Study', *Accounting Organizations and Society*, 13(1): 1–24.

Dent, J. (1991) 'Accounting and Organizational Cultures: A Field Study of the Emergence of A New Organizational Reality', *Accounting, Organizations and Society*, 16(8): 705–32.

Denzin, N.K. (1970) *The Research Act*. Chicago: Aldine.

Denzin, N.K. (1978) *A Theoretical Introduction to Sociological Methods*, 2nd. edn. New York: McGraw-Hill.

Ezzamel, M. and Willmott, H. (1993) 'Corporate Governance and Financial Accountability: Recent Reforms in the UK Public Sector', *Accounting, Auditing & Accountability Journal*, 6(3): 109–32.

Faircloth, A. (1988) 'The Importance of Accounting to the Shakers', *The Accounting Historians*, 15(2): 99–129.

Gendron, Y., Cooper, D.J., and Townley, B. (2001) 'In the Name of Accountability – State Auditing, Independence and New Public Management', *Accounting, Auditing & Accountability*, 14(3): 278–310.

Glaser, R. (1978) *Theoretical Sensitivity*. California: Sociology Press.

Gray, A. and Jenkins, B. (1993) 'Codes of Accountability in the New Public Sector', *Accounting, Auditing & Accountability Journal*, 6(3): 52–67.

Gummeson, E. (1991) *Qualitative Methods in Management Research*. London: Sage.

Guthrie, J. (1990) 'The Adoption of Corporate Forms for Government Business Undertakings: Critical Issues and Implications' in J. Guthrie, L.D. Parker and D. Shand (eds), *The Public Sector: Contemporary Readings in Accounting and Auditing*. Sydney: Harcourt Brace Jovanovich.

Hines, R (1988) 'Financial Accounting: In Communicating Reality, We Construct Reality', *Accounting, Organizations and Society*, 13(3): 22–44.

Hopwood, A.G. (1987) 'The Archeology of Accounting Systems', *Accounting, Organizations and Society*, 12(3): 207–34.

Horton, J., Macve, R. and Struyven, G. (1996) 'Qualitative Research into Changes in Insurance Accounting: The Use of Semi-Structured Interviews', *Proceedings of the ICAEW Beneath the Numbers Conference*, January, Portsmouth.

Humphrey, C., Miller, P. and Scapens, R. (1993) 'Accountability and Accountable Management in the UK Public Sector', *Accounting, Auditing & Accountability Journal*, 6(3): 7–29.

Humphrey, C. and Scapens, R.W. (1996) 'Methodological Themes: Theories and Case Studies of Organisational Accounting Practices: Limitation or Liberation?', *Accounting, Auditing and Accountability Journal*, 9(4): 86–106.

Irvine, H. (1996) 'Pass the Plate Around Again: A Study of Budgeting in Local Church', *Proceedings of the Fourth Critical Perspectives on Accounting Symposium*. New York.

Jorgensen, H. (1989) *Participant Observation: A Methodology for Human Studies*. California: Sage Publications.

Kalberg, S. (1994) *Max Weber's Comparative-Historical Sociology*. Cambridge: Polity Press.

Karim, R.A and Ali, A.E. (1989), 'Determinants of The Financial Strategy of Islamics Banks', *Journal of Business Finance and Accounting*, 16(2): 193–212.

Karim, R.A. (1990) 'The Independence of Religious and External Auditors: The Case of Islamic Banks', *Accounting, Auditing and Accountability*, 3(3): 34–44.

Karim, R.A. (1995) 'The Independence of Religious and External Auditors: The Case of Islamic Banks', *Accounting, Auditing and Accountability*, 3: 34–44.

Lapsley, I (1997) 'The New Public Management Diaspora: The Health Care Experience', *International Association of Management Journal*, Forum on Research in Health Care Financial Management, 9(2): 1–14.

Lapsley, I. (1999) 'Accounting and the New Public Management: Instruments of Substantive Efficiency or a Rationalising Modernity?', *Financial Accountability and Management*, 15(3–4): 201–7 .

Laughlin, R. (1988) 'Accounting in its Social Context: An Analysis of the Accounting Systems of the Church of England', *Accounting, Auditing and Accountability*, 1(2): 19–42.

Laughlin, R. (1990) 'A Model of Financial Accountability and the Church of England', *Financial Accountability and Management*, 6(2) (Summer): 93–115.

Locke, K. (2001) *Grounded Theory in Management Research*. London: Sage Publications.

Meyer, J. (1998) 'Forward' to O. Olsen, J. Guthrie, and C. Humphrey (eds), *Global Warning: Debating International Developments in New Public Financial Management*. Oslo: Cappelen Akademisk Forlag.

Miller, P and T. O'Leary (1987) 'The Construction of Governable Person', *Accounting, Organizations and Society*, 12(3): 235–65.

Nahapiet, J. (1988) 'The Rhetoric and Reality of an Accounting Change: A Study of Resource Allocation', *Accounting, Organizations and Society*, 13: 333–58.

Olsen, O., J. Guthrie and C. Humphrey (eds) (1998) *Global Warning: Debating International Developments in New Public Financial Management*. Oslo: Cappelen Akademisk Forlog.

Osborne, D. and Gaebler, T. (1993) *Reinventing Government: How the Entrepreneurial Spirit is Transforming the Public Sector*. New York: Penguin.

Osman, M.T. (1985) *Malaysian World-view*. Singapore: Institute of South East Asian Studies.

Parker, L.D. (1998) 'Financial Management Strategy in a Community Welfare Organisation: A Boardroom Perspective', *Proceedings of the Second Asian Pacific Interdisciplinary Perspective on Accounting Conference*. Osaka, Japan.

Parker L.D. (2001) 'Reactive Planning in a Christian Bureaucracy', *Management Accounting Research*, 12: 321–56.

Parker, L.D. (2002) 'Budgetary Incrementalism in a Christian Bureaucracy', *Management Accounting Research*, 13: 71–100.

Parker, L.D. and Roffey, B.H. (1997) 'Methodological Themes: Back to the Drawing Board', *Accounting, Auditing and Accountability Journal*, 10(2): 212–47.

Parsons, T. (1951) *The Social System*. New York: Free Press.

Preston, A. (1986) 'Interactions and Arrangements in the Process of Informing', *Accounting, Organizations and Society*, 11: 521–40.

Rosenberg, D., Tomkins, C. and Day, P. (1982) 'A Work Role Perspective of Accountants in Local Government Service Departments', *Accounting, Organizations and Society*, 7: 123–38.

Rowe, T. and Giroux, G. (1986) 'Diocesan Financial Disclosure: A Quality Assessment', *Journal of Accounting and Public Policy*, Spring: 57–74.

Russell, J. (1996), 'An Approach to Organizational Ethnographic Research: Strategy, Methods and Processes', *Discussion Paper in Accounting and Management Science*, University of Southampton, March, 96–122.

Schein, E.H. (1985) *Organizational Culture and Leadership: A Dynamic View*. San Francisco: Jossey-Bass

Sinclair, A. (1995) 'The Chameleon of Accountability: Forms and Discourses', *Accounting, Organizations and Society*, 20(2/3): 219–237.

Strauss, A. (1987) *Qualitative Analysis for Social Scientists*. Cambridge, UK: Cambridge University Press.

Strauss, A. and Corbin, J. (1990) *Basics of Qualitative Research: Grounded Theory Procedures and Techniques*. California: Sage Publications.

Strauss, A. and Corbin, J. (1998) *Basics of Qualitative Research: Grounded Theory Procedures and Techniques*, 2nd edition. California: Sage Publications.

Swanson, G.A. and Gardner, J.C. (1986) 'The Inception and Evolution of Financial Reporting in the Protestant Episcopal Church in the United States of America', *The Accounting Historian*, 13(2): 55–63.

Turner, A. (1983) 'The Use of Grounded Theory for the Qualitative Analysis of Organisational Behaviour', *Journal of Management Studies*, 20(3).

Wan-Muhammad, W.A. (1990) 'Comments on: Enhance the Quality of Accounting Practices in Islamic Religious Agencies in Malaysia', *International Forum on Accounting, Auditing and Reporting in the Public Sector*. Kuala Lumpur.

Weber, M. (1947) *The Theory of Social and Economic Organization*, translated by A.M Henderson, and T. Parsons. New York: Oxford University Press.

Weber, M. (1949) ' "Objectivity" in Social Science and Social Policy', in *The Methodology of Social Sciences*, trans and ed. E.A. Shils and H.A. Finch. New York: Free Press.

Weber, M. (1968) *Economy and Society*, edited by G. Roth and C. Wittich. New York: Bedminster.

Zietlow, J.T. (1989) 'Capital and Operating Budgeting Practices in Pure Nonprofit Organizations', *Financial Accountability and Management*, 5(4): 219–32.

9

The Development of Audit Objectives in the Context of the People's Republic of China

Julia Brandl and Florentine Maier

Introduction

In the People's Republic of China (PRC), audits are becoming increasingly significant in many contexts. As the literature on audits deals primarily with practical concerns, this chapter seeks to explain the development dynamics of auditing. We develop a typology that distinguishes three primary objectives of audits – namely, fraud detection, legitimating and management decision support. We argue that audit objectives develop cumulatively in this order, and we illustrate this argument with examples from organizations in the PRC. With respect to the current state of auditing in China, we conclude that the presently dominant audit objective of fraud detection will remain relevant in the future, but will be increasingly supplemented by the other two objectives of legitimating and management decision support. On a more general level, our explanations contribute to an understanding of the worldwide expansion of managerial knowledge.

The word 'audit' resounded throughout the People's Republic of China (PRC) in summer 2004, when the National Audit Office (NAO) revealed the widespread misuse of public funds in its 2003 Audit Report and, for the first time, published it on the Internet. The Chinese media quickly coined the phrase 'Audit Storm' to describe this and the following campaigns initiated by the NAO and wrote headlines such as 'Heroes Wielding Calculators' and 'The Iron-fisted Auditor' (China Internet Information Center, 12 and 15 July 2004). At the end of the year, Auditor General Li Jinhua was elected 'Person of the Year' by some of China's most important newspapers and TV stations. Not only government audit, but also the auditing of commercial enterprises and subsequent fraud detection regularly attracts public interest. Government author-ities and academic circles are busy exploring ways to disseminate and improve audit practices. Audits and auditing can truly be said to be rapidly gaining relevance in the PRC in many aspects of life.

However, in the PRC, as in other countries, the academic discus-sion of auditing has focused almost exclusively on audit methods and procedures, while audit objectives have attracted far less attention. This is regrettable because representatives of a more critical audit research tradition have highlighted the critical role played by audit objectives in explaining the audit boom, taking place in many societies (see, for example, Power, 1997). According to Power, the objectives related to auditing describe expectations as well as hopes, which are crucial to the various audit methods and procedures as they provide sense and legitimacy to them. While methods and techniques have always been heterogeneous and changing over time, the objectives of auditing and the programs involved aim to integrate audit methods and practices from various areas of life and, by so doing, preserve the concept of auditing in the long term. This function becomes conspicuous in situ-ations where the principle of auditing as a distinctive way of problem solving is still seen as useful and legitimate, even though particular audit practices have failed.

Critical auditing researchers regularly address the diffuse and chan-ging nature of audit objectives. Power (1997), for example, describes with regard to financial auditing the historical development from fraud detection to management decision support. However, so far little is known about the conditions that promote changes in audit objectives and to what extent developments follow distinctive dynamics. Consid-ering the PRC as an example, the purpose of this chapter is to introduce a theoretical model of the dynamics of audit objectives.

The PRC provides an exciting research site for the analysis of audit objectives. Auditing in the PRC is a developing field, as indicated by the enthusiasm of the Chinese population, the growing number of audit associations in recent years, and the discussion on auditing issues in the public press. We think that many aspects of auditing, which are less visible in western countries, where auditing has a longer tradition and has become culturally supported so that it is less evident as a field of analysis, can be observed in the PRC. On the other hand, the PRC is a complex terrain for the analysis of audit objectives. Critical accounting research generally is a difficult area for empirical studies, as the field access depends on the investigated companies and/or accounting firms' readiness to cooperate with researchers. In the PRC, empirical research in management sciences is in its infancy, and researchers mainly depend on publicly available data. Thus, this chapter argues on a conceptual level; empirical data from the PRC is used to illustrate the points. To develop our arguments, we first outline a conceptual framework of the auditing architecture. Then we introduce a typology of audit objectives and explain their development dynamics with consideration of the situation in the PRC. Finally, we delineate the current development stage in the PRC and discuss consequences at the societal and individual level.

The architecture of auditing

Our definition of auditing draws on the concept proposed by Hasselbladh and Kallinikos (2000), who distinguish between ideals, discourses and control techniques for defining institutions. Institutions consist of 'basic ideals that are developed into distinctive ways of defining and acting upon reality (i.e. discourses), supported by elaborative systems of measurement and documentation for controlling action outcomes' (Hasselbladh and Kallinikos 2000: 704). Ideals express a general idea that should be realized; their importance is validated through their relation to major concepts of a society. Since ideals are vaguely defined, they need to be specified in order to become practically relevant and to function as guidelines for concrete behaviour. Control techniques specify the relationships they seek to regulate. In order to become relevant for action, the value of an ideal has to be specified in the concrete instruments and reachable objectives, which are related to the general idea. Therefore, the analysis of practices is only partially helpful for examining the rise of auditing. Practices are forms of behaviour but also have symbolic meanings (Blumer 1973). They gain legitimacy through their aptitude for legitimate objectives (Miller and Rose 1998). On the other hand, legitimate objectives can only be expressed by materializing them in concrete practices. Auditing, thus, consists of material practices and symbolic constructions.

Berger and Luckmann (1995) argue that practices gain meaning from the context in which they were generated (that is, the solving of practical problems). But as practices persist and are transferred to various contexts, this meaning can be replaced. Zilber (2002) showed that symbolic meanings of material practices are changeable as new groups move into the organization. Thus, a specific practice can be legitimized by or related to various rationalities. Since former goals are not replaced by institutional transformation, the rational base for auditing expands. This expansion of meanings, in turn, contributes to the persistence of a practice because it now can be reflected by various institutional logics and serves the interests of various stakeholders.

A literature-based typology of audit objectives

Various notions of audit functions can be found in the literature as well as in practice. Although this problem has been discussed for years (with respect to internal audit, see, for example, San Miguel *et al.* 1977) and numerous attempts to clarify the objectives of audits have been made, no systematic account of audit objectives has been given so far. Power (1997) argues that it may in fact be functional to leave auditing mysterious, because this increases the attractiveness of the audit concept. Nevertheless, we shall try to shed some light on the mystery.

In order to grasp as broad a range of audit objectives as possible, we examine auditing from the perspective of various traditions of organizational research (see Table 9.1). We focus on approaches that account for audit objectives by referring to the relationship between the organization and the environment – namely the economic, the strategic management and the institutional approach – because this enables us later to discuss the transformation of audit objectives in connection to the change of the organizational environment (macro level). For the same reason, theories examining the micro level of organizations (e.g. micro politics) are not included in this discussion.

The various traditions of audit research can best be characterized by what they view as the primary audit objective, whether the auditor is located inside or outside the organization, whether the initiative for auditing comes from management or external stakeholders, and by the typical characteristics of the audit method. By stakeholders, we mean individuals or groups that are interested in the results of audits; they

Table 9.1 Audit objectives from various theoretical perspectives

Theoretical perspective	Primary Audit objective	Initiative for auditing	Audit execution	Audit method
Functionalism, economics	Fraud detection	External	External	Formal, highly-structured
Strategic management	Management decision support	Internal	External	Flexible, informal
Institutionalism	Legitimating	Internal	Internal	Formal, highly-structured

can be part of the organization or its environment. Audit objectives are reflected in the audit method. According to Dirsmith and Haskins (1991), a distinction can be made between mechanistic and organic audit methods. The former are seen as highly structured and formal, while the latter are flexible and informal.

From an *economic* point of view, detecting and preventing fraud is the central objective of audits. Agency theorists, who assume fraud and opportunism, explain audits with a need for control (Flint, 1988). Agency theory argues that the demand for audits arises in a relationship of accountability between two parties (for example, management and shareholders), where one party – the agent – is accountable to the other – the principal – and the principal is unable to personally check the activities of the agent. The demand for auditing emerges primarily in situations where trust is problematic because the agent is assumed to engage in selfish behaviour. Parties outside the organizations (for example shareholders) are the primary addressees and beneficiaries of audits for fraud detection purposes.[1] Audits of this type are geared to scrutinize the reliability of programmes and behaviours, as well as their compliance with specified regulations. In doing so, the auditor needs to be independent from the audited organization. Audit methods are highly structured and formalized. The demand for fraud detection audits has been fuelled by the outsourcing of public functions by New Public Management, and by cases of fraud exposure, such as the misuse of assets by management.

From the perspective of *strategic management*, auditing supports management decision-making. Here the scope of auditing in particular extends to strategically relevant aspects of the organization, which the management finds hard to see through and where decisions have far-reaching consequences (for example, the long-term distribution of resources). Audits enable rational decision-making by providing a basis and rationale. Audits can be understood as an instrument of the strategic management cycle, where they are used in particular for the control of strategy implementation (see Steinmann and Schreyögg, 2000). While decision-making is at the forefront of the management concept, the main emphasis of strategic control is on decision support. Decision support is necessary because management decisions are made under conditions of uncertainty and constantly need to be revised in an ever-changing environment. Audits embody the idea of monitoring activities and conditions in an organization according to strategically relevant criteria and intervention if necessary (see Radcliffe, 1998). Under the decision support objective, audit practices are tailored to the management's needs and are constantly adapted to strategic (re-)orientations. Consequently, audit methods need to be flexible and informal. Auditors are primarily located within the organization in order to ensure instantaneous feedback and extensive knowledge of the auditing processes (with respect to education programs, see Fischer, 1996).

Economic and management-related explanations of auditing represent what Rose and Miller (1992) call programmatic approaches. They are the basis of the normative functionalist management literature and of method books on audits. In contrast, the *institutionalist* perspective on auditing questions the rationalist assumptions of the other two approaches. It argues that in every society there are assumptions about what rational organizations should be like (Scott and Meyer, 1994). It examines the social and cultural background of audit practices (for an overview of empirical studies, see Power, 2003). It argues that organizations can only survive if they are viewed as legitimate by their environment (see Scott and Meyer 1994). To achieve this purpose, organizations employ management practices that make them appear attractive and modern in the eyes of their stakeholders (for example customers, potential employees). Auditing is therefore viewed as a management instrument contributing to the organization's legitimacy by enhancing its image and reputation with relevant stakeholders (for example, commune industrial development zones getting ISO certification to attract foreign investors). From an institutionalist point of view, the very act of carrying out an audit already fulfils the purpose of an audit. Auditing does not have to lead to control or decision support to serve its point. Consequently, if circumstances demand it, for example if audits are perceived as incompatible with the organization's processes, auditing can also be decoupled from management decisions and can assume a purely symbolic character (Meyer and Rowan, 1977). In the implementation of audits, the institutionalist perspective emphasizes auditor reputation, certification, and the presentation of certificates to the public (for example in advertising). Highly structured and formalized methods and procedures, for example written documentation, promote the fabrication of legitimacy (Power, 2003: 387; Fogarty, 1996).

The development of audit objectives in the PRC

We argue that audit objectives in organizations develop along a certain path, beginning with fraud detection, to legitimating, and ending with management decision support. This sequence can be understood as a

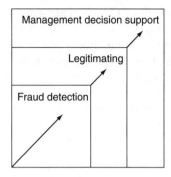

Figure 9.1 Development path of audit objectives

process of increasing understanding, acceptance and internalization of audit practices. This process is cumulative, that is, the various audit objectives supplement rather than replace each other (see Figure 9.1).

In this chapter we illuminate this argument and discuss the consequences of each developmental stage for the creation of an institutional order and the consequences for individuals.

Fraud detection

Since its very conception in the West, the first priority of auditing has been fraud detection (Power, 1997). The main clients of this kind of audit are parties outside the organization (for example, shareholders and government authorities). Audits for fraud detection are usually conducted by external auditors. Consequently, little knowledge about audits is generated within the respective organization, and attitudes towards audits tend to be hostile. Nevertheless, audits for fraud detection are the basis for more advanced kinds of auditing. Organizations are made 'auditable' (Power, 2003) by developing standards and references for further audits.

The historical origin of auditing in China can also be traced back to the fraud detection function. The first written proofs of auditing in China are from the Western Zhou dynasty (1100–771 BC), when a system of government auditors was put in place to conduct a regular review of the accounts of all officials in the country and to report any irregularities directly to the ministry of state or even to the emperor (Chen and Zhou, 2004: 61). From then on, virtually up to the present, government auditing to detect and prevent fraud has been the dominant form of auditing in China. It even survived through the Mao period, when the government introduced the 'Movement Against the Three

Evils' (1951–52) and the 'Four Clean-Up Movements' (1963–66) (Chong and Vinten, 1998). However, during the ensuing Cultural Revolution (1966–76), government auditing almost ceased altogether. It was with the introduction of the Reform and Opening policy (1978) that government auditing was brought back to the agenda. This resulted in the establishment of the Audit Administration, renamed National Audit Office (NAO) in 1983, which is led by an Auditor General and reports all findings directly to the National People's Congress.

In Chinese academic discussion, fraud detection is widely acknowledged as a crucial, if not the most crucial, objective of auditing. For example, Chen and Zhou (2004) name three basic audit functions, namely supervision, evaluation and reflection – certification. This delineation is in line with our description of audit objectives, the first serving fraud detection, the second legitimating and the third management decision support. They state: 'Auditing has a supervisory, an evaluative and a reflection-certification function. Out of these, the supervisory function is the fundamental function.' (Chen and Zhou, 2004: 13).

The biggest demand for audit for fraud detection purposes comes from the government. Government audit institutions are supposed to audit all enterprises that are actually state-controlled, even if state assets occupy less than 50 per cent of the total assets, in a periodic and planned way (Article 20, Implementation Rules of the Audit Law of the PRC, 1997). They can also delegate this audit work to private audit firms that hold a specific license. For enterprises, the Audit Law and Implementation Rules do not specify any fixed interval for the audit. In practice, most state-controlled enterprises are not audited annually because of limited resources. Governments above country level are required to provide annual audit reports to the People's Congress at the corresponding level. Moreover, they are required to report how they correct irregularities, and what results they have achieved in doing so (Audit Law of the PRC, 2006 amendment, paragraph 4).

Apart from external financial audits, the government strongly promotes internal audits. All large and medium-sized state-owned enterprises are required to set up internal audit units and to conduct systematic internal audits. For administrative organs and public institutions the regulations are less rigid. Relevant rules and regulations state that they should be audited and have to accept auditing by the NAO or its respective local bureaus, but it is not stated that the audits should be conducted in a 'periodic and planned way'. Moreover, certain administrative organs and large and medium-sized public institutions are required to establish internal audit units. Social organizations and NGOs that receive state financial aid or donations from society at large also have to accept that they will be supervised by the NAO or its local bureau, but there is no legislation requiring them to conduct internal audits.

Local or provincial tax bureaus conduct targeted tax audits of enterprises and individuals in order to increase tax collection. Some of these tax audits have been highly publicized in the media with the aim to raise public awareness and deter taxpayers from engaging in any non-compliant tax practice.

Audits for fraud detection in the private sector are a comparatively new phenomenon. Professional public accountants first occurred around 1918, when a relatively large number of private corporations had emerged (Zhang, 1987). The number of certified public accountants did not increase greatly, and with the socialization of all enterprises in 1956/57, the private demand for audits disappeared altogether. It was only in the early 1980s that private demand for financial audits in China re-emerged as a result of the growing number of foreign-invested enterprises. All foreign-invested enterprises are required to be audited annually by a certified public accountant registered in the PRC.

Audit for fraud detection purposes is less widespread in private wholly-Chinese owned enterprises and collective enterprises. Most private wholly-Chinese owned enterprises are small-scale, often family-run, and regard audit for fraud detection as unnecessary. Fraud detection in collective enterprises is usually achieved by close personal monitoring of managers by the local government and community members rather than by formal audits. However, along with the expansion of many collective enterprises as they become more successful, the traditional close ties among the community members may loosen (Perotti *et al.*, 1999) and fraud detection may become a more important audit objective.

Legitimating

The transition from fraud detection to legitimating as the dominant audit objective is caused by a change in the nature of the Chinese macroeconomy. State-controlled organizations in the PRC face increasing competition, undergo corporatization, or are even already partly privatized. As the organizational field changes, new competitors emerge. Legitimating plays an important role for organizations that operate in a competitive market and need to justify themselves to their stakeholders. Legitimating audits deal primarily with market-relevant aspects of the organization, such as products, where stakeholders regard audits as indicators of quality. This development is furthered by an increasingly western-orientated population, including the members of the organization themselves. However, organization members don't necessarily have to regard audits as sensible for themselves. It suffices that managers believe that audits are viewed as sensible by stakeholders (collective legitimacy, Weber, 1985). In fact, it is rather unlikely that organization members regard audits as sensible, considering their previous experience with audits as instruments of control. Legitimating audits are introduced into organizations via isomorphism (DiMaggio and Powell, 1983). Market success is attributed to audits and reconfirms the use of audits as means of legitimating. Other organizations apply successful practices and thereby contribute to a further spread of auditing. While legitimating gains importance, fraud detection still remains an important audit objective, not least because it continues to be prescribed by public authorities. This inertia is reinforced by the tendency of organizations to keep existing norms and established routines.

The most important target of legitimating audits are probably the organization's customers. One prominent example in this respect is ISO certification. In 2004, China was the number one country for ISO9001:2000 certification worldwide (ISO, 2005). ISO certification is crucial for Chinese firms hoping to win export orders, as most multinational companies require their suppliers to be certified with ISO9000 and/or ISO14000. On the domestic market, ISO9000 certification is used as a marketing argument to signal superior quality; ISO certification emblems can be found on many Chinese consumer products. This is a good example of impression management: Even though ISO9000 certification by definition does *not* tell anything about the quality of the product but only about the quality capability of the enterprise, it is used for marketing purposes because customers *interpret* it as a quality symbol. In 1994, the government introduced a China Environmental Label based on the ISO14000 series. Up to now more than 9,000 products have been granted this label, and reportedly many consumers look for it when shopping (China Daily, 2003).

Enterprises can also legitimate themselves in the eyes of shareholders. This is achieved by hiring large and renowned auditors to conduct financial audits and thereby signalling firm value (Beatty, 1989). Legitimating themselves in the eyes of shareholders is relevant for companies with a significant number of individual investors who prefer credible financial information. In the current Chinese stock market, few companies fit this description. Government entities effectively own more than 50 per cent of the stock of 85 per cent of all listed companies (DeFond *et al.*, 2000: 274). In these companies there are few incentives for managers to conduct audits for legitimating purposes. Audits are mainly conducted because they are prescribed by law. Evidence suggests an effective 'flight from audit quality', that is, a preference for small and local auditors that are less independent and less likely to issue modified opinions (DeFond *et al.*, 2000). However, Bertin and Jaussaud (2003) report a new reverse trend: Chinese companies that have issued 'A' shares only, and therefore would only need to be audited by Chinese standards, increasingly wish to be additionally audited by international standards.

For most enterprises, legitimating towards civil society within China is of minor importance, since environmental organizations, civil rights groups, and so on don't play a large role in Chinese society. However, such pressures are present in developed countries and influence the operations of enterprises located in China. Evidence shows that multinational companies and local companies exporting a large proportion of their output to developed countries are more likely to adopt ISO14000 than other firms. The same is true for local companies that sell a large proportion of their output to multinational customers within the China (Christmann and Taylor, 2001).

Legitimating does not only matter for enterprises, but can also be important for administrative organs. For example, 49 so-called key development zones in China are applying for or have already passed ISO 14000 certification to attract more investors (China Daily, 2004). Government audit can be seen as a means of legitimating towards the citizenry. Auditor-General Li Junhua describes government auditing as 'the key to rooting out corruption and resolving issues that cause dissatisfaction among the citizens' (China Internet Information Center, 2004). The NAO has started publishing its annual reports, as well as bulletins on certain issues, such as the use of funds for fighting against SARS, on their website. It has announced that, by 2008, all Chinese government audits, including those of financial institutions and banks, will be made public (People's Daily Online, 2005). In the meantime, local administrative organs in some areas of China have already started making their government audit results available to the public (China Internet Information Center, 2004).

Like administrative organs, public institutions have a small, but growing demand for legitimating audits. Certain public institutions in fields like education, health and entertainment face increasing competition from the private sector. Particularly in the case of private non-profit organizations, ISO certification is a way to attract customers and to reassure the supervising government departments that quality standards are being met (see for example People's Daily Online, 2001).

The government strongly promotes audits in all its variations (see, for example, China Daily, 2004). It views audits as a way to curb corruption, improve efficiency, raise exports, and – in the case of ISO14000 – improve environmental protection. It encourages organizations to adopt internal and voluntary external audit practices that go beyond what is required by law. It can be assumed that some organizations also practice audits for the purpose of impression management towards the government.

The use of audit practices for legitimating purposes does not necessarily mean that the practices are understood thoroughly. Audits can be practiced even if management does not carefully occupy itself with the content and meaning of audits (Meyer and Rowan, 1977). For that reason, the spread of audit practices due to institutional pressures from the organizational field precedes the thorough understanding of audits.

Management decision support

The shift of audit emphasis from legitimating to decision support takes place in a second step. When audits are already practiced within an organization, this also creates the opportunity to use them for management decision support. Endogenous and exogenous factors influence this process of transition: First, rules tend to develop an increasingly binding character in the course of time once they are established. They become separated from their creators and turn into objective facts (see Berger and Luckmann, 1969). Secondly, the transition is supported by human resource management. Recruiting new employees that are experienced in the use of audit techniques contributes to the development of competences, which in turn enables the use of audits for decision support. Moreover, audits have a more binding character for newer employees, who tend to take the controlling norms beneath the practices more serious.

As a result, previously unconnected aspects of audits are integrated into a system of meaning. The management now regards audit objectives it used to view as contradictory as mutually supportive and matching. Internal and external controls are now considered to be related, and both are seen to contribute towards legitimating the organization towards its stakeholders.

In Chinese academic discussion, management decision support is widely recognized as an important audit objective. However, from the frequent calls for a stronger use of audits for this purpose, it can be inferred that it is not yet very widespread in practice. Most organizations in the PRC are currently in the stage of transition from fraud detection to legitimating.

In government auditing, there is a lack of emphasis on efficient and effective resource use. In this respect, China differs from the value-added government auditing emphasized by government audit offices in many other Asian countries like India, Indonesia, Malaysia, Pakistan and Singapore, where auditors are expected to assess the effectiveness of internal control systems and procedures of the audited parties (Chong and Vinten, 1998, Khan, 1994). However, leaders of the NAO seem to have acknowledged this problem. After publishing the 2003 audit report, Auditor-General Li Junhua stated that 'the performance audit is what we need to improve. The focus of our audit is gradually moving toward that. It is expected that half of our resources will be devoted to performance audits by 2007' (China Internet Information Center, 2004).

Large and medium-sized state-owned enterprises, administrative organs and public institutions are required by law to set up internal audit units, which are supposed to provide management decision support. However, since all of these organizations are state-controlled, internal audit is also called upon to supplement the government audit system for fraud detection. Internal auditors are often faced with a dilemma, because the interests of enterprises and the state are not always compatible (Cooper *et al.* 2002).

Very little is known about auditing for management decision support in private enterprises in China. To the authors' best knowledge there has been no study on this issue yet. The majority of local private enterprises are small and do not practice auditing at all. Foreign-invested enterprises usually transfer management accounting practices from their foreign parent companies (Firth, 1996; O'Connor *et al.*, 2004), which is presumably also the case for management audits.

One factor that could lead to the greater utilization of audits as instruments for decision support is the mobilization of human resources. In this respect, improved education and training opportunities (for example, MBA programmes) and increasing internationalization through the exchange of students and managers between developed countries and China play an important role.

Conclusion

In this chapter we have proposed a model of the development dynamics of audit objectives in the PRC. We have argued that audit objectives follow a development path, starting from fraud detection, then to legitimacy, and finally ending at management decision support. These development dynamics describe an increasing internalization of audit practices and an accumulation of audit objectives.

The internalization of auditing practices starts in the stage of fraud detection, when organization members get to know audit practices. They experience auditing as a practice imposed on the organization by stakeholders and conducted by external auditors. Initial references and standards for audits are developed. During this first stage, organizations learn that good audit results are a means of gaining and retaining resources. If organizations extend the application of auditing to fields where auditing is not compulsory, this indicates the beginning of the next stage, where audits are used for legitimating purposes. Audits are conducted by external auditors to create an impression of independent judgement, which is instrumental for legitimating the organization. Thus, auditing practices can be applied by organizations, even if they lack expert knowledge about auditing. At this stage, the initiative for conducting audits has already moved into the organization, which indicates the first step towards internalization. At the next stage, the internalization is completed, as the initiative and the execution of audits are both conducted by the organization itself. At this stage, the organization is both willing and able to conduct audits.

Audit objectives develop cumulatively rather than consecutively. This is because the situations that have led to the emergence of earlier audit objectives persist (for example, governmental and shareholder control). With regard to the current situation in the PRC, the spread of audit objectives can be characterized as follows: An overarching importance of fraud detection in public awareness as well as in practice; a wide spread of legitimating, without adequate theoretical awareness; and a strong theoretical awareness of management decision support accompanied by rather weak but developing practice.

Because of the cumulative development of audit objectives and the expansion of the methodological base, the complexity of auditing as a management instrument increases. At the societal level, auditing becomes a widely accepted and unquestioned (that is, culturally supported) principle for problem-solving in the organizational context (Power, 1997: 4). Auditing becomes more and more irreversible, also because its practices can be justified by a variety of objectives which can be switched if the macro-order changes.

The increasing complexity of audit methods is a fundamental reason for the growth of related consulting services. The demand for audit consulting rises because organizations require support for the implementation of audit methods. Audit consulting services are already available in the PRC, even though they currently focus on fraud detection. The expected liberalization of the Chinese consulting services market will allow consulting firms to expand their audit product range (for example, by providing audit methods from more industrialized countries), which will further stimulate demand for consulting services.

At the individual level, auditing is reflected in normative orientations and cognitions. The integration of auditing into normative orientations means that people use audit techniques to evaluate others, for example through individual performance appraisals. This implies that conformity to audit measures becomes important for the careers of individuals in organizations. The integration of auditing into the cognitive level means that auditing becomes a general, unquestioned way of reflection about issues, which Scott (1995) describes as taken-for-grantedness.

In this chapter, we have taken the perspective that the expansion of auditing is part of a worldwide modernization process. Once implemented, auditing gains a state of irreversibility because it structures the interests of stakeholders and is manifested in the institutional order (Power 1997). In other words, it becomes an unquestioned element of management, a rationalized myth (Meyer and Rowan 1977). Therefore, we expect that the 'travel' (Czarniawska and Joerges 1996) of the audit idea described for China can also to be found in other transition countries in Asia. Meyer *et al.* (1989) argue that different local environments may lead to variations of rationalized myths. Since auditing contains a broad spectrum of practices, and practices need to be related to specific institutional contexts (that is, integrated with other practices), audit instruments are likely to be heterogeneous and differ between countries. The Meyer *et al.* (1989) argument is also relevant for understanding why the institutionalization of auditing occurs at different time horizons in Asian countries, since institutional contexts can facilitate or slow down the expansion of management knowledge (Sahlin-Andersson and Engwall 2002). As outlined above, the growing presence of western companies and the centralized bureaucracy facilitate the expansion of auditing knowledge in the PRC.

The model for the development dynamics of audit objectives in the PRC presented in this chapter was developed at a conceptual level. The data used to illustrate our arguments only allow a superficial analysis of the current situation of the PRC in this field. Empirical research is necessary to provide deeper insights into which audit objectives currently dominate in the PRC and to test the empirical relevance of the proposed development dynamics. In order to analyse variations in the speed of development of audit objectives and in the adoption of audit instruments, it is also necessary to compare the PRC with other transition countries. The arguments in this chapter are not limited to auditing, but apply to the spread of other types of management knowledge as well. Thus, we also suggest transferring them to study the adoption of other rationalized myths in the Asian context such as human resource management (see chapter 10) and corporate social responsibility (see chapter 6).

References

Audit Law of the People's Republic of China (2006 amendment) [zhonghua renmin gungheguo shenji fa (2006 xiuding)] (2006) Homepage of the Supreme People's Court of the PRC, http://www.chinacourt.org [last retrieved on 13 July 2006].

Beatty, R. (1989) 'Auditor Reputation and the Pricing of Initial Public Offerings', *The Accounting Review*, 64(4): 693–709.

Berger, P.L. and Luckmann, T. (1995) *Modernity, Pluralism and the Crisis of Meaning*. Gütersloh: Bertelsmann Foundation.

Berger, P.L. and Luckmann, T. (1969) *Die gesellschaftliche Konstruktion der Wirklichkeit: Eine Theorie der Wissenssoziologie*. Frankfurt am Main: Fischer.

Bertin, E. and Jaussaud, J. (2003) 'Regulation of Statutory Audit in China', *Asian Business & Management*, 2(2): 267–80.

Blumer, H. (1973) *Der methodologische Standort des Symbolischen Interaktionnismus*, in Arbeitsgruppe Bielefelder Soziologen (eds), *Alltagswissen, Interaktion und gesellschaftliche Wirklichkeit. Bd. 1: Symbolischer Interaktionismus und Ethnomethodologie*. Reinbek bei Hamburg, pp. 80–146.

Chen, Z. and Zhou, S. (2004) *Zhongguo shenji wenhua yanjiu*. Beijing: zhongguo shidai jingji chubanshe.

China Daily (2003-12-15) 'Going Green Gets Popular Support at Home'. http://www.china.org.cn/english/2003/Dec/82479.htm (last retrieved on 13 July 2006).

China Daily (2004-01-06) 'Manufacturers Urged to Live up to International Standards'. http://www.china.org.cn/english/government/84053.htm (last retrieved on 13 July 2006).

China Daily (2004-08-04) 'Zone Harbouring Ambitions for Growth'. http://www.chinadaily.com.cn/english/doc/2004-09/30/content_378915.htm (last retrieved on 13 July 2006).

China Internet Information Center (2004-07-12) 'Audit Report 2003: Heroes Wielding Calculators'. http://www.china.org.cn/english/BAT/100980.htm (last retrieved on 13 July 2006).

China Internet Information Center (2004-07-15) The Iron-fisted Auditor. http://www.china.org.cn/english/2004/Jul/101377.htm (last retrieved on 13 July 2006).

Chong, H.G. and Vinten, G. (1998) 'Harmonisation of Government Audits in the People's Republic of China', *Managerial Auditing Journal*, 13(3): 159.

Christmann, P. and Taylor, G. (2001) 'Globalization and the Environment: Determinants of Firm Self-Regulation in China', *Journal of International Business Studies*, 32(3): 439–58.

Cooper, B.J., Chow, L. and Tang, Y.W. (2002) 'The Development of Auditing Standards and the Certified Public Accounting Profession in China', *Managerial Auditing Journal*, 17(7): 383–9.

Czarniawska, B. and Joerges, B. (1996) 'Travel of Ideas'. in B. Czarniawska and G. Sevon (eds), *Translating Organizational Change*. Berlin: De Gruyter, pp. 13–48.

DeFond, M.L., Wong, T.J. and Li, S. (2000) 'The Impact of Improved Auditor Independence on Audit Market Concentration on China', *Journal of Accounting and Economics*, 28(3): 269–305.

DiMaggio, P.J. and Powell, W. (1983) 'The Iron Cage Revisited: Institutional Isomorphism and Collective Rationality in Organizational Fields', *American Sociological Review*, 48(2): 147–60.

Dirsmith, M. and Haskins, M. (1991) 'Inherent Risk Assessment and Audit Firm Technology: a Contrast in World Theories', *Accounting, Organizations and Society*, 16(1): 61–90.

Firth, M. (1996) 'The Diffusion of Managerial Accounting Procedures in the People's Republic of China and the Influence of Foreign Partnered Joint Ventures', *Accounting, Organizations and Society*, 21(7/8): 629–54.

Fischer, M.J. (1996) 'Realizing the Benefits of New Technologies as a Source of Audit Evidence: An Interpretative Field Study', *Accounting, Organizations and Society*, 21(2–3): 219–42.

Flint, D. (1988) *Philosophy and Principles of Auditing*. London: Macmillan.

Fogarty, T.J. (1996) 'The Imagery and Reality of Peer Review in the US: Insights from Institutional Theory', *Accounting, Organizations and Society*, 21(2–3): 243–67.

Hasselbladh, H. and Kallinikos, J. (2000) 'The Project of Rationalization: a Critique and Reappraisal of Neo Institutionalism in Organization Studies', *Organization Studies*, 2: 697–720.

Implementation Rules of the Audit Law of the People's Republic of China (zhonghua renmin gungheguo shenji fa shishi tiaoli) (1997) Homepage of the Supreme People's Court of the PRC, http://www.chinacourt.org (last retrieved on 9 November 2004).

ISO (2005) *The ISO Survey – 2004*. http://www.iso.org/iso/en/prods-services/ otherpubs/pdf/survey2004.pdf (last retrieved on 14 July 2006).

Jensen, M.C. and Meckling, W.H. (1976) 'Theory of the Firm: Managerial Behaviour, Agency Costs and Ownership Structure', *Journal of Financial Economics*, 3: 205–360.

Khan, M.A. (1994) 'Value-for-Money Studies in Revenue Auditing', *International Journal of Government Auditing*, 21(4): 7–8.

Meyer, J.W., Boli, J. and Thomas, G.W. (1989) 'Ontology and Rationalization in the Western Cultural Account', in G.M. Thomas, J.W. Meyer, F.O. Ramirez and J. Boli (eds), *Institutional Structure: Constituting State, Society, and the Individual*. Newbury Park, CA: Sage, pp. 12–38.

Meyer, J.W. and Rowan, B. (1977) 'Institutionalized Organizations: Formal Structure as Myth and Ceremony', *American Journal of Sociology*, 83(2): 340–63.

Miller, P. and Rose, N. (1998) 'Governing Economic Life', in C. Mabey, G. Salaman and J. Storey (eds), *Strategic Human Resource Management: A Reader*. London: Sage, pp. 46–57.

O'Connor, N.G., Chow, C.W. and Wu, A. (2004) 'The Adoption of "Western" Management Accounting/Controls in China's State-owned Enterprises During Economic Transition', *Accounting, Organizations and Society*, 29(3–4): 349–75.

People's Daily Online (2001-06-04) 'China Seeks ISO Authentication for Better School Education'. http://english.people.com.cn/english/200107/04/eng20010704_74159.html (last retrieved on 13 July 2006).

People's Daily Online (2005-02-02) 'All Gov't Audits to be Made Public from 2008'. http://english.people.com.cn/200502/05/eng20050205_173071.html (last retrieved on 13 July 2006).

Perotti, E.C., Sun, L. and Zhou, L. (1999) 'State-owned versus Township and Village Enterprises in China', *Comparative Economic Studies*, 41(2–3): 151–79.

Power, M. (1997) *The Audit Society: Rituals of Verification*. Oxford: Oxford University Press.

Power, M.K. (2003) 'Auditing and the Production of Legitimacy', *Accounting, Organizations and Society*, 28(4): 379–94.

Radcliffe, V.S. (1998) 'Efficiency Audit: an Assembly of Rationalities and Programmes', *Accounting, Organizations and Society*, 23(4): 377–410.

Rose, N. and Miller, P. (1992) 'Political Power beyond the State: Problematics of Government', *British Journal of Sociology*, 43(2): 173–205.

Sahlin-Andersson, K. and Engwall, L. (2002) 'The Dynamics of Management Knowledge', in K. Sahlin-Andersson and L. Engwall (eds), *The Expansion of Management Knowledge: Carriers, Flows and Sources*. Stanford: Stanford University Press, pp. 277–96.

San Miguel, J.G., Shank, J.K. and Govindarajan, V. (1977) 'Extending Corporate Accountability: a Survey and Framework for Analysis', *Accounting Organizations and Society*, 2(4): 333–47.

Scott, R.W. (1995) *Institutions and Organizations*. Thousand Oaks, CA: Sage.

Scott, R.W. and Meyer, J.W. (1994) *Institutional Environments and Organizations: Structural Complexity and Individualism*. Thousand Oaks, CA: Sage.

Steinmann, H. and Schreyögg, G. (2000) *Management: Grundlagen der Unternehmensführung. Konzepte – Funktionen – Fallstudien*. Wiesbaden: Gabler.

Weber, M. (1985) *Wirtschaft und Gesellschaft: Grundriss der verstehenden Soziologie*. Tuebingen: Mohr.

Zhang, Y.K. (1987) *Company Auditing*. Beijing: China Business Publishing.

Zilber, T. (2002) 'Institutionalization as an Interplay between Actions, Meanings and Actors: the Case of a Rape Crisis Center in Israel', *Academy of Management Journal*, 45(1): 234–54.

10
Overt Age Discrimination in Employment in Thailand: The Ethical Role of Multinational Corporations in Human Resource Practices

Chutarat Inma

Introduction

Given the immediate global interest in the socioeconomic challenges of an ageing population, the issue of age discrimination in employment in Southeast Asia, in countries such as Thailand, is still being treated as a topic of low priority. This chapter underlines the significance of the impact of the ageing workforce in less developed countries by investigating the extent to which overt age discrimination took place through job advertisements in Thailand between the months of April and May 2004. The findings indicate that the candidates' age is still being stipulated in job advertisements and in a hiring process of which the older candidates are the group most disadvantaged. Some of the multinational corporations' management practice on equal employment opportunities were anticipated to be transferred to their subsidiaries. However, the overt age-discriminatory practice was found in both multinational corporations and local firms. This calls for urgent attention from the public policy-makers to acknowledge the future socioeconomic challenge of the ageing workforce. Serious attention should also be given to the role of multinational corporations in translating equal opportunity practices to their subsidiaries, especially to those in less developed countries.

At the beginning of the twenty-first century, developed countries face a great challenge involving the issue of an ageing society and workforce. Due to the large 'baby boom' generation, longer life expectancies, and lower fertility rates (FTR), there have been concerns that the demographic structure of the current workforce would be inadequate to support the whole economic structure of the society in the near future. The ageing population would increase the burden on health and welfare provisions due to an increase in the number of people aged 60 years or older. This demographic challenge has been predicted to cause an immense problem to societies where the dependency ratios of youth and old-age persons to one single working adult aged between 15 and 64 years are high. In developed countries, the number of dependents to 100 persons of the working population was 49 persons in 2000. This ratio is anticipated to increase to 73.4 dependents per 100 persons in 2050 (see Table 10.1). In some countries, such as Japan and Spain, the effects from the dependent ratio were predicted to be overwhelming. The ratio will increase to 95.8 dependents per 100 persons for Japan and 96.2 for Spain (United Nations, 2002). This prediction indicates that high old-age dependent ratios (75.3 dependents per 100 persons in Japan and 73.8 in Spain respectively), will impact on the capacity the nations have to care for their citizens in the future.

The proportion of the older population is increasing, while the proportion of the younger age group is reducing. By 2050, for the first time in history the number of older persons in the world is projected to exceed the younger generation (United Nations, 2002). People would live longer than their ancestors, while their fertility rates would still remain below the rate of the replacement level of 2.1 children per woman. Specifically, in developed countries, the average age of deaths for males would be close to 80 years of age, while their female counterparts would live on average close to their 90s (see Table 10.1). These socioeconomic trends of the ageing workforce are also predicted to have strong implications for the demographic profiles of the workforce and the human resource policies of the organizations.

The issues of population ageing and the ageing workforce have not only been topics of concern in developed countries. Currently, several governments in Southeast Asia have started to express concern about the proportion of the working-age population (aged 15 to 59 years), which may result in future shortages. Among the governments contemplating these issues are: Indonesia, the Lao People's Democratic Republic, Malaysia, Myanmar, the Philippines, Singapore, and Thailand. Specifically, two countries in the region, Singapore and Thailand, are currently specifying the issues of future labour shortages and population ageing to be at a level of high concern in their population policies (see United Nations 2003).

The demographic challenge in Asia Pacific, specifically in Southeast Asia, may be the consequence of past social trends and government

Table 10.1 Projected total fertility rates, dependency ratio and life expectancy of selected developed countries and ASEAN countries

Countries	Fertility rate		Dependency ratio			Life expectancy at birth, 2000–2005		Life expectancy at birth, 2045–2050	
	2000–05	2045–50	2000	2025	2050	Males	Females	Males	Females
Australia	1.8	2.0	48.8	57.0	67.0	76.4	82.0	80.3	85.7
Canada	1.6	1.9	49.8	59.2	69.6	76.2	81.8	80.1	85.6
Denmark	1.7	1.9	46.5	58.0	68.4	74.2	79.1	79.0	83.9
France	1.8	1.9	53.2	63.1	74.6	75.2	82.8	78.6	85.3
Germany	1.3	1.6	46.9	58.3	76.4	75.0	81.1	80.7	86.2
Italy	1.2	1.6	47.8	57.9	89.8	75.5	81.9	77.9	84.0
Japan	1.3	1.8	46.8	69.6	95.8	77.8	85.0	81.3	89.9
New Zealand	2.0	2.1	53.0	56.0	66.9	75.3	80.7	77.8	83.1
Spain	1.1	1.6	46.4	53.0	96.2	75.4	82.3	79.4	85.9
Switzerland	1.4	1.7	48.5	58.9	73.3	75.9	82.3	79.9	86.0
UK	1.6	1.9	53.2	58.9	73.3	75.7	80.7	79.0	84.0
USA	1.9	2.1	51.5	58.9	65.6	74.6	80.4	78.4	83.7
Developed countries	**1.5**	**1.9**	**48.3**	**57.0**	**73.4**	**71.9**	**79.3**	**79.0**	**85.1**
Brunei	2.5	2.1	54.1	50.5	57.4	74.2	78.9	78.7	83.7
Cambodia	4.8	2.1	87.5	62.5	46.5	53.6	58.6	69.3	75.0
Indonesia	2.3	2.1	55.2	45.7	57.1	65.3	69.3	75.1	79.8
Lao PDR	4.8	2.1	86.0	59.2	47.2	53.3	55.8	70.2	74.3
Malaysia	2.9	2.1	61.9	48.4	54.4	70.6	75.5	77.3	82.2
Myanmar	2.8	2.1	60.5	45.2	54.9	53.8	58.8	69.2	75.0
Singapore	1.5	1.9	41.0	55.4	73.9	75.9	80.3	80.5	85.3
Thailand	2.0	1.9	46.8	44.8	61.9	74.2	79.4	76.5	81.7
The Philippines	3.2	2.1	69.7	46.6	52.0	68.0	72.0	76.0	80.8
Viet Nam	2.3	2.1	63.2	47.0	58.6	66.9	71.6	75.7	80.7
ASEAN Countries	**2.5**	**2.1**	**58.9**	**46.7**	**56.1**	**64.8**	**69.2**	**74.8**	**79.8**

Source: United Nations (2002).

policies that promoted a high fertility rate. For example, in Thailand, the high fertility rate in the early 1950s (FTR $\approx$ 6.4) was facilitated by a prenatalist government policy, which included bonuses for large families and incentives for early marriage (Prachuabmoh and Mithranon, 2003). When the fear that rapid population growth might lead to serious food shortages and social and political unrest, many countries curbed their population policies. India made the first move in 1952 by setting up the population policy in an effort to reduce the fertility rate. In 1972, China implemented the One-Child Policy to control rapid population growth. Subsequently, most developing countries followed suit (Population Reference Bureau, 2003). In Thailand, the national family planning programme, introduced in the 1970s, resulted in a large decline in the fertility rate from 4.0 in 1975–1980 to 1.9 in 2002 (United Nations, 2002). Nevertheless, the prolonged effects of the low fertility rate and the trend towards the retirement age of the 'baby boomers' are gradually reversing the conventional demographic trend in the region. In Thailand, the number of people in the labour force (15 to 24 years) is declining (Asian Development Bank, 2004), which illustrates that Thailand will soon face the problems of a high ageing population and future labour shortages. This issue of an ageing population is currently being experienced by most developed countries.

The increasingly changing trend of the ageing population and workforce may suggest that the accommodation of ageing workers within an organization may become more desirable. New government directions in several developed countries are now promoting the late retirement policy and encouraging the full utilization of the older workforce, for example: the Netherlands (Ekamper, 1997; Remery *et al.*, 2003), the United States (Hogan and Kerstein, 1999; Anderson and Hussey, 2000; Collins, 2003) and the United Kingdom (Hogan and Kerstein, 1999; Anderson and Hussey, 2000). In Australia, recent government policies are being directed toward retaining older workers and reducing health costs of retirees (Commonwealth, 2003). However, the trend towards age diversity at work in the less developed countries is being less acknowledged and to some extent, is in jeopardy. More often, the ageing workers are being openly discriminated against in these countries.

The discriminatory practice in Thailand is still being treated as a topic of low priority in terms of public policies and human resource practices. Specifically, age discrimination is considered to be a relatively inconsequential concept and is likely to be taken for granted. In addition, this concept has received little attention from the mass media and academic researchers in the region. Nevertheless, the elimination of such forms of discrimination is likely to prepare the less developed countries to accommodate the future demographic challenge. The human rights and equal employment opportunities of their citizens will also be extensively promoted.

Overt age discrimination is defined as the less favourable treatment of a person compared to others on the basis of their chronological age for a particular position in an organization where the requirement specified for the candidates is often based on stereotypes, rather than on more relevant position criteria (De Cieri, 1998). The propensity of employers to engage in discriminatory practices in their hiring procedure may depend upon their cultural and ethical values, which may vary extensively from those of local organizations to multinational corporations

(Rawwas, 2001). Ethical values of firms can also vary from country to country (see Enderle, 1997; Mcdonald and Kan, 1997; Baker and Veit, 1998). It is anticipated that discriminatory practice in local Thai firms involves human resource practices which manifest through organizational culture. However, in the multinational corporations (MNCs), the discriminatory practices may have been transferred from the home countries to the host countries of the corporations (Selmer and De Leor, 1993). This chapter is based on an empirical study of the extent to which overt age discrimination in employment took place in the less developed country. Thailand is the host country, while the MNCs from Asia, America and Europe are the home countries. Another form of inequitable practice in employment, sex discrimination in association with age discrimination will also be investigated.

Overt employment discrimination

The discrimination and disadvantages experienced by older people in employment are well documented in gerontology and management literature (for example, Singer and Sewell, 1989; McGoldrick and Arrowsmith, 1993; Bennington, 2001; Bennington and Wein, 2003; Gunderson, 2003; Duncan and Loretto, 2004). The age-discriminatory practice towards older workers is often derived from the tastes or preferences of employers and, to a large extent, of customers and societies (Walker and Taylor, 1993). Employers may hold strong stereotypical views on age rather than an employee's capability to do the job (Rickard, 1999). Customers may also possess the same pessimistic assumptions, perceiving older workers to be less productive and unable to portray a youthful company or industry image (Sheen, 2001). Societies which are in a stage of cultural lag may be unable to recognise that older workers can potentially remain physically fit and mentally active longer in employment due to improvements in health and working conditions (Paul and Townsend, 1993; Taylor and Walker, 1998). Thus, older workers were often being viewed as lacking ability to perform tasks, being resistant to change, having a higher risk of sickness and absence due to illness and injury and likely to increase costs of hiring, insurance and maintenance to employers (Paul and Townsend, 1993; Rickard, 1999; Brooke, 2003). These pessimistic views were argued to be tenuous and unfounded (that is, Giniger, Dispenzieri *et al.*, 1983; Haltiwanger, Lane *et al.*, 1999; Ceniceros, 2001). Nonetheless, these assumptions may lead to an exclusion of the older people from entering or re-entering the workforce (Bennington, 2001).

In the more developed countries the term 'older workers' may refer to those who are 45 years of age or older (Brooke, 2003). However, the 'older workforce' in less developed countries like Thailand seems to extend to those who are much younger than 45. Possibly, the view on the ageing benchmark was based upon an earlier era when the standard of health care and quality of life were still poor, and life expectancies were relatively moderate. The life expectancy at birth of Thai males and females were 49.8 and 54.3 years in 1950, and has increased by 70 per cent (71.1 years) and 71.35 per cent (76.1 years) respectively by 2000 (ASEAN, 2003). Employers might classify persons who are over 30 years (which was an approximate of middle age males and females in 1950s) as older workers as a result of the cultural lag. Although the definition of the older workers in the Thai employment market is still inconclusive (Duncan and Loretto, 2004), age discriminatory practice in Thailand is likely to occur to a much younger person across gender and industries when compared to the age-discriminatory practice in the more developed countries.

Employment discrimination is prohibited in Thailand under the Labour Protection Act 2541 (LPA, 1998), which states the grounds for discrimination against race, sex, ethnic origin, colour, religion, marital status, disability, sexual orientation, and age. However, the LPA (1998) places more emphasis on sex discrimination and child labour practice whilst other areas of equal employment opportunities are less specified. When cases of discrimination practice in employment occur, legal institutions are often avoided for dispute resolution in Thailand by employees, as legal resources are heavily skewed in favour of employers (Vause, 1992). Relationships between Thai employers and their employees tend to be paternalistic where individual employees rarely have significant bargaining power and the unionization in the country has remained fragmented and fractionalized (Vause, 1992). Thus, the LPA (1998) towards employment discrimination practice is deemed to be only a *'paper tiger'* in the Thai labour market with a lack of mechanisms to establish fairness between employers and employees.

Discriminatory practices may begin in the initial recruitment and selection process when the employers are placing their preferences on candidates' identity in job advertisements, thus discouraging candidates from non-preferred categories (McGoldrick and Arrowsmith, 1993). There are two forms of employment discrimination. *Covert discrimination* occurs when employers intentionally or unintentionally use subtle and indirect language to express their preferences for job candidates based on their identity rather than their ability to do the jobs. In contrast, *overt discrimination* is more open with a direct language that specifies employers' preferences (Oswick and Jones, 1991). Overt discrimination rarely occurs in developed countries where employment discrimination is illegal and the policy of equal employment opportunities is strongly encouraged – for example, in Australia, United Kingdom, and the United States (Sheen, 2001). This is in contrast to the practice in Southeast Asia, specifically in Thailand where overt discrimination in job advertisements is likely to be detected in spite of its labour law prohibiting discriminatory practice in employment.

MNC management practice and employment discrimination

With stable social, economic and political environments, Thailand is one of the most popular economic hubs in Southeast Asia and provides a home-base to multinational corporations from different cultures and regions (Pornpitakpan, 2000). The extensive investment by multinational corporations may have both positive and negative effects for the host nation: for example, the effects on socioeconomic structure and value systems (see Lawler and Bae, 1998). The MNCs operating in Thailand largely constitute a large portion of companies from developed countries such as the United States and Japan which are likely to be distinctive in their cultures. A culture is defined by the belief, attitudes, norms and role expectations, and values widely shared by the members of a particular group (Lawler and Bae, 1998: 129). In a domestic environment dominated by a homogenous national culture, the organizational culture reflects national culture which is displayed by a common notion of shared beliefs, values and norms (Weiss, 1978; Hofstede, 1983). However, when the MNCs operating in the subsidiaries of host countries hold dissimilar cultures, the cultures of the MNCs may influence work values of local subsidiaries and vice versa (Selmer and De Leor, 1993). For example, research conducted by Swierczek and Onishi (2003) found that Japanese managers adapted more to Thai culture and that Thai subordinates adapted to the Japanese style of management and human resource system.

Lawler and Bae (1998) suggested that the culture of the MNCs could be linked to the likelihood of employment discrimination of their subsidiaries mainly in three ways (Lawler and Bae, 1998). First, the parent company may transfer its management practice to its subsidiaries, which has become entrenched from the law prohibiting employment discrimination in the home country. Secondly, the expatriate managers of

subsidiaries, which have been influenced by the cultural predisposi-
tions of their home country, may pass their tastes and preferences with
regard to employment discrimination to the subsidiaries. Thirdly, the
host-country nationals employed in managerial positions are likely to
have been socialized to MNC home-country standards and values, and
may absorb those attitudes and values with regard to equal employment
opportunities. In addition, the culture, laws, and economic environments dominant in the host countries might also moderate the degree
of influence of MNCs home countries' culture (Hofstede, 1980). This
may be the consequence of the experience of MNCs in the international
market or/and their globalization strategy to adapt to the local taste and
practice (Schuler, Dowling *et al.*, 1993).

National cultural traits may manifest the management practice of
organizations (Hofstede, 1980). Hofstede (1983) suggested four traditional scales of cultural traits. *Power distance* represents the degree to
which members of organizations accept and expect that the power is
not allocated equally. *Masculinity,* as opposed to *femininity,* represents
a culture of being assertive and competitively orientated to which the
male is dominant in the power structure. *Individualism,* as opposed to
collectivism, represents a tendency of individuals primarily looking after
themselves and their immediate families.

Uncertainty avoidance focuses on the degree to which the society rein-
forces, or does not reinforce, uncertainty and ambiguity within the
society. Of these four scales, Power Distance and Uncertainty Avoidance
are claimed to be closely related to how organizations operate. As quoted
by Hofstede (1983: 87): 'organisations are devices to distribute power,
and they also serve to avoid uncertainty, to make things predictable'.
However, uncertainty avoidance suggests a strong theoretical argument
regarding cultural linkages to employers' tendencies to discriminate
against older employees. With the current pessimistic stereotyped views
of older workers, the employers may believe that the promotion of an
ageing workforce in organizations increases the risks of achieving low
levels of performance. Hiring of older workers is translated in association
with a strong uncertainty as their abilities to perform are ambiguous.
For example, the costs associated with health and safety insurance of
the older workers are relatively high and the duration of their service
to organizations are somewhat shorter than younger workers (i.e., Szalai
1998). Therefore, the home countries that have a strong scale of uncertainty avoidance will be likely to stipulate the age barrier in job advertisements.

Hypothesis: The likelihood of overt age discrimination will increase with the parent company's home-country average value on Hofstede's uncertainty avoidance scale

Method

Data collection

The data source for this study consisted of a sample of job announcements for white-collar positions advertised electronically in six of Thailand's principal sources for job searches. The Four electronic job search databases examined were: *JobsDB* (www.jobsdb.com), *Job top gun* (www.jobtopgun.com), *Jobthai* (www.jobthai.com) and *Jobbee* (www.jobbees.com); and two of the sources affiliated with the principal newspapers are the *Nationjobs* (www.nationejobs.com) and the *Thane* (www.thannews.th.com). The electronic databases used in this study were increasingly popular and widely accessed by job applicants (Feldman and Klass, 2002). Internet searches also represent familiarity with technology and are therefore viewed positively by the employers. In 2000, Thailand reported 3.6 per cent Internet penetration in the population, of which 55 per cent of the access was in Bangkok, the location of the sampling frame (Attetanan, 2001). Recently, the younger generation has also been exposed early to the new media technology via formal education. In 2000, 5.8 per cent of schools in Thailand connected to the Internet, while all 82 Thai universities have access (Attetanan, 2001). The majority of the internet users (81 per cent) covered those who were 20 to 49 years, which represent the majority of the job seekers.

The database was drawn at random between the months of April and May 2004. Ten to twenty jobs were randomly selected from the eight-week period. Only one job found in each company was used. A hundred job advertisements each were drawn from *Nationjobs*, *JobsDB*, and *Jobthai* (n = 300) as they had a larger database. Fifty job advertisements each were drawn from *Thane, Job top gun* and *Jobbees* (n = 150). The total sample consists of 450 usable cases. Both Thai and English language advertisements were used to cover a wide level of jobs across industry.

Dependent variable

The dependent variable involves determination of a candidate's age relating to positions advertised (see Table 10.2). Age requirements may fall into one of three categories: (i) age was not mentioned; (ii) an age barrier on persons who are younger than a certain age; and (iii) an age barrier on persons who are older than a certain age. All together there

Table 10.2 Average Hofstede scores and distribution of job advertisement by firms' country of origin (n = 375)

Country	No. of Ads	Percent 'Age bar for older workers'	*Percent 'Age bar for younger workers'	Percent 'Male only'	Percent 'Female only'	Uncertainty Avoidance score
Australia	2	100	0	0	0	51
Belgium	1	100	0	0	0	94
Canada	3	100	0	0	0	48
China	3	100	0	0	0	40
Denmark	1	100	0	0	0	23
France	6	100	0	0	33.3	86
Germany	10	100	10	20	0	65
Italy	3	66.7	33.3	66.7	0	75
Japan	37	91.9	8.1	24.3	13.5	92
South Korea	1	100	0	0	0	85
Malaysia	4	100	0	0	50	36
Netherlands	2	100	0	0	0	53
Singapore	2	100	0	0	0	8
Sweden	1	100	0	0	0	58
Switzerland	2	100	0	0	50	58
Taiwan	1	100	0	0	100	69
Thailand	262	96.9	3.1	11.5	11.5	64
UK	4	100	0	25.0	0	35
US	30	100	0	6.7	10	46

Note: Age bar for younger workers referred to those advertisements that required candidates who were more than 45 years (advertisement contained age barrier of more than 21 years and 25 years were discarded).

were seven categories of age requirement found in the database. These were: age not specified (32.4 per cent), age less than 30 (33.3 per cent), age less than 35 (8.9 per cent), age less than 45 (5.8 per cent), age more than 21 (4.4 per cent), age more than 25 (12.2 per cent), and age more than 35 (2.9 per cent). Concurrently, there were 32.8 per cent of cases which did not specify the age limit, 48 per cent which did specify a lower age limit and 19.2 per cent which specified a higher age limit. It should be noted that most Thai people look to secure an undergraduates degree before entering the workforce for white-collar jobs. The average age of Thai undergraduates will be 22 years, and that of postgraduates will be 25 years. The requirements stating the higher age limit of more than 21 and more than 25 merely emphasize the congruence between qualifications and the average candidate's age – rather than their intention to discriminate against younger people. Only those advertisements specifying the requirement for a candidate who was more than 35 years of age (13 cases) represented those actual requirements that favoured older candidates. Therefore, 77 cases from 'more than 21' and 'more than 25' were eliminated from the analysis. Age requirement of those who are 'more than 35' represented only a small proportion of the sample size (11 case = 2.89 per cent), thus it was treated as an outlier. In total, 362 cases were used to test the proposed hypothesis. The dependent variable is a categorical variable consisting of cases falling in yes (1), stating the age requirement for younger candidates and (0), not stating the age requirement.

Independent variables

Independent variables comprise the scores on Hofstede's Uncertainty Avoidance, gender, education, and experience of candidates, and types of language used, positions and industry advertised. The average scores for uncertainty avoidance on each national home country were used (see Table 10.3).

Altogether MNCs from 18 countries and local Thai firms were found to express their interests for job candidates in the job search database. The national origin of the firms was checked through reference to Thai business directories, and through their company websites to determine ownership and control. MNCs were classified into four main groups: Japan, USA, Europe and Australia, and other Asian countries except Japan. Japan constituted the largest proportion of MNCs (33.6 per cent) that expressed their interest in job candidates in the database. Japan also

Table 10.3 Four main categories of MNCs and local firms on age advertised (n = 375)

Categories	*Age bar within category*		*Age bar within total samples*	
	No	Yes	Yes	No
Thailand	59.9	40.1	68.6	71.9
Japan	83.8	16.2	13.3	4.1
USA	46.7	53.3	6.1	11
Europe/ Aus	60	40	9.2	9.6
Asian countries accept Thai & Japan	54.5	45.5	2.6	3.4

Note: * Age bar for younger workers referred to those advertisements that required candidates who were more than 45 years (advertisement contained age barrier of more than 21 years and 25 years were discarded).

used a high proportion of age discriminative language when compared to the other main categories (see Table 10.3).

The discriminative language on gender was also used as one of the independent variables. Initially, the language specifying the requirements on age were divided into four categories: female only (12.2 per cent), male only (11.6 per cent), both male and female (37.8 per cent), and not specified (38.4 per cent). Since advertisements directed towards equal opportunities could not discriminate against sexes, therefore the four gender categories were merged into two groups: as (1) = stating gender requirement as in 'female only' and 'male only': and (0) = not stating gender requirement as in 'both male and female' and 'nil'. Past work experience measured as a unit per year, was determined by some of the employers. Minimum qualifications specified fall into 5 main categories: *high school* (2.2 per cent), *diploma* (15.2 per cent), *bachelors degree* (75.1 per cent), *master degree* (3.6 per cent) and *not specified* (3.9 per cent). It should be noted that the minimum qualification requirement was highly skewed towards a bachelors' degree. This requirement to request a candidate who has a minimum undergraduate qualification is common for a white collar job in Thailand

Types of language use in job advertisements fall into two categories: Thai and English. Most multinational corporations sometimes require English as a means to communicate in the subsidiaries. Thus, some advertisements were placed in English to find a suitable candidate who is fluent in English language. Position and industry advertised were classified under the Australian industry classification indices. The sample falls into 10 industries and 7 levels of positions, ranging from a very senior level, managers & administration' to junior level 'elementary clerical, sales & service workers'.

Given a dichotomous dependent variable, logistic regression analysis with SPSS 12 was used to assess the impact of the home countries' culture and other independent variables on the dependent variable (n = 362). A test of the best fit model with three predictors: uncertainty avoidance, experience required and gender, against the dependent variable was statistically reliable, χ^2 (3, n = 362) = 33.46, p < .001). Four independent variables were omitted from the model to increase the model explanatory power – namely type of language, education, position and industry. Overall classification was satisfactory. On the basis of three independent variables, 100 per cent of the observed cases that specified age requirement were correctly predicted (yes), whereas 0 per cent of the cases that did not specified age requirement (no) was correctly predicted. The overall correct classification rate was 59.7 per cent. After the regressors had been included in the model, the classification ratio showed significant improvement to 64.9 per cent. 87.5 per cent were correctly classified on the category specifying age limit (yes), and 31.5 per cent on the category that did not specify age limit respectively.

Table 10.4 displays regression coefficients, Wald statistics, odds ratios and 95 per cent confidence intervals for odds ratios for each of the three predictors.

According to the Wald criterion, the home-countries' Uncertainty Avoidance scale ($z = 4.61$, $p < 0.05$), experience required ($z = 4.01$, $p < 0.05$) and gender ($z = 17.29$, $p < 0.001$) reliably predicted the use of discriminative language on older job applicants. As the level of Uncertainty Avoidance of the home-country cultural traits increases, the probability of a company imposing an age requirement also increased. The overt discrimination on the older people occurred together with the probability of the advertisements that required candidates with little or no work experience. In addition, age barriers on older candidates were predicted to increase with the probability of non-gender discriminative language. The results confirmed the hypothesis that the likelihood of overt age discrimination would increase with the company's home-country average value on Hofstede's Uncertainty Avoidance scale.

Discussion

The findings of this study indicate that a candidates' age is still being used as a key criterion in decision-making for employment, to which the older candidates are the group at a disadvantage. The issue of an ageing workforce has been taken lightly by local Thai firms. The majority (72 per cent) of the firms found in this study used discriminative language

Table 10.4 Logistic regression analysis of job advertisement of MNCs and local firms as a prediction of overt age discrimination (n = 362)

Variables	B	Wald Test (z-ratio)	Odds ratio	95% confidence interval for odds ratio	
				Upper	Lower
Uncertainty Avoidance	.019	4.61*	1.020	1.002	1.038
Experience	−.095	4.01*		.829	
Gender	−1.272	17.288***	.910		.998
(Constant)	.349	.292	.280	.154	.511

Note: *p < 0.05, **p < 0.01, ***p < 0.001.

against job candidates, probably due to their low awareness of the issue. It should also be noted that the terms, 'ageing workers' or 'older workers', in the Thai job market referred to those who are at a very young age (age above 30 years). However, the category of the ageing workers specified within the Thai business environment is of concern, as it will only escalate the predicted intensified effects of the ageing workforce.

Given the experience of some MNCs from developed countries with regard to the issue of an ageing workforce, it is anticipated that these countries would transfer a standard practice of equal management opportunities to their subsidiaries. For example, Japan is one of the developed nations that is facing immediate concerns regarding an ageing population and workforce (see United Nations, 2002). The evidence from this research displays that most of the Japanese corporations, which had a higher tendency to discriminate overtly against older candidates in the Thai subsidiaries, held their recruitment and selection policies in the areas of equal employment opportunities similar to most of the Thai firms found in the study. In addition, the employment laws of Australia, the United Kingdom and the United States strongly prohibit overt and covert discrimination within their countries. Nevertheless, all the job advertisements of these corporations in the database overtly displayed a preference for younger candidates. The propensity to discriminate against older candidates in the Thai employment market was found not only in local Thai firms but also extensively in the MNCs of developed countries.

Rational explanation for the findings may rest with the national cultural trait of the MNCs associated with their level of risk avoidance (Hofstede, 1980). The MNCs' tendencies to become less ethnocentric in the management practice of equal employment opportunities in their subsidiaries may lie in their inclination to be competitive in the local market (Schuler, Dowling *et al.*, 1993). MNCs with strong Uncertainty Avoidance scores tend to prefer relatively young candidates to avoid the unambiguous outcomes relating to the risks envisaged from recruiting older job seekers (for example, low performance, high cost of maintenance, and resistance to change from the older workers), or seek to retain a youthful image favoured by customers and society. The inclination to avoid business risk and promote performance may also lie with the endorsement from academic research. Past research has shown that MNCs' business performance increased when management practice of the MNC were congruent with the national culture of host countries (Hofstede, 1980; Wilkins and Ouchi, 1983; Newman and Nollen, 1996).

Whilst, this may be true to some extent, the basic standard of international human rights and human development promotes universally applicable values in areas concerning employment discrimination

Ethically, the multinational corporations operating in less developed countries could develop their management practices in line with guidelines on human rights and human development proposed by several international human rights agencies (i.e., United Nation Development Program, 1995; Organisation for Economic Co-operation and Development, 1976/200; International Labour Organization, 1977; and United Nations Global Compact, 2000) (see Lozano and Boni, 2002). Countries have different work standards and employment laws (Rawwas, 2001). However, labour laws and conditions of equal employment opportunities in the less developed countries are not as favoured as those in developed countries (Asgary and Mitschow, 2002). Nevertheless, the organizational practice of international human rights and human development which governs the promotion of social equity and labour rights in an organization, should be considered a minimum standard in MNCs' subsidiaries, regardless of differences in their national cultural traits.

The results also indicate that the tendency to discriminate against age does not concur with the propensity of the employers to discriminate against gender. The issue of sex discrimination in Thailand could be improving since this issue has been policed by international human rights organizations (for example, the United Nations). When compared with past research on overt sex discrimination conducted by Lawler and Bae (1998), sex discriminative language in job advertisements reduced by 13.7 per cent. This demonstrates that issues relating to equal opportunities and human rights practices are attainable, if public policy-makers and business corporations give it consideration.

Conclusions

The socioeconomic issue of an ageing workforce has become a topic of concern in the developed countries. The results of this study displays that MNCs who hold high values regarding equal employment opportunities can be influenced by management practice which manifest through the national culture of the host countries. It should be noted that the variables used in the study are those restricted from the job advertisement database. Incorporating other variables such as size and age of the companies may be able to offer more details for the investigation.

More specifically, several governments in Southeast Asia have expressed serious concerns about the increasing proportion of the working-age population and the issue of population ageing. This issue encourages a change in human resources policy and practice to accommodate and plan for the future demographic trend. The ageing workforce is a strategic issue that requires strategic direction and vision, both from within the local and across multinational organizations. It requires immediate attention from human resource managers to maintain long-term organizational competitiveness (Seyed, 2003). The changing trend towards an ageing workforce, especially in the less developed countries, suggests the benefits of a close scrutiny on human resource structure and strategy to match the socioeconomic challenge.

It is recommended that MNCs take the lead in promoting age equality, especially in the less developed countries. For example, corporations should avoid giving age limits, age ranges or language-specified restrictions such as '*new graduate*' with their job announcements. Their human resource policy and procedures should also be age positive and free from any discrimination related to employees' age. The positive role of MNCs regarding age-discriminatory practice in their subsidiaries will not only set an example to local Thai firms, but will also increase their chance of recruiting the best candidates. The management practices of MNCs could affect the host nation's public policy of human rights practice and equal employment opportunities (Payne, Raiborn *et al.*, 1997). Thai organizations should also recognise that older workers are beneficial to them as a human resource investment.

References

Anderson, G., F. and P. Hussey, S. (2000) 'Population Aging: A Comparison Among Industrialized Countries.' *Health Affairs* 9(3): 191–212.

ASEAN (2003) *ASEAN Statistical Yearbook*. Jakarta: The ASEAN Secretariat.

Asgary, N. and M.C. Mitschow, (2002) 'Toward a Model for International Business Ethics', *Journal of Business Ethics* 36(3): 239–46.

Asian Development Bank (2004) Thailand: Country strategy and program update 2002–2004, Asian Development Bank: 11.

Attetanan, P. (2001). *Country Report: Thailand*. The 12th International Workshop for Information Policy and Management in the Public Sector, Japan, The Institute of Administration Information Systems (IAIS).

Baker, K., H. and T. Veit, E. (1998) 'A Comparison of Ethics of Investment Professionals: North America versus Pacific Rim Nations', *Journal of Business Ethics* 17(8): 917–37.

Bennington, L. (2001) 'Age Discrimination: Covering Evidence from Four Australian Studies', *Employee Responsibilities and Rights Journal* 13(3): 125–34.

Bennington, L. and R. Wein (2003) 'Does the Resumé Open the Door to Age Discrimination for Older Workers?', *Australian Journal of Ageing* 22(2): 70–5.

Brooke, L. (2003) 'Human Resource Costs and Benefits of Maintaining a Mature-age Workforce', *International Journal of Manpower* 24(3): 260–83.

Ceniceros, R. (2001) 'Adapting Injury Risk Management to Aging Workforce', *Business Insurance* 35: 33.

Collins, G., A. (2003) 'Rethinking Retirement in the Context of an Ageing Workforce', *Journal of Career Development* 30(2): 145–57.

Commonwealth (2003) *Intergenerational Report 2002–03*. Canberra: Commonwealth of Australia.

De Cieri, H. (1998) 'Issues of Occupational Health and Safety', in L. Hartmann (ed.), *Managing an Ageing workforce*. Warriewood, NSW: Business & Professional Publishing, p. 263.

Duncan, C. and W. Loretto (2004) 'Never the Right Age? Gender and Age-based Discrimination in Employment', *Gender, Work and Organization* 11(1): 95–155.

Ekamper, P. (1997) 'Future Age-conscious Manpower Planing in the Netherlands from Early Retirement to a New Perspective on the Elderly?', *International Journal of Manpower* 18(3): 232–47.

Enderle, G. (1997) 'A Worldwide Survey of Business Ethics in the 1990s', *Journal of Business Ethics* 16(4): 1475–83.

Feldman, D.C. and B. Klass, S. (2002) 'Internet Job Hunting: a Field Study of Applicant Experiences with On-line Recruiting', *Human Resource Management* 41(2): 175–92.

Giniger, S., A. Dispenzieri, *et al.* (1983) 'Age, Experience, and Performance on Speed and Skills Jobs in an Applied Setting', *Journal of Applied Psychology*, 68(3): 469–75.

Gunderson, M. (2003) 'Age Discrimination in Employment in Canada', *Contemporary Economic Policy* 21(3): 318–28.

Haltiwanger, J., C., J. Lane, I., *et al.* (1999) 'Productivity Differences Across Employers: the Roles of Employer Size, Age, and Human Capital', *The American Economic Review* 89(2): 94–8.

Hofstede, G. (1980). *Culture's Consequences: International Differences in Work-related Values*. Beverly Hills, CA: Sage Publications.

Hofstede, G. (1983) 'The Cultural Relativity of Organisational Practices and Theories', *Journal of International Business Studies* 14 (Fall): 75–89.

Hogan, R., G. and S. Kerstein, J. (1999) 'Employer Retirement Obligations in a Changing World', *Journal of Financial Service Professionals* 53(6): 62–7.

Kessapidou, S. and N. Varsakelis, C. (2002) 'The Impact of National Culture on International Business Performance: The Case of Foreign Firms in Greece', *European Business Review* 14(4): 268–75.

Lawler, J., and J. Bae (1998) 'Overt Discrimination by Multinational Firms: Cultural and Economic Influences in a Developing Country', *Industrial Relations* 37(2): 126–53.

Lozano, F., J. and A. Boni (2002) 'The Impact of the Multinational in the Development: An Ethical Challenge', *Journal of Business Ethics* 39(1/2): 169–78.

Mcdonald, G.M. and P.C. Kan (1997) 'Ethical Perceptions of Expatriate and Local Managers in Hong Kong', *Journal of Business Ethics* 16(15): 1605–23.

McGoldrick, A.E. and J. Arrowsmith (1993) 'Recruitment Advertising: Discrimination on the Basis of Age', *Employee Relations* 15(5): 54–65.

Newman, K.L. and S.D. Nollen (1996) 'Culture and Congruence: The Fit between Management Practices and National Culture', *Journal of International Business Studies* 27(4): 753–79.

Oswick, C. and P. Jones (1991) 'The Age Factor in Work Performance: Age-ism or Realism?', *Management Services* 35(12): 12–15.

Paul, R., J. and J. Townsend, B. (1993) 'Managing the Older Worker: Don't Just Rinse Away the Grey', *The Academy of Management Executive* 7(3): 67–74.

Payne, D., C. Raiborn, *et al.* (1997) 'A Global Code of Business Ethics', *Journal of International Business Studies* 16(16): 1727–35.

Population Reference Bureau (2003). 'World Population Data Sheet', Population Reference Bureau.

Pornpitakpan, C. (2000) 'Trade in Thailand: a Three-way Cultural Comparison', *Business Horizons*, 43(2): 61–70.

Prachuabmoh, V. and P. Mithranon (2003) 'Below-Replacement Fertility in Thailand and its Policy Implications', *Journal of Population Research* 20(1): 35–50.

Rawwas, M.Y.A. (2001) 'Culture, Personality and Morality: a Typology of International Consumers' Ethical Beliefs', *International Marketing Review*, 18(2): 188.

Remery, C., K. Henkens, *et al.* (2003) 'Managing an Aging Workforce and a Tight Labour Market: Views Held by Dutch Employers', *Population Research and Policy Review*, 22(1): 21.

Rickard, S. (1999) 'Future Employment', *Foresight*, 1(5): 427–40.

Schuler, R., P. Dowling, *et al.* (1993) 'An Integrated Framework of Strategic International Human Resource Management', *International Journal of Human Resource Management*, 4 (Summer): 717–64.

Selmer, J. and C. De Leor (1993) 'Organizational Acculturation in Foreign Subsidiaries', *The International Executive*, 35(4): 321–48.

Seyed, M.A. (2003) 'The Future of Human Resource Management', *Work Study* 52(4): 201–7.

Sheen, V. (2001) 'The Ageing Work Force: Policy Lessons from the United States', *CEDA Bulletin* (March): 42–4.

Singer, M.S. and C. Sewell (1989) 'Applicant Age and Selection Interview Decisions: Effect of Information Exposure on Age Discrimination in Personnel Selection', *Personnel Psychology* 42: 135–54.

Swierczek, F.W. and J. Onishi (2003) 'Culture and Conflict: Japanese Managers and Thai Subordinates', *Personnel Review* 32(1/2): 187–210.

Szalai, G. (1998) 'Employee Tenure in Increasing as Workforce Ages: Study', *Business Insurance*, 32(35): 2–4.

Taylor, P. and A. Walker (1998) 'Policies and Practices Towards Older Workers: A Framework for Comparative Research', *Human Resource Management Journal* 8(3): 61–76.

United Nations (2002) *World Population Ageing: 1950–2050*. P. Division, Department of Economic and Social Affairs. New York: United Nations.

United Nations (2004) *World Population Policies 2003*, Department of Economic and Social Affairs. New York: United Nations.

Vause, G.W. (1992) 'Labour Relations in Thailand', *East Asian Executive Reports* 14(11): 9–13.

Walker, A. and P. Taylor (eds) (1993) *Ageism vs Productive Ageing: The Challenge of Age Discrimination in the Labour Market. Achieving a Productive Ageing Society.* London: Auburn House.

Weiss, H.M. (1978) 'Social Learning of Work Values in Organisations', *Journal of Applied Psychology* 63(6): 711–18.

Wilkins, A.L. and W. Ouchi (1983) 'Efficient Cultures: Exploring the Relationship between Culture and Organizational Performance', *Administrative Science Quarterly* 23(3): 468–81.

11
Competition in Globalizing Markets, and the Relationships between the Korean State and Corporate Power

Doo-Jin Kim and Young-Chan Kim

Introduction

This contribution provides a discussion of the relationship between international competitiveness and the shifting contours of state and corporate power through a case study of Korean state-corporate power, or *chaebol* governance. This chapter explores the issue of why Korean big business can be regarded as a political power rather than merely as a market agent. It shows how Korean corporate power has emerged as the countervailing force against Korean state power. In particular, in conjunction with the increasing significance of international trade barriers in the advanced markets since the early 1980s, the growing importance of international competitiveness has tended to have an influence in government–industry relations in terms of increasing the market power of indigenous big corporations. Alongside what we have termed knowledge-intensive industries, the importance of technological factors has tended to increase the influence of big business on government–industry relationships. The chapter concludes by suggesting that under the pressures of globalization, market power that mainly originated in the Korean private sector gradually gave rise to economic power as well as *political* power in relation to public authority or state power. The issue of government–industry relations has long been an interesting topic for academic discussion and a subject of concern for public policy-makers. Globalization has freed large firms from the constraints of national government even though over the past few years firms have been almost entirely dependent on national political institutions and regulations for domestic access and influence (Coen, 1997: 97). As for newly industrializing economies, the new international trade regimes that appeared after the early 1980s, it seems apparent that latecomers needed to pay much more attention to the compelling significance of international competitiveness that governs the wealth of nations. As a consequence, this had triggered a reconsideration of the nature of the seemingly successful development states in terms of market-shaping activities. This chapter reconstructs the historically evolving interaction of state, market and firm by paying much more attention to the significance for the phenomenon of governance of Korean big business in the process of globalization. We argue that Korean big businesses have emerged as political actors, whether in world markets responding to a new international trade regime, or, more specifically, in the process towards European integration. Individual MNCs incorporating knowledge-intensive technology have began to emerge as market coordinators, individually or collectively. The nature of industry or industrialization has transformed the 'nature of market'. By implication, it appears that Korean corporate power is both politically and economically at odds with Korean state power in terms of shaping market institutions and the workings of markets. 'Market power' originated by Korean major MNCs has tended to pave the way for political power, because multinational companies intrinsically translate economic activities in international markets into political leverage. The interpretation of market power provides a preliminary explanation of how Korea's *chaebol*-governance gives rise to 'market power' (economic actor) as well as 'political power' (political actor), to the extent that Korean MNCs invariably led to an entanglement of political and economic power in relation to the Korean state power.

Big business and global competition: knowledge-based industry and 'market power'

We argue that government–business relations have tended to shift strongly in favour of the latter over time, even when taking into account variations between industrial sectors, such as electronics, or the steel industry. In addition, government's role is a controversial and still unresolved issue in arguments about international competitiveness, as reflected in the form of strategic trade policy or industrial policy. In the more immediate past, the importance of international competitiveness and the market-making function have been emphasized less by interventionist governments than the newly emerging governance of big business in conformity with the globalizing markets.

Depending upon his corporatist explanation of bargains between the EC and major firms, Cawson's (1992) concept of micro-corporatism (at the firm level) suggests that major European MNCs–for example, Philips– are of no less significance in the EC-level decision-making process, as illustrated by the Europeanization of an industrial sector, for example, the consumer electronics industry. However, Cawson considers that the big firms remain invariably perceived by being subject to market forces. As in orthodox economic theory, firms are still interpreted as polit- ical actors in terms of 'lobbyists' (Cawson, 1997: 185). While Cawson describes the notion of firms as political actors, it is not suggested that we can identify the market power of big business as the *cause* of political power. In terms of the 'market power', we assume that the concept of market power *cannot be simply seen as the extent, or amount of market share likely to be existent in particular marketplace(s)* in the context of commercial, or business activities whether at the level of the domestic, the international marketplaces or in-between. Whether the market can be regarded as mechanism, or a marketplace, or a geographical area, we need to present new perspectives on the definition of market power. By contrast with conventional understanding of market phenomena, we argue that market power should not be characterized by being simply confined to economic activities representing profit-seeking busi- ness or benefit-maximizing management of particular corporations, *but* rather 'politico-economic' phenomena that have existed *historically* in social structure incorporating political and economic activities centring around marketplaces (see Zysman, 1983).

In conjunction with the increasing significance of international trade barriers in the advanced markets since the early 1980s, the government has not appropriately resolved the problem of international compet- itiveness. Against such a background, while the emerging governance of corporate power needs to be examined from a new international competitive perspective, we would like to focus much more atten- tion on the reformulation of initial premises surrounding government– industry relations. Alongside what we have termed knowledge-intensive industry, the importance of technological factors has tended to increase the influence of big business in the government–business relationship. The existing discussion has perceived the growth of the economic and political role of big business as capable of challenging the state that had unexpectedly enjoyed autonomy from the private sector in Korean society. Until recently, however, there seems to have been little explor- ation of what really has given rise to the changing pattern between the developmental state and big business.

Concerning knowledge-products as distinct from 'general purpose technologies', we can consider knowledge-intensive products as 'knowledge-like goods' that encompasses many of 'the same physical and economic properties as knowledge itself' such as computer software, new media, and information technology, including semiconductors, thus providing typical examples of the developments of a 'weightless economy', to borrow the term from Quah (1999). This does not always mean, however, that 'the resulting goods continue to be knowledge-intensive'. Subsequently, for a meso-market at the production level, the market structure may be determined by particular knowledge-intensive products resulting overall from the firm's innovative capability. That is to conjecture that severe competition among the leading firms targeting industrial markets may determine the market structure for a sustained period of time, or periodically. In this regard, contrary to the perspectives of classical economic theorists on the reformulation of the correlation between firm behaviour and market structure, with the compelling importance of knowledge factor in international competitiveness, we posit that the *market-making* behaviour displayed by business can meaningfully determine the structure of industrial markets in some cases.

Correspondingly, in terms of spillover effects on the national economy, new technology alongside knowledge-intensive industry has evoked new perceptions or interpretations of the firm which is traditionally perceived and analysed *only* at the micro-level in the context of 'level of analysis' by classical economists, (compared to 'the industry' at the meso-level, and 'the economy' at the macro-level, see Cawson *et al.*, 1990: 15 and Mattsson, 1999: 242). In contrast, when it comes to international competitiveness concerning knowledge-intensive products, it is undeniable that individual big business, or MNCs with global corporations, have tended to represent and restrain to a substantial extent the industry at the international level, or sometimes to the extent that the national economy, in macro-aspects, is overwhelmingly affected by behaviour or actions of *individual* big business in terms of 'economic (market) power'.

The state and big business: strategic finance

Finance, as Woo-Cumings (1999: 10) contends, is above all one of the most important engines that 'binds state to industrialization in the developmental state'. The financial factor in the historic relationship between the Korean developmental state and Korean large firms is a case in point. Critical of the notion of a market-conforming path, scholars such as Johnson (1982), Amsden (1989) and Wade (1990) consider government intervention as having been indispensable in achieving the East Asian miracle. In particular, Amsden (1994) goes so far as to suggest that the 'unfettered regulation by the world markets' could lead to *under*development instead of development.

Despite the background of such achievements of the Korean economy, it is apparent that the growth of Korean *chaebol* has eventually tended to significantly restrain such state capacity emanating from the developmental state. As Field (1995: 48) put it:

> [T]here was a gradual shift from the state dominance over the chaebol to a relationship of symbiosis to, most recently, increasing friction and animosity... the size and complexity of the economy and its chaebol engines have limited the Korean state's capacity to dictate the chaebol's developmental path.

For developing countries, e.g. NIEs, we need to present a convincing explanation of how big business has emerged as a countervailing social force against government, even though it has been almost subordinate to the developmental logic primarily pursued by the strong state for a considerable time. Whilst the growth paths of the Korean big business system are seen as dependent on pre-existing configurations of financial factors originally structured by Korean economic and political institutions, it appears that with regard to government–industry relations finance has come to be perceived as a lever no longer to be wielded permanently by a strong state.

Moreover, when it comes to globalization, Korean big business systems seem to have developed considerable organizational capacity and adaptability to the major changes prompted by globalization, given that the nature of business systems has in some cases remained almost untouched, and in others has been able to adapt. Yeung (2000: 402) argues that Asian business systems prominently exhibit adaptive capability and organizational flexibility. Given that the 'withering away' of the state is really inconceivable, governments, in particular, in industrializing countries have become *relatively* weaker in terms of government–business relations in the context of international competitiveness following liberalization and deregulation originating significantly from the newly emerging world economic order (Woods, 2000: 11–12). In this regard, as Underhill (2000: 22) maintains, the role of non-state actors such as 'international business, or organized business' that traditional international relations scholars have until most recently been unconcerned with tend to have gradually attracted much attention in the context of regional integration as well as the changing global market economy.

As Woo-Cumings (1999) emphasizes, it is evident that finance has become central in analysing the developmental state in East Asia. Inspired by Johnson (1982: 10–11), as far as state–industry relations are concerned, government control of finance has constituted a major reason for considering economic policy in Japan, South Korea and Taiwan as typically finance-related, while the remaining major issues, such as labour relations, autonomy of bureaucracy, and so on, have been given less significance in the academic analysis of national industrial policy.

According to Lee (1997), with regard to the role of the state in relation to big business, even though the Korean government intended to exercise a crucial influence in orchestrating economic development, the Korean state, in reality, seemed to have enjoyed autonomy from Korean conglomerates, in other words, the capitalist class in Neo-Marxist terms, as argued, amongst others, by Poulantzas (1972). That is to say that the Korean government was not willing to serve to secure the domination of the capitalist class regardless of the government's support of Korean *chaebol*, even though such a relationship is said to be invariably extended to Chun and Roh's democratizing and liberalizing regimes, let alone the period under the Park Jung Hee regime.

As for state autonomy, whilst Lee's (1997) argument is to some extent persuasive, it is important also to examine other analyses of what really caused the Korean state to establish its autonomy in relation to big business or the capitalist class in terms of socioeconomic background or class structure. Some scholars have attempted to characterize state autonomy as being derived from a particular Korean government's state capacity in light of state apparatus – that is, the presence of the Economic Planning Board (EPB), which is very similar to the role of the Japanese MITI, in terms of overseeing foreign capital and initiating the 'administrative guidance', and so on. The concentration of decision-making in the government branch, especially in relation to economy-related issues as a whole, was one major factor that allowed the state to remain independent of societal powers by virtue of its institutional cohesion and responsiveness related to expertise. Subsequently this led to enhanced state autonomy and strong state capacity (Ravenhill, 1995: xxiv).

Until recently, the Korean banking system was largely state-owned. As a consequence, loans from state agencies and state-regulated banks have allowed for the expansion of Korean big companies. This illustrates the point that loans have been offered at interest rates far lower than those commonly available in domestic or international financial markets. This has necessarily given way to subordination of Korean *chaebol* corresponding with state policy directive and national economic goals, coupled with industrial policy and strategic trade policy (Henderson, 1993; Wade and Veneroso, 1998).

Government–industry relations: new context

The steady growth of the *chaebol* permitted the state to reduce subsidies and thus allowed the *chaebol* to become more independent of the state. Historically, it cannot be denied that the firms have eventually emerged as social forces, economically and politically. Based on what Cawson terms 'corporate power' in his analysis of big firms as political actors in the European consumer electronics industry, it is useful to investigate how the different character of power exerted by big business in each country tends to affect government's relations with large corporations, or inter-firm relationships in three different dimensions: first, power exercised in relation to *other firms* through the process of competition; secondly, power exercised in relation to *government and public authorities*; and, thirdly, power relations *within firms* (Cawson *et al.*, 1990; Cawson, 1997: 186–92). In a similar context, to understand big firms as exercising political power, Zysman (1983) has attempted to see political power as related to the market itself. Political power is interrelated with the operation of the market mechanism and, consequently, market position itself automatically gives rise to political power. In addition, Penrose (1995: 197) also emphasized that 'market and firms are interacting institutions, each being functionally necessary to the existence of the other' for resource allocation. Overall, we can see that government and firms simultaneously interact in the market, economically and politically. Under these conditions, the particular arrangements of the financial system stipulated by government help to constrain both the marketplace choices of firms, sometimes both being in accordance with each other, or cooperative, while business is plausibly subordinate to government in the context of competitiveness in the marketplace (Zysman, 1983: 16).

As Johnson (1995) observes, in most of the East Asian NICs, until recently, that is, prior to the Asian financial crisis, government's exclusive control of finance might have been understood as one of the most distinctive features in leading and controlling the private sector. Johnson added that 'these financial measures are often *unorthodox* by Anglo-American standards, particularly in their emphasis on the supply of capital to industry primarily through the banking system' (53). Specifically, with regard to Korea, direct government ownership and control of the banking system have been one of the most conspicuous features of the industrial policies that characterized the 1960s and 1970s. However, 1979 saw a departure from the traditional pattern of banking ownership when there was an attempt to privatize the state banks and to liberalize government control over the financial sector.

Moreover, with reference to state autonomy, it is important to acknowledge that one should distinguish between the East Asian capitalist states and Latin America countries. In terms of public–private relations, Asian states have tended to develop independent economic development options in contrast with their Latin American counterparts wherein the state's goals are noticeably subordinate to private interests. Whilst the Asian states cannot unilaterally disregard the interests of big business, it is also clear that the strength of economic bureaucracy helped to maintain government autonomy in pursuing national policy objectives to a greater extent than in other industrializing countries (Chai, 1993). According to Kim (1988: 106) and Soh (1997: 254), state power is not constant over time, and the state–business relationship at the same time varies 'over time and across industry'. Soh (1997), in particular, contends that the aims of government initiatives *vis-à-vis* the industrial realm have changed over the last thirty years. The conventional hypothesis that the developmental state in Korea has considerably affected the nation's *entire* industries must be reformulated (see Kim, 1988). The state–corporate power relationship has shifted from a subordinate to a symmetrical one (Soh, 1997: 257), in a sense, 'from state dominance to interdependence and symbiosis to competition' (205). Even when the initial phase of economic development in the NICs was orchestrated and initiated by the state, big business also emerged as a powerful, independent actor in relation to government as national goals of economic development have been identifiably achieved (Kim, 1988: 120–1). In his comparative study of the steel industry and semiconductor sector, Soh (1997: 255) maintains:

By the 1980s, ... semiconductor production was initiated by the chaebol rather than by the state. The role of the state in the semiconductor industry has been less significant than that of its involvement with the steel industry ... did the 1980s witness a change in the state-business relationship.

Specifically with regard to Korea, government-industry relations also have to be analysed in the context of both *market size* and *external factors*. The implication is that Korea has a small local market resting 'excessively on export (even more than Japan)', which is to say that Korea firms need to be well equipped to cope with international competition (Woo-Cumings, 1999: 12). Korean firms have been required to respond to external shocks in terms of fluctuations in trade and in world markets, for example, those arising from the advent of new international regimes. These circumstances have acted to re-condition Korean industrial policy or strategic trade policy, thereby contributing to a reconsideration of relations between state power and corporate power. Thus, in response to changing circumstances in the world, whilst big business has been the beneficiary of industrial finance, new conditions necessarily may give Janus-faced big corporations a new opportunity to redefine the pattern of relations between the state and corporate power. Given that the role of the Korean developmental state was due mainly to finance, it might be expected that state–corporate power relations would tend to become more vulnerable and more unstable, relatively allowing big business to increase to a greater extent bargaining power directed to a larger market *vis-à-vis* government, along with the gradual retreat of state power in dealing with market creation. Thus, we contend that control and influence deriving from *strategic* finance provided by government seems to be time-limited in terms of government–business relations, when faced with recent changing international conditions surpassing domestic market mechanism and national government's jurisdiction.

In exploring Korea's economic achievement, although the Heavy and Chemical Industry (HCI) Policy pursued by the Korean government in the 1970s turned out to be a failure, it gave Korean conglomerates a momentum to increase to a certain degree their leverage vis-à-vis the Korean government (Ravenhill, 1995: xxvi). This trend seems to have intensified following the social, economic and political upheaval accompanying the Chun Doo Hwan regime (1980–88). For example, what is termed a 'Chaebol Republic' has represented the reality of Korean corporate power (see Kim, 1997a, 1997b). This is also to argue that the *chaebol* have undeniably shifted from the 'private agency of public purpose' towards '*quasi-state* organizations' (Woo-Cumings, 1999: 17) exercising power, politically or economically, thus going beyond the indigenous domain of economic organizations. It is implied that business organizations remain no longer mere business firms in many ways subordinate to the state. Moreover, the pursuit of hegemony between state and corporate power has become pervasive and has culminated in some frictions displayed by the *chaebol* founders and the presidents of big business groups. For example, the founder of Hyundai, Chung Ju-yung, formed his own political party (Unification National Party) and unexpectedly captured 25 per cent of the National Assembly seats in the March 1992 election. Surprisingly, Chung's further challenge to contest the presidential election even with no prospect of success against powerful political leaders such as Kim Young Sam is an indication of the deteriorating relationship between big business and the state. In addition, the announcement of Daewoo's Kim Woo Chung and seemingly forced consequent retraction of his decision to run for president in the 1992 election was also seen as a sign of the growing rift and competition in conventional state–business relations in Korea. Moreover, on the 13th of January 1995, in front of press reporters, Lee Kun-Hee, the president of the Samsung Group, during his visit to China criticized the political class for being incompetent by grading Korean politics as fourth-class lagging far behind the administration as third-class, and the business group as second-class (Chang, 1999: 38). Even though Lee had to apologise publicly and withdraw this remark, the event signifies more than any other episodes or scandals, the changing relations between corporate power and the state.

The *chaebol*-governance: beyond the Japanese 'MITI paradox'

The Korean government owned commercial banks, while the Korean state maintained tight controls on foreign currency, broadly acquiring foreign capital together with its strict control on inward FDI at the international level. Since the 1980s, the liberalization of the financial market has focussed on the privatization of commercial banks and liberalization of interest rates, followed strategically by the re-orientation of financing objectives from large firms-centred towards more emphasis on small and medium-sized firms. This was due, on the one hand, to the internationalization of entire economic spheres, and on the other hand – mainly by virtue of liability – to a change in the status of Korea in parallel with its participation in the OECD in 1996. In the end, domestic financial markets have been forcibly or unwillingly opened and become more adaptable to foreign investors as well as FDI, inward or outward, following the settlement of the Uruguay Round of Trade Negotiations.

Unlike the bank-centred Japanese *keiretsu*, until recently the large Korean companies have been excluded from the banking business. In this regard, the Korean government exercised a more influential leverage over its industry than did its Japanese counterpart by unilaterally controlling the financial system, such as loan funds, and foreign exchange. With regard to finance, this has made Korean conglomerates heavily reliant upon the Korean government since the Korean banks were nationalized in 1961, following the military coup. It was only in the early 1980s that the Korean government came to consider the privatization of banks and the creation of related measures directed towards specialized areas, such as small and medium-sized business financing. Conventionally, as in the Japanese financing system, investment policy directives and credit expansion have been understood as a result of cordial discussion between the government and industry, especially in the case of the *keiretsu* groups. By contrast, the Korean financial system, characteristic of 'bank-loan capitalism' (see Plummer, 1999: 233), has been greatly vulnerable to a 'highly-centralized top-down conduit' originating with government, accompanied by 'policy loans' targeting specific sectors of a particular industry as well as 'general loans' directed towards preferential financing (Plummer, 1999: 234–5).

From the early 1990s, the Korean government sought to loosen its regulation of the financial sector and, under the Kim Young Sam government, which came to power in 1993, the presumed five-year financial liberalization plan was announced by Kim's government, and accordingly put in place by substantial policy measures. In fact, state power in the former Korean model was related to its power to orchestrate financial options partly through the coordination of a pilot agency such as the Economic Planning Board (EPB), and partly through government control over strategic finance. From the mid-1990s, and by the time of the Asian currency crisis, such policy instruments had been all but abolished. The Economic Planning Board was absorbed into the Ministry of Finance and Economics, but strategically the latter was deprived of the formerly strict control of the EPB over economic policy objectives (Mathews, 1998: 757).

Compared with the leverage of the Japanese MITI (Ministry of International Trade and Industry) over the industry, despite the fact that outwardly Korean corporate circles have been placed in the process of corporate restructuring aggressively designed by state as well as international finance institutions, we hypothesize that Korean corporate power has been more autonomous vis-à-vis [Korean] state power in light of the Japanese 'MITI paradox'.

More generally, the prevailing view of MITI was that it exerted influence via a 'not-so-invisible guiding hand' likely to be seen as part of the shaping of the long-term structural change in the Japanese economy. Specifically, MITI was mainly concerned with the prospective trend of technical change and the development of various technologies, combined with the Japanese choice of rejecting the traditional development strategy that depended upon the notion of comparative advantage. MITI focused upon the promotion of the most advanced technologies identifying the world market potential in the long term (Freeman, 1988: 331). Here, one critical point is that strategic finance, as we have seen it in Korea's government role, is one of the key functions of its role, whereas the Japanese MITI has had a significant degree of control on distinctive features of the entire Japanese industry *even* without relying considerably upon finance. With reference to national technology policy, as with key government institutions, such as the Ministry of Education, or the Science and Technology Agency, what Fransman (1995) has termed the 'MITI paradox' indeed relates to how MITI can be the most powerful ministry in the technology area, given that its power and influence may originate from *non*-financial sources rather than from control of the budget. It is in this context that the Japanese ministry's control of industry, in specific cases or generally, came to become considerably dependent on the Japanese 'administrative guidance' rather than finance itself. Unlike its Korean counterpart, Fransman (1995: 116) argues that MITI continues to play an important role even though MITI's *financial* leverage over Japanese firms has considerably diminished. As he put it:

> MITI is indeed the most powerful ministry in this area but that its power and influence come, not from its budget, but from two related sources : the companies which fall under its jurisdiction, and the highly effective global information network that it controls.

On the domestic dimension, MITI has been able to ensure its indispensable role in the most dynamic sector of the Japanese economy, while simultaneously this role is applied in the international arena, where it is the co-ordinator of numerous information networks in other major economies of the world. Apart from its technology-related role, with technology's growing importance for trade, MITI has also come to play a crucial role in dealing with Japan's international economic relations with its major trading partners. Relative to other key government institutions, MITI's role has been extensively connected with two closely related issues – that is, technology and trade (Fransman, 1995: 117–18), notwithstanding financial resources manipulated by MITI at national and international levels.

We would like to contend, however, that Korean corporate power has eventually tended to become more autonomous *vis-à-vis* state power in accordance with a gradual diminution of finance-oriented leverage dominantly exercised by the Korean government. In contrast, as exemplified by MITI's role, even though the role of government is likely to be interpreted as 'auxiliary', and 'complementary' in terms of government control of the private sector (Kikkawa, 1983: 262), it could be increasingly assumed that relations between state power and Japan's corporate power have consistently remained intact. This means that the entire industry of Japan, especially the knowledge-intensive industry, seems to be subject to MITI's guidance regardless of the amount of Japanese MITI-sponsored finance available for particular industries. Concerning Japanese corporate autonomy, it is *not* the size of finance that counts but government's conventional leverage in guiding strategic industries and sectors. In contrast, with respect to Korean government–industry relations, for a definite period, it was indeed the *size* of finance that mattered, but Korean state strength in relation to corporate power gradually shifted to a modest level and then took on the role of a catalyst in real terms. With reference to the Japanese case, state–corporate power relations have not steadily changed following the emergence of knowledge-intensive industries, whereas the Korean case has shifted significantly in favour of corporate power. Moreover, it is argued that this tendency seems to have intensified since the Asian currency crisis, despite the fact that corporate restructuring was an enormous help to the Korean government in enforcing *re-regulation* through widespread intervention over the entire industry, or the Korean big firms. It is more important to recognize, however, that the Korean government can behave as a naïve political actor rather than as the typical *marketplace player* (see Zysman, 1983) with regard to the more powerful role in what Wade (1990) called the 'governed market'.

The emergence of new technology has triggered a significant transformation in 'old' modes of industrialization possibly led by the state in some industrializing countries, consequently tending to focus on the agenda of 'knowledge-intensive development' in the main, pertaining to big corporations in terms of international competitiveness (Chataway and Wield, 2000). Under these conditions, over time a change in the nature of development in which 'state and big businesses work together' eventually gives birth to a considerable transformation in relations between state and corporate power (see Kim, 1997a).

Big business as market agent has developed and enhanced its private sector market process to the point where the private sectors have become an 'integral part of the pattern of market governance' (see Underhill, 2000: 822). Thus, the state and markets coexist in symbiosis with private interests. On the one hand, at national level, *chaebol*-governance can be viewed as comprising two kinds of power: one is market power (as an economic actor) and the other political power (as a political actor). We assume that both kinds of power may be mutually reinforcing. In practical terms, market power as such, especially in world markets, tends to strengthen a firm's bargaining power in dealing with political power in relation to government, and vice versa. At the international level, we need to understand the governance of Korean conglomerates within the context of world markets underpinning new protectionist regulations in the form of anti-dumping duties among the industrial economies such as the US and the EU.

On the other hand, *chaebol*-governance can be regarded as stemming from an *organization* in its own right, rather than from *individual* members of a group. That is not to say that the demise of particular conglomerate(s), or power shift among the *chaebol*, following forceful corporate restructuring since the Asian currency crisis, is likely to make *chaebol*-governance more vulnerable in relation to the Korean government. Basically, *chaebol*-governance is defined by a collectivity of *chaebol*, in the sense that the *chaebol* as a whole is more than the sum of the individual member *chaebol*. It is assumed that individual *chaebol* as part of *chaebol* can speak on behalf of the *chaebol*, given that the Big Five *chaebol* should be responsible for the *chaebol* as a whole. From a holistic perspective, we need to treat the *chaebol* as an industrial system rather than a mere sum of firms (see Jacobson and Andreosso-O'Callaghan, 1996: 3) through the FKI (Federation of Korean Industries) formally representing the overall *chaebol*. In 1997, FKI revealed that the top five *chaebol* – Samsung, Hyundai, Daewoo, LG and SK – accounted for 32 per cent of total corporate sales, 29 per cent of assets, and 30 per cent of debt in Korea. In particular, the Samsung Group alone accounted for 28 per cent of overall Korean exports in 1997 (*Far Eastern Economic Review*, 19 November 1998).

The rationale of a competitive state in the IMF era

Since Korea embarked on *segyehwa*-connotated policies, it has transformed itself into a 'competition state' away from the developmental state or regulatory state. Competition state theory is regarded as 'the first serious and comprehensive attempt' to go beyond the market-state dualism in international political economy (Palan and Abbott, 1999: 36). As Dent (2003: 263) suggests, *segyehwa* was understood as 'a "one-way" globalisation strategy primarily seeking to improve Korea's export competitiveness and extending *chaebol* transnationalisation'.

Under the Kim Dae Jung administration Korean development adopted the style of a 'competition State' as proposed by Cerny (2000). Cerny (2000: 30–1) maintains that the competition state focuses on 'marketization' as well as the 'commodification of the state', indicating (i) a shift from macroeconomic to *micro*economic interventionism, embodied in both deregulation and industrial policy; (ii) the pursuit of 'competitive advantage' as distinct from 'comparative advantage'; and (iii) a commitment to 'the promotion of enterprise, innovation and profitability in both the private and public sectors'. The paradox of the competition state is that 'the actual *amount* or weight of government imbrication [*sic*] in social life can increase while at the same time the power of state to control specific activities and market outcomes continues to diminish' (Cerny, 2000: 34).

Following the IMF bail-out from the 1997–98 financial crisis, it was Kim Dae Jung's economic priority that enabled the Korean state to transform itself into a potential 'competition state' to face further globalization. As a consequence of this policy, there had been an increase in large private sectors and their globalization. The competitive state policy allowed Korea's policy-makers to opt for a *firm-driven* economic promotion strategy. Thus, the Korean state has emerged to become a competitive state since the IMF era. The Korean government-led competitive state attempt had considerably increased the leverage of the Korean corporate power in response to the Korean state, even though the Korean government drastically forced economic and corporate restructuring of Korean *chaebol* during the IMF era.

In that context, we acknowledge the notion of an 'individual' MNC as 'the key economic actor and commercial actor' (Sally, 1994), that is, the competitive advantages of MNCs within the context of the changing international economic environments. According to Sally (1994), we can sense that the various approaches towards MNCs have mainly tended to view the existence of MNCs as a phenomenon strongly subordinate to 'state power', or to an MNC-related 'international regime' without an exclusive focus upon the MNC itself.

The global strategies of *individual* MNCs as well as multinationals (MNCs) collectively, have to be incorporated as an enabling variable in the explanation of the country's economic development and in exercising a considerable influence over the direction of the world economy and shaping of the public policy agenda (Sally, 1994: 163). Thus global corporations of this kind have propelled individual countries to depend more upon their 'MNC-centred policy network' than ever before. Drawing on this, the outcome of market co-ordination derived from the Korean conglomerates *alone*, be they *chaebol*, or individual, should not be underestimated.

With the new mode of knowledge-driven industrialization, the challenging logic of competitive advantage has propelled Korean *chaebol* to respond rapidly to new paradigmatic innovations. We argue that the Korean individual MNCs, in some cases, even 'individual' *chaebol* as an industrial system have a significant impact on meso- (industry-) market at the international level, as prominently exemplified by Samsung Electronics. Thus the concept of market power resulting from the Korean MNCs serves to provide an account of the reason why Korean corporate power has emerged as the countervailing force against market mechanism and, especially, state power.

Conclusion

This chapter has examined how Korean corporate power has emerged as the countervailing force to Korean state power in terms of *chaebol*-governance. Following changing global market situations, the growing significance of international competitiveness tends to have influenced a shift in government–industry relations in terms of the market power of indigenous big corporations. Following the IMF bailout, the Korean state began to accelerate the translation of the orthodox model of a developmental state into one of a competition state. The move to a competition state is regarded as indicating a shift from macroeconomic to *micro*economic interventionism with a focus on competitive advantage deriving from large private sectors directed towards global markets. It is undeniable that advanced technologies have had an impact on the power relations between states and firms. Moreover, global MNCs have emerged to exercise leverage in response to the very state from which they emerged.

Specifically, within the context of 'knowledge-intensive develop-ment', the emergence of new technology has caused a significant trans-formation in 'old' modes of industrialization, thereby leading to a retreat of state power in the light of the governed market when confronted with a world trade regime.

Under these conditions, as Korean state power was mainly the result of strategic finance, state–corporate power relations tended to become unstable and more vulnerable. Meanwhile, this enabled big business to create to a great extent market power directed to the interna-tional markets, given the gradual fading of state power in dealing with 'market shaping' in the context of a globalizing market. Compared with the Japanese government, especially MITI, Korean state control seems to be time-limited, heavily finance-reliant, and transitory, invari-ably reflecting the structural weakness of the developmental state in the world system. The state and markets coexist in symbiosis with the private sector. In a highly competitive advanced market, market posi-tions derived from Korean large firms give rise to economic power, furthermore also *political* power, on the assumption that political power is interrelated with the workings of the market mechanism and market institutions, as addressed by some scholars – for example, Zysman (1983). In this context, it might be that Korean big business has shifted significantly from a private agency of public purpose conventionally vulnerable to state power *towards* a collection of quasi-state organiza-tions able to challenge the state to a greater degree. Thus, this chapter helps to examine how and to what extent the *nature* of industry has transformed state–corporate power relations, in political and economic terms, combined with the recent paradigmatic agenda of knowledge-intensive development. This argument also contributes to providing an answer to why we have to characterize big firms as exercising *political* power rather than being merely exercising economic power.

References

Amsden, A. (1989) *Asia's Next Giant: South Korea and Late Industrialisation.* New York: Oxford University Press.

Amsden, A. (1994) 'Why isn't the Whole World Experimenting with the East Asian Model to Develop in 'Review of "The East Asian Miracle" ', *World Devel-opment,* 22(4): 627–33.

Cawson, A. (1992) 'Interests, Groups and Public Policy-Making: the Case of the European Consumer Electronics Industry', in Justin Greenwood *et al.* (eds) *Organized Interests and the European Community.* London: Sage.

Cawson, A. (1997) 'Big Firms as Political Actors: Corporate Power and the Governance of the European Electronics Industry', in H. Wallace and A.R. Young (eds), *Participation and Policy-Making in the European Union*. Oxford: Clarendon Press.

Cawson, A. *et al.* (1990) *Hostile Brothers: Competition and Closure in the European Electronics Industry*, Oxford: Clarendon Press.

Cerny, P. (2000). 'Structuring the Political Arena', in Ronen Palan (ed.), *Global Political Economy*. London and New York: Routledge.

Chai, D. (1993) 'Korean Banking: Skeletons in the Closet', *Asiamoney*, September, 67–9.

Chang, Kyung-Sup (1999) 'Compressed Modernity and its Discontents: South Korean Society in Transition', *Economy and Society*, 28(1): 30–55.

Chataway, J. and Wield, D. (2000) 'Industrialization, Innovation and Development: What Does Knowledge Management Change?', *Journal of International Development*, 12: 803–24.

Coen, D. (1997) 'The Evolution of the Large Firm as a Political Actor in the European Union', *Journal of European Public Policy*, 4(1): 91–108.

Dent, C.M. (2003) 'Transnational Capital, the State and Foreign Economic Policy: Singapore, South Korea and Taiwan', *Review of International Political Economy*, 10(2): 246–77.

Far Eastern Economic Review (1998) 19 November.

Field, K. (1995) *Enterprises and the State in Korea and Taiwan*. Ithaca and London: Cornell University Press.

Fransman, M. (1995) 'Is National Technology Policy Obsolete in a Globalised World? The Japanese Response', *Cambridge Journal of Economics*, 19: 95–119.

Freeman, C. (1988) 'Japan: a New National System of Innovation', in Giovanni Dosi *et al.* (eds), *Technical Change and Economic Theory*. London and New York: Pinter Publishers.

Henderson, J. (1993) 'The Role of the State in the Economic Transformation of East Asia', in C.J. Dixon and D.W. Drakakis-Smith (eds), *Economic and Social Development in Pacific Asia*. London: Routledge.

Jacobson, D. and Andreosso-O'Callaghan, B. (1996) *Industrial Economics and Organization: European Perspective*. London: McGraw-Hill.

Johnson, C. (1982) *MITI and the Japanese Miracle*. Stanford: Stanford University Press.

Johnson, C. (1995) 'Political Institutions and Economic Performance: the Government-Business Relationship in Japan, South Korea, and Taiwan', in J. Ravenhill (ed.), *China, Korea and Taiwan*, vol. 1. Adlershot and Brookfield: Edward Elgar.

Kikkawa, M. (1983) 'Shipbuilding, Motor, Cars and Semiconductors: The Diminishing Role of Industrial Policy in Japan', in G. Shepherd *et al.* (eds), *Europe's Industries*. London: Frances Pinter.

Kim, Eun Mee (1988) 'From Dominance to Symbiosis: State and Chaebol in Korea', *Pacific Focus*, 3(2): 105–21.

Kim, Eun Mee (1997a) *Big Business, Strong State*. Albany: State University of New York Press.

Kim, Eun Mee (1997b) 'Shifting State–Chaebol Relations and Their Implications for Globalization'. 1st International Conference on International Cooperation in the Age of Globalization, 23–4 May, Institute of International Trade and Cooperation, Graduate School of International Studies, Ewha Womans University.

Lee, Yeon-ho (1997) *The State, Society and Big Business in South Korea*. London and New York: Routledge.

Mathews, J. (1998) 'Fashioning a New Korean Model Out of the Crisis: The Rebuilding of Institutional Capabilities', *Cambridge Journal of Economics*, 22: 747–59.

Mattsson, Lars-Gunnar (1999) 'Dynamics of Overlapping Networks and Strategic Actions by the International Firms', in A.D Chandler, Jr., P. Hagstrom, and O. Solvell (eds), *The Dynamic Firm: The Role of Technology, Strategy, Organization, and Regions*. Oxford: Oxford University Press.

Palan, R. and Abbott, J. (1999) *State and State Strategies in the Global Political Economy*. London and New York: Pinter.

Penrose, E. (1995) *The Theory of the Growth of the Firm*, 3rd edn. Oxford: Oxford University Press.

Plummer, M. (1999) 'Corporate Interaction, Direct Investment and Regional Cooperation Industrializing Asia', in A. Rugman and G. Boyd (eds), *Deepening Integration in the Pacific Economics*. Cheltenham and Northampton, MA: Edward Elgar.

Poulantzas, N. (1972) 'The Problem of the Capitalist State', in R. Blackburn (ed.), *Ideology in Social Science: Readings in Critical Social Theory*. London: Fontana.

Quah, Danny (1999) 'The Weightless Economy in Economic Development', WIDER (World Institute for Development Economics Research), The United Nations University, Working Paper no. 155, pp. 1–28.

Ravenhill, J. (ed.) (1995) *China, Korea and Taiwan*, vol. 1. Aldershot and Brookfield, VT Edward Elgar.

Sally, R. (1994) 'Multinational Enterprises, Political Economy and Institutional Theory: Domestic Embeddedness in the Context of Internationalization', *Review of International Political Economy*, 1(1): 161–92.

Soh, Changrok (1997) *From Investment to Innovation*. Seoul: Global Research Institute, Korea University.

Underhill, G. (2000) 'State, Market, and Global Political Economy: Genealogy of an (Inter- ?)Discipline', *International Affairs*, 76(4): 805–24.

Wade, R. (1990) *Governing the Market: Economic Theory and The Role of government in East Asia*. Princeton, NJ: Princeton University Press.

Wade, R. and Veneroso, F. (1998) 'The Asian Crisis: The High Debt Model Versus the Wall Street–Treasury–IMF Complex', *New Left Review*, 228: 3–23.

Woo-Cumings, M. (1999) 'Introduction: Chalmers Johnson and the Politics of Nationalism and Development', in M. Woo-Cumings, *The Developmental State*. Ithaca and London: Cornell University Press.

Woods, N. (2000) 'The Political Economy of Globalization', in N. Woods (ed.), *The Political Economy of Globalization*. London: Macmillan.

Yeung, Henry Wai-chung (2000) 'The Dynamics of Asian Business Systems in a Globalizing Era', *Review of International Political Economy*, 7(3): 399–433.

Zysman, J. (1983) *Governments, Markets, and Growth*. Oxford: Martin Robertson.

Index